Reviews of the author
THE GRIP O

For more information on *The Grip of Death*, see the last page of this book.

Goodbye America!

Globalisation, debt and the dollar empire

Michael Rowbotham

JON CARPENTER
CHARLBURY

ENVIROBOOK
SYDNEY

In the **UK and Europe**, order post free from
Jon Carpenter Publishing (address below)
Credit card orders should be phoned or faxed to 01689 870437
or 01608 811969
E-mail: joncarpenterpublishing@compuserve.com

In **Australia**, order from Envirobook (address below).
Tel 02 9518 6154, fax 02 9518 6156
E-mail: editor@republican.com.au

In **South Africa**, order from New Horizon Distributors, PO Box 44585,
Claremont 7735. Tel 021 683 0360, fax 021 683 8666
E-mail: wizards@cis.co.za

Distributed in the **USA and Canada** by Paul and Company
PO Box 442, Concord, MA 01742. Tel 978 369 3049, fax 978 369 2385
E-mail: paulinc@tiac.net

First published in 2000 by
Jon Carpenter Publishing
Alder House, Market Street, Charlbury, Oxfordshire OX7 3PH
☎ 01608 811969

and

Envirobook
38 Rose Street, Annandale, NSW 2000, Australia
☎ 02 9518 6154

© Michael Rowbotham

Cover illustration by Heather Tamplin

ISBN 1 897766 56 4 (Jon Carpenter)
ISBN 0 85881 177 4 (Envirobook)
Printed in England by J. W. Arrowsmith Ltd., Bristol

Contents

Acknowledgements

No work on Third World debt should begin without acknowledging that this province of economics is no academic issue. We write and argue whilst in the impoverished nations, people die. For this reason my first statement of gratitude and respect must go to the many outstanding writers who have fought on behalf of the developing nations over the years, and whose work it has been my privilege to study. They have stood up for the dispossessed of the Two-Thirds World who have suffered so long under the merciless rule of unjust economic conventions. My admiration in particular to Cheryl Payer, Jeffrey Sachs, Susan George, Hans Singer, Bade Onimode and Michel Chossudovsky.

The support of my family has been especially important during the writing of this book. It was a hard year. Thanks then to Pete, Barbie, Judy, Jocelyn, Dinah and Rosie. Thanks also to the confidence shown in me by those colleagues who have become my friends and given me invaluable support; Tracy, George, Frances and Mark.

I have great pleasure in acknowledging also the Christian Council for Monetary Justice, who gave me the honour of electing me their secretary for two years. My gratitude, finally, to two people without whom this book would in all likelihood never have been written. Jon; professional, kind and brilliant. And Eroica.

*This book is dedicated
to Africa*

1

After Seattle, no jubilee

When the World Trade Organisation met at Seattle in November 1999, pictures of the protest riots were shown all over the globe. The story remained in many national headlines for weeks. Whatever the level of public awareness before the conference, there is a post-Seattle consciousness that issues of vital importance were under discussion. All over the world, people realised that in a remote city in an all-powerful country, economic and political decisions affecting their future were being determined without prior consultation, without democratic involvement and without the opportunity for redress. The reality of globalisation had begun to dawn.

At precisely the same time, the millennium countdown was closing in on the Jubilee 2000 campaign. Since 1994, Jubilee 2000 had worked to address the debt issue, focusing on the dawning of the millennium as the moment of forgiveness. It didn't happen. Although the general public could be forgiven for celebrating the American, Canadian and British leaders for their generosity, the amount of money actually pledged by Presidents Clinton, Blair and Chretien amounted to less than 1% of the total of international debt. The way the media portrayed this gesture, praising Blair and Clinton especially for 'ending Third World debt', is a salutary lesson in the superficiality of the press and the political manipulation of public opinion. As the next chapter discusses, the media misrepresentation of the debt issue has been a consistent feature in recent years whilst the problem remains completely unresolved.

Unfortunately, we have now lived for so long with an awareness of Third World debt that, even if compassion fatigue has not set in, the passage of time has exacted a perhaps heavier price. Familiarity has bred a subtle form of acceptance. Major disasters set against a back-cloth of perpetual grinding poverty have, over the years, fostered a deeply depressing judgement; there is a resignation that nothing direct and immediate can be done. The best international economists have struggled for years over the 'development conundrum' and still the debt totals mount and the tragedies recur. Third World debt is clearly so complex a problem that there are 'no easy solutions'.

A similar impotence and futility is felt by those concerned at the direction in which globalisation is leading us. When Tony Blair famously declared globalisation to be 'inevitable', he was merely giving voice to the popular perception. The pressure of international markets; the move towards political integration; the accelerating pace of technology – all seem part of a combined process that is so powerful it is beyond restraint. It almost appears that a complex scenario is being played out which, whether the outcome is seen as good or bad, is surely irresistible.

Globalisation and debt … debt and globalisation … are there really no answers and no alternatives? This book is written in the conviction that the tangled developmental disaster of Third World debt can be tackled, and that this can be done directly and rapidly. Third World debts, the bulk of which lack both economic and moral validity, could be cancelled at a stroke, but only by breaking with certain aspects of current economic orthodoxy.

As for globalisation, far from this being a separate and distinct issue from debt, the two matters are intimately related. Globalisation is a direct product of the debt crisis; it is also the price we all now pay for the inequities in international trade and finance that created the scandal of Third World debt. And far from being inevitable, globalisation is best described as a deliberate policy. The debt crisis is discussed more fully in subsequent chapters. First, it is important to appreciate the nature and the enormity of the issue termed globalisation.

Globalisation

Debt is a relatively simple concept but globalisation is rather like the word 'civilisation'. G. K. Chesterton once complained that either to define or defend civilisation was almost impossible. Where do you start with something so big and so complex? Civilisation is about quite ordinary things, such as having pavements, policemen and lamp-posts, every bit as much as it is about literature, politics and manners. Civilisation means different things to different people. And it is not that any of these perceptions is in any important sense wrong. Civilisation simply covers a lot of ground. So too with globalisation. Globalisation is about Coca-Cola and cars. It is about international power-politics, trade and democracy. And as the street riots in Seattle in November 1999 showed, it is also about policemen and pavements and manners.

In the years prior to the Seattle Conference, public awareness of globalisation had been informed and motivated by a succession of events. Books had been published warning of the internationalisation of economics and politics.[1] As giant multinationals continued their practice of demanding investment sweeteners from national governments, playing one country off against another, the excessive power of corporate business had become apparent. There was an attempt by the OECD (Organisation for Economic Cooperation and Development) to draw up a quiet, backroom agreement on a vital international charter – the MAI (Multilateral Agreement on Investment). This was exposed and thrown out after world-wide lobbying by pressure groups concerned with economic justice and the environment.[2] The integrity of institutions such as the OECD and WTO was badly tarnished as a result and their supposed neutrality called into question. Meanwhile, in the United Kingdom and Canada, public concern was fuelled as much as anything by the debate over genetically engineered food. People could finally understand what globalisation was about – and they didn't want to eat it.

The agreed feature of globalisation is that, whatever one perceives as being globalised, the process involves some form of international standardisation and the narrowing of differences. Beyond this point, the disagreements begin. Is globalisation a good or a bad thing? Global free trade and foreign investment have resulted in such a proliferation of the Western lifestyle that it is possible to live in the Far East, eating, shopping, working and being entertained just as if one had never left Los Angeles or London. But whilst some critics bemoan the loss of cultural distinctiveness, others see this spread as a democratic entitlement driven by consumer choice. Globalisation creates many such conflicting perspectives, as well as ironies. The voluntary organisations and non-governmental organisations (NGOs) that collaborated so bravely and successfully to contest the MAI did so largely via the internet – undoubtedly a prime example of the globalisation of communication.

Despite the varied opinions and lack of definition as to what the process of globalisation actually amounts to, the principal concerns are clear. The first area of concern is political. There is considerable alarm that a tier of un-elected, unaccountable international governance is becoming consolidated that is assuming excessive power. Institutions such as the North American Free Trade Agreement (NAFTA), the European Union (EU) and the World Trade Organisation (WTO), although they consist of delegates from elected national governments, are demonstrating increasing detachment from their member states. Along with the World Bank, International Monetary Fund (IMF) and OECD, these institutions are attempting to take detailed and complex decisions of far-reaching consequence for citizens in all nations. The concern is not just with the lack of democratic accountability, but that the entire edifice is over-centralised, unwieldy and inherently incompetent by virtue of its drift towards a cumbersome global government.[3]

To this must be added the power of corporate influence. The supposedly neutral organisations listed above have frequently been accused of various forms of corruption. One of the most worrying is the abundant evidence of excessive political lobbying and representation by powerful commercial interests at this tier of international governance.[4] But the most subtle and damaging form of corruption is mental; there is an inevitable tendency for international political delegates to view the world and its progress through the eyes of corporate business, since these are the 'big players' and this is 'big government'. The interests of individual citizens, the details of democracy and the health of smaller businesses are assumed to be incorporated in the 'big decisions', either as a spin-off or because the greater good and the bigger picture is being embraced.

The excessive power of multinational corporations is itself a component of the globalisation debate and a clear cause for concern. Multinational corporations, many of which possess a turnover exceeding that of the majority of the world's nation states, have been accused of a catalogue of crimes; blackmailing national governments to grant them subsidies; exerting pressure to change government economic policy; asset-stripping; exploitation of the developing world; transfer pricing to avoid taxation; acquiring by patent law rights that ought not to belong to any single private interest – the list is endless. The fact that these issues have not been addressed, indeed are not even on the agenda, lends support to the concern that the tier of international governance is pro-corporate.

The upsurge of international trade, from 9% of global output in 1965 to 25% in 1999, is another focus of concern.[5] Such is the modern emphasis on exporting that similar goods are increasingly being exchanged between countries. There is now an extraordinary global transfer of products. The components of a car may be manufactured in twelve separate countries, before being assembled in a yet another country and then exported as widely as modern marketing skills will permit. Near-identical products are exchanged between nations and foodstuffs that could easily be produced more locally are grown in remote corners of the planet, often displacing impoverished populations, and then bulk-transported throughout the world.[6]

Orthodox economics has no concept of the cost and loss involved in the proliferation of such pointless trade. Just as all economic activity is perceived as inherently productive, the annual increase in trade is viewed as an indisputable mark of progress. But the damage to the environment, the remorseless increase in transport demands, the waste and the blatant inefficiency involved ought to impress upon the minds of our economists that all is not well. They have only to recall that both the power of monopoly and the effect of hidden subsidies have the capacity to render free trade theory completely invalid.

There is also a cultural dimension to globalisation. The loss of distinctive national and regional cultures and their replacement with a brash consumer ethic born in a thousand corporate ad-campaigns is epitomised by the global spread of McDonald's, Pepsi-co and Nike. One does not want to be over-puritanical. There is no reason why India should not have fast food. But why McDonald's? Why not an Indian company? And why not a company that offers eastern delicacies?

The decline of culture is a broad and contentious issue, but the economics of this cultural homogenisation has clearly not been a simple matter of consumer demand and free choice. The history of this demise of diversity is also a record of cynical commercial aggression. This has taken place against a back-cloth of the most appalling impoverishment within the emergent nations, the prior destruction of their self-esteem and sense of direction and the blatant manipulation of their citizens' desires by mass advertising and image fostering.

The impoverishment and cultural decline within the emergent nations brings the discussion back to the issue of Third World debt. I have suggested that globalisation and the debt crisis are not separate issues, but closely linked problems. Exploring the connections reveals more of the economic dimension of globalisation.

Globalisation and Third World debt

The tie-in between globalisation and Third World debt is underlined by the fact that, with each issue, many of the institutions are the same. The multinational corporations that dominate and drive forward the process of globalisation have for decades proved the *bête noire* of debtor nations. Corporate investment has long been relied upon as a vital factor in development, bringing employment and new technology and mobilising resources. But many developing nations are left wondering what they have actually gained after the minerals have been extracted and exported, the profits repatriated and any corporate tax revenues swallowed up by debt repayments.

The multilateral lending institutions, the IMF and World Bank, are also key players in both debt and the progress of globalisation. In advancing loans, they have always demanded that the developing nations adhere strictly to an economic programme that is deliberately and avowedly corporate-friendly. Debtors are obliged to follow a rigorous diet of demand restriction, free market deregulation, currency devaluation and privatisation. This orthodoxy, representing the development views and priorities of economists within the wealthy nations, means that virtually the entire planet now follows a single economic ideology, founded on the concept that foreign investment is inherently and unquestioningly desirable.

Larry Summers, former President of the World Bank, demonstrated his contempt for the notion that a nation might wish to pursue its own economic priorities during an address in India: '[Third World governments] need to realise that there is no longer such a thing as separate and distinct Indian economics. There is just economics'.[7] As the final chapter discusses, although claiming to embrace social priorities, the World Bank's current HIPC initiative for debt relief is founded upon precisely the same economic tenets.[8] In ensuring this rigid orthodoxy is applied globally, the IMF and World Bank have done more to further the interests of corporate power and provide the conditions for globalisation than any other institution.

The very existence of endemic Third World debt itself promotes globalisation. The ubiquity of debt, coupled with deregulated economic conditions, means that multinationals are presented with vistas of investment opportunities. The acute financial pressure on debtor nations and the sheer number of countries in this desperate position devalues all Third World assets. Land, labour, minerals, primary commodities, manufactured goods and state assets undergoing privatisation are all available at what Susan George has described as 'fire-sale prices'.[9]

Debt always provides a corporate opportunity. The opportunity to purchase 'land at acres per dollar, rather than dollars per acre' is the type of opportunity commerce will never ignore. The multinationals driving forward the process of globalisation can thus operate in the 'development gap' between the developed and underdeveloped worlds, able to use debtor nations as cheap agricultural and manufacturing outposts and secure profits in more wealthy markets.

Debt also promotes the growth of global trade. Only by a perpetual surplus of exports over imports can debtor nations hope to manage their interest payments. The obligation on debtor nations to direct an increasing proportion of their resources and economic effort to the export market has long been recognised as one of the primary causes of poverty and lack of internal development in the emerging nations. Meanwhile, the volume of exports from the developing to the developed world increases constantly – though never sufficiently to settle the debts.

Who pays?

The suffering throughout the developing world due to the debt crisis has been well documented. However, in her seminal book, *The Debt Boomerang*,[10] Susan George notes a host of ways in which Third World debt also impacts negatively on the standard of living of citizens in the wealthy nations. Instead of pursuing a programme of true cancellation, bank profits are protected and the debt burden transferred to citizens in the wealthy nations, who find themselves funding debt relief programmes through their taxes. As corporations seek low-cost opportunities in the debtor nations, the wealthy nations experience a loss of employment abroad and suffer an influx of cheap products that destroy home markets. There is also the need constantly to step in when famine occurs due to over-emphasis on export crops; the obligation to act when, as so often, debt has caused civil or regional wars and cope with immigration in flight from poverty and conflict. Considerable damage to the global environment has been caused by the large number of destructive, ill-suited economic projects that debtor nations have constantly undertaken in their efforts to earn export revenues. These factors are all associated with Third World debt. They are what we in the North pay for the poverty and instability in the South.

The boomerang principle emphasises that there is general economic loss due to debt in the form of social and economic chaos, waste and destruction. This principle applies equally, and even more obviously, to globalisation. Economics is supposed to be about efficiency and the optimal use of resources. A supposed 'misallocation of resources' has justified the most disgraceful 'adjustment' policies by the IMF and World Bank. The ethic of deregulation in support of free trade holds as its most sacred tenet the notion that this will lead to a more efficient global economy. But globalisation can almost be defined as the epitome of abuse, wastage and inefficient use of resources and neglect of human priorities. What greater and more obvious misallocation of resources could there be than the monopolisation of land in poverty-stricken nations to produce food for the industrialised nations – food that loses its nutritional value during transport and storage – whilst the indigenous population go hungry, and acres of land suitable for growing quality foodstuffs lie neglected within the northern hemisphere?

Ten per cent of land in the European Union has been taken out of production under the EU set-aside programme and many European farmers face bankruptcy, whilst global corporations monopolise land in Africa, Asia and South America to grow crops for export from nations many of whose citizens suffer from malnutrition. As Ed Mayo of the New Economics Foundation comments, a child can see the stupidity involved.[11]

The rational geography of production and supply at the local, national and regional level is increasingly breaking down as multinationals seek the latest low-price investment opportunities around the world. The trafficking of goods over ever-greater distances between producer and consumer, amounts to a blatant misuse – indeed the profligate waste – of resources throughout the global economy. To this must be added the gross wastage and inefficiency of modern junk-produce. Globalisation has added significantly to the remorseless drift of recent years towards the production of low-price, mass-produced goods and services of poor quality and durability. Produced in remote locations and bulk-transported around the world, cheap goods and services persistently drive out better quality, more durable products, promoting centralisation and transport and generating pollution. The loss and waste are immeasurable, as are the potential gains of a more benign, efficient and stable world economy.[12] The connection between debt and globalisation and the inter-related damage they both cause thus provides a real incentive to citizens in the wealthy, developed nations to seek a genuine and rapid solution to the international debt crisis.

There is yet another connection between debt and globalisation which is an important aspect of this book and also contributes to the escalation of trade described above. The financial system is increasingly being viewed as a major and critical flaw amongst modern economic institutions.[13] Chapter 10 argues that the present debt-based financial system, which is ultimately responsible for the intractability of third world debt, is also responsible for much of the impetus behind globalisation. The huge domestic debts of even the most wealthy nations mean that, just as in the Third World, governments are frequently obliged to adopt policies that favour global corporate interests. Fiscally weakened by burgeoning national debts, all governments now find themselves dwarfed, out-manoeuvred and subject to the power of multinationals and international finance.

Goodbye America!

The title of this book was not chosen merely to be provocative. Still less was it chosen to either injure, insult or foster resentment against the citizens of a nation, most of whom are no less tied than other peoples by the dictates of modern economics. Nonetheless, the conclusion of this book is that powerful American economic and political interests have undoubtedly been persistently and deliberately furthered by the same institutions that have so disadvantaged the developing world, and which are now key players in the drive behind corporate globalisation.

The brief survey of developing country debt before Bretton Woods, in Chapter 4, reminds us that pre-war debt crises were recurrent, with causes and patterns very similar to today's. It also emphasises the historical role of debt as a tool of imperialism and political influence. The theme of imperialism is underscored in the review of the Bretton Woods Conference where two competing proposals, one from the USA and the other from Britain, were considered. The rejection of Keynes' proposal and his warnings that endemic debt would be a consequence of the US plans for a World Bank and IMF are salutary evidence that Third World debt was both foreseeable and avoidable. It also confirms that Third World debt was the direct product of America's post-war political and economic aspirations.

The years after Bretton Woods and the very biased policy-demands of the World Bank, IMF, GATT and WTO present the inescapable conclusion that these institutions, and the trading accountancy conventions associated with them, are at least co-responsible for the backlog of debt now accrued. The economic status of Third World debt, and the fact that such debt is inherently un-repayable, is discussed in Chapter 8. In the final chapter, the doubtful legal status of such debt is discussed with reference to financial contract law. This raises the option both of a legal challenge to the validity of international debts and the opportunity for an alliance of debtor nations to stand together and seek economic justice.

The complaint of this book is not principally about the material wealth enjoyed by Americans which, as has often been pointed out, is for many Americans more mythical than real. In the end, the issue being discussed here is power. It is the power to control and direct economic activity, and thereby, ultimately, people. This is the power of money and of banking, the power of the Federal Reserve and especially the dollar, the power of the IMF and World Bank, the power of the World Trade Organisation, the power of a few hundred Chief Executive Officers of the most powerful multinational organisations and the power of dominant governments. It is today's imperialism. And in the end, the apex of this power can with full justification be identified with America, American history, American corporate interests and American political influence.

Goodbye America! looks to a future where international corporations, the US dollar and powerful multilateral institutions based in America no longer dominate world economic policy. A future where the 'Washington Consensus' has been replaced with a more benign, democratic and accountable economic ethic. The right and the obligation to seek this freedom lies with people in the wider community of nations to assert this right, and so regain their own sense of identity, culture, economic independence and destiny. With any degree of popular conviction and determination, and commitment by politicians to their own citizens, the Washington Consensus, the empire of the dollar and the power to dominate and draw an unjust profit from the world's economic activity will simply vanish.

Endnotes

1   David Korten. *When Corporations Rule the World*. Earthscan. 1995.
2   Tony Clarke, Maude Barlow. *MAI*. Stoddart Publishing (Canada). 1997.
3   William Greider. *One World, Ready or Not*. Penguin Books. 1997.
4   David Korten. *Op cit*.
5   *World Economic and Social Survey*. United Nations. 1996.
6   Helena Norberg Hodge. *Small is Beautiful, Big is Subsidised*. International Society for Ecology and Culture. 1999.
7   Susan George, Fabrizio Sabelli. *Faith and Credit*. Penguin Books. 1994.
8   Anthony R. Boote, Kamau Thugge. *Debt Relief for Low Income Countries. The HIPC Initiative*. International Monetary Fund. 1997.
9   Susan George. *The Debt Boomerang*. Pluto Press. 1992.
10   *Ibid*.
11   Foreword to Richard Douthwaite. *Short Circuit*. Green Books. 1996.
12   Michael Rowbotham. *The Grip of Death*. Jon Carpenter. 1998.
13   See Michael Rowbotham, *op cit*. and Richard Douthwaite, *The Ecology of Money*, Green Books. 1999.

2

A lasting jubilee

There can be little dispute that Third World debt was the greatest economic, cultural and humanitarian disaster of the twentieth century. Not even the horror of two world wars and numerous lesser conflicts can stand comparison with the scale and depth of the unrelenting tragedy that has swept through the developing nations over the last four decades.

But it is worth reminding ourselves that, with the exception of a small number of astute commentators, Third World debt was not a problem that was anticipated. Quite the contrary. Little more than a generation ago, the emergent nations of Africa, Asia and Latin America, with a tremendous wealth of natural resources and many geographical advantages, were predicted as having a prosperous future. Technology and expertise from the advanced Western economies would build on these natural advantages and it was confidently expected that these nations would enjoy a period of sustained and beneficial post-colonial development. E. Wayne Nafziger writes of this optimism;

> Africans entered the last half of this century with high expectations. Kwame
> Nkrumah, Ghana's President, 1957–66, prophesied in 1950, 'If we get self-
> government, we'll transform the Gold Coast into a paradise in ten years'.[1]

This early vision of prosperity now reads like a child's fairytale. Sub-Saharan Africa's development, like that of so much of the Third World, has been a horrifying tragedy in which 'progress' has been accompanied and countered by the most appalling suffering, starvation and wretchedness. Millions now find themselves marginalised within their own society, existing in the midst of an economic degradation so profound that it not only fails to supply them with food, water and shelter, but has destroyed their culture, their past, their future and all hope. Nafziger bleakly observes; 'The great ascent expected in the 1960s has, in Africa, become the great descent'.

What went wrong? Is it because the original vision was unrealistic? Is it because of population growth? Or economic incompetence? The conclusion of this book is a categorical 'No' to all such suggestions. The nations of the Third World have been robbed, and the debts they now carry are both a measure of this robbery and its continuing cause. This has been effected by the interplay of key economic and political institutions that operate to the advantage of the wealthy nations and their powerful corporations.

The early predictions of gathering prosperity were not over-idealistic. There was no need for the development of the Third World to have followed the pattern we have witnessed. The expectation that the resources, abundant raw materials and commodities produced by the South, and the technological expertise and capital of the North, would form the basis of trade for mutual benefit between the two hemispheres was both realistic and justified. All that was required were the economic institutions to promote this.

Third World nations have been robbed in material terms. In addition, their cultures have been destroyed and the process of development diverted from serving the welfare of their people by a process of subtle but brutal expropriation. This has led to gathering poverty, triggering social and economic chaos, as well as political corruption. The first purpose of this book is to attempt to explain how this has been done, and how it is still being done, through the institution of Third World debt. The second purpose is to outline a number of straightforward accountancy methods by which these debts can be cancelled, allowing the emergence of more humane, constructive and sustainable patterns of development within the poorer nations.

The popular consensus

Many of these statements conflict sharply with, and challenge, an opinion that has achieved the status of a popular consensus. With a new millennium and a rise in public consciousness over the depth of suffering within debtor nations, Third World debt became a headline issue. In the UK, a coalition lobbying for major action on debt relief emerged. Jubilee 2000 and Christian Aid managed to exert sufficient pressure to draw the parties of influence – leading politicians, financiers and representatives from the World Bank and IMF – into discussions. Out of their dialogue, and through much media coverage, the new consensus is emerging.

According to this consensus, not all developing nations actually need debt remission; many have debt totals that are 'sustainable'. As for the 'Highly Indebted Poor Countries' (HIPCs), these cannot possibly expect to have all of their debts cancelled; and these debts are due primarily to their own 'corruption and economic mismanagement'. The politicians, economists, and financiers have agreed that there should be some cancellation, but only of 'unpayable debts', to the point where the debt of all Third World nations becomes 'sustainable'. And such debt forgiveness should be conditional on sound economic, social and environmental policies.

Regrettably, the Jubilee 2000 coalition accepted this response, which is now enshrined in the World Bank's HIPC initiative.[2] The consensus is now being marketed as a responsible position; it is the best the debtor nations can hope for – a reasonable compromise.

The thesis of the next four chapters is that this popular consensus is misinformed. In fact, this consensus can only be described as rubbish. It represents an abject failure to respond to the suffering within the debtor nations and a total failure of analysis. As Chapter 11 demonstrates, economic incompetence, corruption, capital flight and excessive military spending are no more than political scapegoats for the glaring injustice of Third World debt.

Throughout the recent media debate, Third World debt has been utterly misunderstood and misrepresented. The suffering has been covered in graphic detail. The statistics have been reported. But the discussion of the causes of the debt stands in defiance of four decades of study and criticism. The catalogue of books on Third World debt and the problems encountered by developing nations forms a massive body of authoritative literature. This includes broad theoretical works, regional case studies, country-by-country analyses, statistical assessments, evaluations of major and contributory causes, possible remedies and policy options to alleviate the suffering that has engulfed two-thirds of the world in a whirlwind of economic disruption and social dislocation.

Out of this vast body of work emerges one consistent message – that the problems of debtor nations are not, primarily, of their own making. In the current media and political 'consensus', however, this established and recorded history of Third World debt has been largely ignored. The actual financial structure of the debt has not been analysed; its relationship to the rest of the world economy has not even been discussed. Third World debt is now just being treated as a series of unpleasant numbers, for which the debtor nations should seek 'forgiveness' at the alter of 'sound economics'. In the current popular consensus, it is almost as if most of the books on development economics had never been written.

The failure of economics

To a large extent, the popular consensus reflects the opinion, and failure, of orthodox economics. It is still not appreciated by the majority of economists that Third World debt constitutes a glaring anomaly. For two-thirds of the planet to be carrying any endemic international debt, let alone debts so onerous that they dominate every micro- and macro-economic policy decision, stands in stark defiance of all orthodox economic theory. Such permanent, increasing and crippling debts ought simply not to exist. They constitute both a profound failure of the terms under which international lending is conducted, and a permanent disturbance in the balance of trade. The institution of flexible and floating exchange rates was specifically designed to avoid such trade imbalances. Endemic and growing levels of developing country debt thus represent a major economic contradiction, casting the gravest doubt upon the adequacy of orthodox theory, advice, and key institutions. Third World debt is certainly not a minor aberration that can be ironed out with the supposedly 'sound economics' of 'structural adjustment' – indeed, it raises serious doubts as to what actually constitutes sound economics.

Unfortunately, the fact that Third World debt does exist is often not accepted as an indication that there are deep fallacies within established trade, development and lending theory, nor within the institutions associated with trade and debt. Quite the reverse. That such levels of chronic debt do exist is taken by many economists as a sign that the canons of neo-classical orthodoxy have not been fully understood and applied. Debt is read as a sign of debtor-nation incompetence; a failure to follow the Golden Rules.

This judgement naturally lends support to the popular consensus, fostered through the media, that the debts of Third World nations are the product of their own economic incompetence and corruption. The discipline of economics is perceived as so complicated that it is hardly surprising that the developing nations 'have not got it right yet'. In fact, there is abundant evidence that it is the discipline of economics – not the Third World – that has not got it right yet. The recurrent failure of the range of remedies proposed by conventional economists, indeed the fact that these policies have compounded the problems of debtor nations, serves only to underline that Third World debt stands as a profound indictment of current economic orthodoxy.

Bretton Woods and banking

It might seem that these are extreme claims to make. The suggestion that the catastrophe of Third World debt was predictable and avoidable; that the blame for this colossal humanitarian tragedy does not lie primarily with the debtor nations themselves; that the accountancy problem of Third World debt is capable of simple resolution – these claims stand in marked contrast to the 'popular consensus'.

In fact, the extensive literature analysing and recording the problems of developing nations certainly bears out the first two claims. The historical record contains a number of clear warnings by the most eminent economists that the Bretton Woods institutions and the accountancy of world trade were, from the outset, fundamentally flawed. The structure of the Bretton Woods institutions is often mistakenly attributed to John Maynard Keynes. In fact, Keynes' proposals for an International Clearing Union were rejected by the dominant American delegation shortly before the conference. After Bretton Woods, Keynes returned to London and a highly revealing correspondence broke out in *The Times*, in which Keynes commented on the inherent weaknesses of the World Bank and IMF as just constituted;

> Some of your correspondents press me to admit (a) that forms of commercial policy, permissible under the Bretton Woods currency proposals, may nevertheless be very foolish; (b) that [these] may be so destructive of international trade that, if they were adopted, Bretton Woods will have been rather a waste of time. Both of these contentions are, in my opinion, correct.[3]

Keynes and others warned that endemic debt and trade conflict would be the consequence of the Bretton Woods agreement. These warnings were ignored.

Bearing out these misgivings, attributing a high degree of blame to the Bretton Woods institutions and clearly exonerating the debtor nations, comments such as the following are recurrent throughout the development literature of the past thirty years;

> … in the last ten years, the whole IMF policy has been nothing but a failure. All its prognoses were proved wrong, and its policies and measures had an opposite effect from what had been expected.[4]

Such numerous assessments, by critics qualified to comment, show the lack of substance behind today's public/media consensus. Chapters 4 and 5 discuss the numerous studies of Third World debt that have, since the 1950s, emphasised the impact of factors over which the developing nations have had little or no control. These range from criticism of World Bank and IMF policies to flaws in the accountancy of trade and the ruthless imposition of an inappropriate free trade agenda on debtor nation economies.

As regards the third contention, that Third World debt is open to a satisfactory accountancy solution, this is perhaps less well established. The main reason for this is the paucity of critical economic study in the area of debt and money. Although every basic economics textbook carries a chapter on banking and the supply of money via the multiplication of debt, one searches in vain for any recognition that this might have serious macro-economic consequences. Yet it stands to reason that if we continually and almost exclusively create and supply money via a process that automatically generates debt, we cannot express great surprise when debt becomes a problem.

By contrast, this book carries at its core a strong critique of the mechanism of fractional reserve banking, and stresses the direct connection between money and debt in modern economic systems. National and international economies now rely almost entirely upon the creation of money by a process that automatically involves the creation of debt. The supply of money is thus directly paralleled by the growth of debt totals that are, in aggregate, quite unrepayable. In fact, the wealthier the nation, the larger its mountain of debt. For example, the American national debt is fast approaching $6 trillion, outstanding US mortgages are in excess of $4.5 trillion and commercial debts exceed £4 trillion. The United Kingdom, Germany, Japan, and all the G8 countries carry similarly staggering national private and commercial debts. No-one even pretends that these can ever be repaid (although political leaders often make grandiose claims to that effect). The fact that the financial system generates unrepayable debts is obviously of the first importance in understanding why the Third World finds itself in this position. Otherwise, what are we saying to the poor nations of sub-Saharan Africa – 'Work hard, follow sound Western economic advice, and one day your debts will be as small as America's – a mere $5.5 trillion dollars of national debt, plus $4.5 trillion dollars mortgage debt, plus $4 trillion dollars commercial debt'? It is simply not acceptable to claim that international, or Third World debts, are of a different economic category from other debts. The world has a debt problem in every category.

But in conventional economics texts, once one ventures outside the chapter on 'the money supply', the peculiar accountancy of modern banking is simply excluded from all consideration. Money is just assumed to 'be there'; present in the quantities required to allow theories to function; a 'given' in the analytical process. Third World debt is a prime example of this failing. Incredible as it may seem, even in the academic field of debt literature and development theory, the vast majority of texts contain no analysis of either debt or money! In one of the few works that does show an awareness of the monetary structure of Third World debt, Lord Lever and Christopher Huhne comment;

> The advanced countries had thrown a single vulnerable sector of their economies, the banking system, into a task it could not bear without official support… in any banking system every loan creates a new deposit in the system as a whole … The original loan can be multiplied many times as the process of lending and depositing continues … [however] debtors inevitably became vulnerable to the disintegration of market confidence…[5]

Awareness of the direct (but ultimately unnecessary) link between money and debt in modern economic systems gives us many penetrating insights into factors that impact directly on Third World debt. At a theoretical level, these debts are clearly a function of the money supply principle adopted by all modern economies. Such debts are not statements of economic failure, nor any justifiable obligation to remit goods and services of equivalent value, as conventional economic theory implies. Indeed, the entire status and legitimacy of Third World debt is called into question when a thorough analysis of money is employed.

At a practical level, the ubiquity of debt in the global economy has a profound bearing on the Third World, by introducing a high degree of aggression into the conduct of international trade. A balance of trade, and anything approaching mutuality, are both quite lost in today's cut-throat world market – in which material abundance is overlain by financial stringency and monetary conflict. With a surplus of goods and services, insufficient buyers and widespread poverty, the disgraceful 1930s spectre of 'poverty amidst plenty' still stalks the planet. It has often been observed that people in the poorer nations starve not for want of food, but for want of money to buy the food that clogs the global market. Third World debt is poverty amidst plenty.

A thorough monetary analysis strongly confirms the dominant conclusion – the documented consensus of history – that Third World debt constitutes a systemic failure involving major economic institutions. This includes the institution of money in its current form. A monetary analysis of the international debts carried by the developing nations shows that these are essentially invalid statements, and do not represent true 'inter-national' debts. Rather, these debts are an expression of the current financial system, and the result of inequitable trading conventions instituted at Bretton Woods and subsequently.

However, the monetary analysis does more than offer accordance; it integrates many of the established ingredients that contribute to the growth of Third World debt and lends deeper understanding to the entire process. A critical understanding of money and debt also, most crucially, allows us to establish a rationale and technically competent accountancy for the cancellation of debts.

A monetary critique also allows us to consider an entirely new theory and practice for international development. Many writers and analysts have faulted applying the theory that 'capital flows from rich to poor' to development loans, and advocated the generation by the emergent nations of their own capital. A monetary reform analysis allows us to build this critique into a new, more flexible model of development. This book also emphasises the need for a range of reforms including new systems of trade accountancy and a new 'financial architecture' covering investment and lending.

A systemic overview

At the time of writing, the total of international debt stands in excess of $2.3 trillion dollars. This figure, which is constantly rising, is divided between many countries. Those defined as 'low income' nations often carry a relatively small debt burden, but nonetheless may be crippled by its effects. 'Middle income' nations generally carry a far larger share of the aggregate international debt. As with low income nations, the burden of debt may be sustainable and under apparent control, or so onerous as to produce a range of very damaging economic and social effects.

Over the years, considerable analytical attention has been paid to monitoring the totals of debt and relating these to key economic variables. Comprehensive data is available for individual countries and major regions, giving details of the ratio of debt to GNP; the ratio of debt to export earnings or per capita income; the reliance of each nation on key export commodities; the distribution of earnings, etc. These ongoing studies have been of enormous value in revealing the range of debt-related economic trends, and the direct and indirect impact of debt within developing countries. They have greatly improved our understanding of Third World debt as well as providing an informed basis for policy decisions.

The studies have had another important result. The abundant evidence and consistent trends that have emerged provide clear justification for taking a step back and adopting a critical overview of the true nature of Third World debt. That is to say, a systemic evaluation is warranted and recent studies are increasingly adopting such a global perspective. One of the most noted writers on Third World debt, Susan George, comments;

> If the goals of the managers of the official institutions that rule over Third World debt were to squeeze the debtors dry, to transfer enormous resources from South to North and to wage undeclared war on the poor continents and their people, then their policies have been an unqualified success. If, however their policies were intended – as official institutions always claim – to promote beneficial development to all members of society and to preserve the planet's unique environment and gradually to reduce the debt burden itself, then their failure is colossal.[6]

Her view is representative of the trenchant protest over Third World debt that emerged during the late 1980s and 1990s. It is representative for a number of reasons. It highlights the plight of debtor nations and also raises a serious question mark over the conduct and the intent of lenders. Such a perspective also stands above the stream of country-specific data and evaluates general trends. Most of all, however, Susan George highlights the astonishing degree of contradiction within the issue of debt and development. Throughout, the lending of money to the developing nations has been intended, or at least portrayed, as an act of assistance and generous support by the industrialised nations – yet the outcome has been counterproductive in the extreme. Indeed, the outcome has been sufficiently disastrous to elicit statements such as the following;

> Do not attempt to do us any more good. Your good has done us too much harm already... Please don't lend us any more money. Not even if we plead for another quick fix. ... If [foreign aid] stops, that will be the greatest service they can do us.[7]

Such comments graphically portray the staggering contradiction of development aid. There has been a wild mismatch between the expressed intent and the damaging effect of lending to the Third World. There is a similarly divergent opinion on the status of their debts. For some observers, the debts are deeply unjust, and represent the chains of a pitiful economic servitude. Other commentators stress the obligation of borrowers to repay lenders, and the need for debtor nations to learn the disciplines of modern economics, if for no other reason than their need to avoid such financial catastrophe in the future. Both public sympathy and professional economic opinion are thus deeply divided by the conundrum of debt – divided over the various causes, where to place blame, the motives of key agents and the possible solutions.

The methodology of the following chapters is to analyse Third World debt as a systemic problem, in an effort to discover the fundamental reasons for the contradiction and failure that it constitutes. The conclusion is that Third World debt does indeed amount to a form of international economic slavery. The argument that debtor nations 'ought' to repay their debts is rendered irrelevant when, as the monetary analysis shows, such debts are inherently unrepayable. No-one should be castigated, punished or exploited for not doing what cannot be done.

Summary

Both the established development literature and a study of the modern financial system present the conclusion that a far greater degree of debt remission is justified than that currently being considered. The historical record and monetary analysis emphasise that the very nature of Third World debt lacks validity and legitimacy; that such debts are 'not safe'. These debts are not a product or measure of debtor nation incompetence or corruption, but an expression of the broad failure of the economic institutions involved in the accountancy of world trade and finance. The call for widespread debt cancellation is a call to acknowledge this institutional failure.

Endnotes

1   E. Wayne Nafziger. *The Debt Crisis in Africa*. The Johns Hopkins University Press. 1993.

2   Anthony R. Boote, Kamau Thugge. *Debt Relief for Low Income Countries. The HIPC Initiative*. International Monetary Fund. 1997.

3   Van Dormael. *Bretton Woods – The Birth of an International Monetary System*. Macmillan Press. 1978.

4   Hans Singer and Soumitra Sharma (eds). *Economic Development and World Debt*. Macmillan Press 1989.

5   Lord Lever and Christopher Huhne. *Debt and Danger*. Harmondsworth; Penguin. 1985.

6   Susan George. *The Debt Boomerang*. Pluto Press. 1992.

7   Cheryl Payer. *Lent and Lost*. Zed Books. 1991.

3
The invalidity of Third World debt

The passion to be found in many books on Third World debt is not the result of simple pity for human suffering. There is genuine anger born of a recognition that the developing nations are not the primary cause of their own destitution, that the debt totals carried by developing nations are unjust, and are to some degree invalid. The build-up of debt has been attributed to a wide range of 'external causes' – factors beyond the control of the debtor nations. These included broad issues such as poor terms of trade, damaging loan conditions and political bias on the part of key international institutions.

Unfortunately, in the public/media discussion attending the debt relief initiative, the grounds upon which debt remission is being sought have narrowed considerably. Today, the challenge to debt generally stresses borrowing undertaken by corrupt rulers, and/or the liberal lending policies of the World Bank and IMF at various periods during the 1970s and 1980s. It is worth examining these rather narrower grounds before broadening the enquiry.

Borrowing by corrupt leaders, who then sequestered revenues for personal gain, forms one of the principal grounds upon which Jubilee 2000 is seeking debt relief. It is argued that commercial banks and the international lending agencies should acknowledge that, at times, loans were made to regimes whose corrupt, self-serving policies ought to have excluded them from consideration as legitimate borrowers. Redress is claimed on the grounds that a lender bears a measure of responsibility for the improper use of a loan. It is not the original borrower but an innocent third party – the nation as a whole – that is now suffering the consequences. Debts associated with such earlier political corruption ought not to constitute a punishing legacy, charged against a country's later efforts to progress.

This claim is not founded purely on moral grounds. It invokes the concept of 'odious debt', which is now part of international law. When Cuba was captured by the Americans in 1898, Spain demanded that the US repay Cuba's debts to her. The US refused, arguing that the debt to Spain had been 'imposed upon the people of Cuba without their consent and by force of arms... The creditors, from the beginning, took the chance of the investment.'[1] The affirmation that odious debts are not the responsibility of a people, nor of successor governments, was later recognised by international legislation. It is deeply ironic, given the role discussed below of American cupidity in the causation of Third World debt, that the first nation to invoke, and take advantage of, the concept of odious debt was America.

It has also been argued by many critics that the liberal lending policies of the World Bank and IMF, particularly during the 1980s, constituted a form of entrapment that in some degree invalidates the total debt that many developing nations now carry. This is clearly a strong basis for claiming debt relief, since the wilful actions of the multilateral lenders are directly challenged, their motives questioned, and a measure of co-responsibility invoked. In *Faith and Credit*, Susan George and Fabrizio Sabelli describe the record of the World Bank 'pushing money out the door' under the Presidency of Lawrence Summers.[2] They draw attention to the lack of 'risk assessment' and 'project evaluation' procedures, and also the fact that Bank staff often received promotion on the basis of the size of their loan portfolios.

But although these arguments, emphasising a lender's responsibility, are a perfectly valid basis on which to seek a measure of debt relief, there are far more substantial grounds. These involve the heavily biased charter and remit of the Bretton Woods institutions, the equally biased terms of trade operating during the periods of debt build-up, the punishing demands by the World Bank and IMF that have persistently damaged the interests of borrowing nations, and an evaluation of the actual monetary structure of Third World debt.

Each of these approaches casts a far higher degree of doubt on the status of developing country debt. Taken in combination, they contribute to the conclusion that the developing nations do not actually owe a true 'inter-national' debt. It also becomes clear that endemic and permanent debt is an automatic product of the funding structures underpinning the world economy. The conclusion is that Third World debt lacks economic, political and moral legitimacy.

Circumstantial evidence

There is considerable circumstantial evidence that Third World debt is deeply lacking in legitimacy. Four distinct lines of enquiry all offer a similar conclusion.

1 Borrow/invest/export/repay

The theoretical model accompanying borrowing from the World Bank and the IMF has, almost without exception, proved to be a failure. The model is that a nation wishing to develop will borrow funds and invest these in agricultural or industrial projects, or infrastructure development. Goods and services resulting from this improved economic capacity can then be exported, and the surplus revenues used to repay the capital loan, the country finally ending up in an improved position with a more highly developed economy.

The theoretical model is perfectly rational in neo-classical economic terms, involving (a) capital advances, (b) investment to develop local resources, (c) export revenues leading to (d) capital repayments, and (e) economic progress accruing from value added by the borrowing country.

The fact that no Third World nation has ever succeeded in restoring solvency once funds have been borrowed from the World Bank and IMF strongly argues that the theoretical model constitutes a flawed paradigm. Not only have debtor nations failed to repay the principal – the original sum borrowed – they have often been unable to manage interest payments. So general and complete has been the failure of the borrow/invest/export/repay model that the majority of debtor nations have been obliged to seek additional loans from the World Bank and IMF, not for purposes of further investment, but simply in order to manage interest repayments on former loans. The revenue borrowed thus channels directly back to the World Bank and IMF, whilst the total debt and annual interest payments both increase.

Not only have debtor nations been obliged to borrow simply in order to manage interest payments, most countries have also been obliged to ask for the time-frame of much of their debt burden to be extended, or 'rescheduled' by the 'Paris Club' of creditors. This perpetual distress-borrowing and rescheduling by virtually the entire world community of debtor developing nations is, on its own, sufficient to merit reviewing the status of these debts. It constitutes a dramatic failure of the development model advanced by the World Bank and IMF. It also raises considerable suspicion that the loans that have been advanced to the Third World are inherently un-repayable. As *Time* magazine commented in January 1983; 'Never in history have so many countries owed so much money with so little promise of repayment'.

The suspicion that Third World debt is inherently unrepayable is deepened by the increasing 'conditionality' accompanying loans from the lending institutions. The history of Third World debt has been marked by growing control over the economies of debtor nations by the World Bank and IMF. The legal conditions that have accompanied loans since the start of structural adjustment have amounted to international economists virtually taking control of these nations. Teams of advisors from the Bank and Fund have defined macro- and micro-economic targets, set social and political agendas, and introduced the most stringent programmes of reform encompassing labour regulations, welfare, education, subsidies, government spending, inward investment and financial deregulation.

Throughout the record of failed repayment, the judgement of the World Bank, IMF and international community has been that the inability to manage repayments of interest and principal is a reflection of economic incompetence on the part of developing nations. Rather than re-examine the development paradigm or the financial terms and conditions of the loans, the stated conclusion has been that loans have, in many and various ways, been miss-spent. Thus the fault lies with debtor nations, not with the economic model. As Susan George, a former member of staff at the World Bank, observes;

> The Bank has explained in any number of publications that adjustment poli-
> cies are certifiably correct: the problem lies, rather, with the adjustees who
> haven't applied the proper remedies hard enough or long enough; their
> hearts simply aren't in it... the development model itself is never seen to be
> at fault; failure is attributed rather to the degree of perseverance and compe-
> tence with which the Bank's borrowers apply it.[3]

The first question of doubt that is raised by this judgement concerns the invari-
ability with which such 'economic failure' has occurred. Is it really credible that
all debtor nations should display such sustained and irreversible economic
incompetence? And what of those developing nations that were deemed to be
investing productively? Cheryl Payer comments;

> Brazil, Chile and the Philippines are three countries whose investment
> projects were – at the time they could still borrow – viewed approvingly by
> nearly everyone who knew anything about them.[4]

Why should such countries find themselves ever deeper in debt? This question
is reinforced by the fact that attempts to gain sufficient export revenues have not
been confined to output from the projects funded, but have included raw materials and products from industries that have received no direct loan assistance.
This has gradually extended to the point where a considerable proportion of the
economic effort of certain nations has been directed solely towards revenue gain.
The doubt thus cast is colossal. Not only is there sustained, irreversible growth of
debt in almost all debtor nations, but this in spite of effort extending far beyond
that envisaged in the model. This was supposed to involve repayment through
exports deriving from funded projects – not the entire economy!

The second doubt has regard to the depth of control exercised over debtor
nations by the World Bank and IMF. Despite the input from those who, by their
position, must lay claim to a high degree of economic competence and who
subscribe to the very economic paradigm being proffered, debts have continued
to mount. Leaving aside the fact that, through these binding conditions, the World
Bank and IMF are thereby at least co-responsible for the mounting indebtedness,
the question mark over the validity of the original paradigm is even larger. If the
borrow/invest/export/repay model does not function with teams from the
World Bank and IMF setting the detailed agenda, when does it work?

It is true that there have often been fluctuations in the economic pressure
exerted by debt in different nations. Some nations have, from time to time, experienced a significant improvement in their economies, with an upsurge in
employment and productivity, and social benefits spreading from this. All too
often, however, the recovery has been short-term.

...in virtually all cases, the impact of these (IMF and World Bank) projects has been basically negative... Even the so-called success stories in Ghana and the Ivory Coast have turned out to offer no more than temporary relief which had collapsed by the mid 1980s.[5]

This has been a recurrent theme. The evidence is that such events constitute a pattern in which recovery from debt is a temporary illusion, often connected with deepening debt in other nations or areas. A single nation or region may experience a temporary recovery by attracting loans, and becoming the target of substantial inward investment. Such monetary influxes can transform the status of a nation in a short time. But inward investment into one country is frequently money withdrawn from another national economy, or region. The success within one developing economy is thus built on the back of decline in another country or region.

In addition, as loans become due for repayment, and as profits are repatriated, the former 'growth area' can just as rapidly move into decline. If investment is then suddenly withdrawn, the levels of debt can rapidly become critical again, at the same time as some other nation or region starts to enjoy a recovery. The 1997 Asian financial crisis clearly revealed both the power and the damage caused by this process, confirming what observers of Third World debt had been saying for years about the unpredictability of finance. We even have confessions 'from the horse's mouth', George Soros commenting freely on the 'international exuberance of capital' and the 'herd-instinct' of investors, and their effects.[6]

It is now clear that we cannot look at the localised, temporary alleviation of distress through this style of economic growth as evidence of even a partial recovery from Third World debt. There are two reasons for this conclusion. First, the assumption that the success of an individual country can automatically be translated into success-for-all is a perfect illustration of the 'fallacy of particularity'. The whole basis of such sudden surges in economic progress is that the country concerned attracts an undue share of world investment, succeeding on the basis of monetary withdrawal from other nations, which are forced into decline. This is a process that cannot, by definition, be generalised.

Second, although in some rare cases the gross total of debt may be marginally reduced, the most common scenario is that the earlier debt total remains static. GNP and exports increase, interest payments are managed and this reduces the immediate pressure of debt. However the backlog of debt remains and, during the economic decline that follows the boom, debt again begins its familiar upwards accumulation. Indeed, distress-borrowing may resume on such a scale that the total of debt rises to what it might have been had the 'recovery' not occurred.

The issue of 'selective recovery' of debtor nations is more fully discussed in relation to free trade and monetary flows in later chapters. At this stage it is worth pointing out that the pattern emphasises the importance of considering

international debt from a global perspective. An analysis that embraces the fluctuating fortunes of the entire community of developing nations, recognising the
connection between temporary economic recovery in one nation and decline in
another, and evaluating the overall debt trends – such an analysis affords a more
complete understanding of the intractable character of developing country debt,
than a simple country-by-country approach.

The evidence contained in the table opposite is absolutely irrefutable. The
borrow/invest/export and repay model that developing countries have been
persuaded to adopt, constitutes a total failure. In not one year since 1960 has the
total of Third World debt decreased. On the contrary, it has increased annually
from $68 billion in 1970 to $2,300 billion in 1998. It has also increased steadily
with respect to the aggregate of debtor nation GNP (from 17% of GNP in 1970
to 33% of GNP in 1998),[7] and shows no sign of decreasing or even levelling off.
This has been despite the closest involvement of the best (orthodox) economists
that money can buy, acting on behalf of commercial creditors and multilateral
lenders who have, between them imposed the most stringent conditions.

2 Debt and money

In the recent public debates over Third World debt, the most obvious consideration has been ignored – that there is something blatantly odd about debt in the
modern world. It is not just the Third World nations that are drifting ever deeper
into permanent insolvency. As stated in the previous chapter, the United States
has a national debt that is approaching $6 trillion dollars – nearly three times the
total of international debt shared between over 100 nations! The UK's national
debt stands at more than £400 billion; Germany's exceeds 600 billion
Deutschmarks. All nations carry mounting debts of such magnitude that they are
clearly just as impossible of repayment as Third World debt. On top of these
national debts, unpaid mortgages in the US total $4.8 trillion dollars; commercial
debts top $4 trillion dollars. In the UK, outstanding mortgages have reached £420
billion and commercial debts exceed £300 billion.[9]

The public in wealthy nations might be forgiven for being baffled by the
constant rise in these debt totals. How can the entire world be in debt – if all
nations are in debt, who owes whom? And how can we be so wealthy yet drifting
ever deeper into debt?

The world of orthodox economics ought not to be complacent on this issue.
For whilst there is abundant fiscal theory that seeks to explain these debts, it is
generally acknowledged that this branch of economics has been in a state of theoretical disarray for years. The Keynesian justification for deficit financing has
given way to post-Keynesian; a splintering of varied models that beg many more
questions than they answer in attempting to explain the pace at which the
community of nations is drifting into irredeemable debt. Increased levels of
commercial debt regularly threaten economic stability in all nations at critical

International Debt of Major Third World Borrowers[8] ($ billion)

	1971	1975	1980	1985	1990	1995	1998
Argentina	2.3	4.3	27	51	62	90	133
Brazil	3.3	22.7	71	106	116	159	258
Chile	2.2	3.6	12	20	19	26	32
Colombia	1.3	2.6	7	11	16	21	19
Egypt	1.4	5.0	21	42	33	34	28
India	7.9	12	21	41	83	92	93
Indonesia	3.0	8.7	21	34	67	108	136
Republic of South Korea	2.1	5.7	29	47	35	n/a	154
Malaysia	0.4	1.7	7	21	18	34	40
Mexico	3.6	16.5	57	97	97	166	153
Nigeria	0.5	1.4	9	20	34	35	39
Philippines	0.9	2.6	17	27	30	39	46
Thailand	0.4	1.3	8	17	28	57	90
Turkey	1.8	3.6	19	26	49	74	93
Venezuela	0.9	2.2	29	35	33	36	27
Yugoslavia	1.4	6.0	18	20	17	14	n/a
Zaire	0.3	1.9	5	6	10	13	15

points in the business cycle. The growth of mortgage debt and the extent of 'equity leakage' from a nation's housing stock are trends that baffle property analysts. The variety of explanations as to the causes and consequences of monetary inflation form part of this theoretical morass. The American Shlomo Maital reported a poll of professors of economics at fifty major American universities, two-thirds of whom responded that they believed there was a 'lost sense of moorings in economics'. Maital concluded that the discipline was at a crisis, since 'evidence contrary to the conventional wisdom of economics continues to accumulate'.[10]

It has been claimed that wealthy nation debt 'does not matter' in the same way as does Third World debt. The suggestion is that since the industrialised nations cope with their debt totals, these are irrelevant to the discussion or comparison. Those evicted through failure to meet mortgage demands, those businesses forced into bankruptcy by their debts, and the general public who see their essential public services subject to recurrent cuts by a government paying billions of dollars in annual interest payments on a national debt that increases like a balloon, despite such stringency, would be fully justified in claiming that debt is neither under control nor innocuous in the industrialised nations.

A full examination of the relationship between money and debt, and a discussion of the monetary reasons behind the growth of Third World debt, are left to a later chapter. At this point it is simply worth asking the obvious question. Why are we trying to address Third World debt in isolation? How can we hope to understand Third World debt when the entire world has 'developed into debt', and we do not know why? How can we hope or pretend to offer sound fiscal or developmental guidance to Third World nations on how to cope with their debt problems when our levels of debt are rising according to identical patterns, for reasons we do not fully understand?

There is of course a distinction between the various categories of debt. Mortgages, commercial debts, national and international debts are all distinct classes of debt, with different structures reflecting their differing function. Third World debt is enormously complicated by an international context that involves trade, investment, currency values etc. But an absolute distinction between Third World international debt and other classes of debt should not be insisted on. Just as the willingness or unwillingness of a government to undertake a generous deficit can significantly affect borrowing levels by home-buyers and commerce, so international debt is affected by other categories of debt. This is not least because quotas remitted to the IMF are generally raised by national governments through their deficits. The categories of debt are linked, as is bound to be the case when one considers that they are all denominated in monetary units and sources of repayment can be through a variety of income, taxation and further borrowing sources.

When we consider the gross debts of the wealthy industrialised nations, the most immediately striking fact is that these present a marked contradiction to the true state of wealth of their economies. Indeed, it is noteworthy that the more advanced the economy, the greater the level of debt that is carried.

How, then, can the advanced industrial nations hope to offer economic guidance to the Third World on its debt problems when their own financial accounts are even worse?

Why, when there is a global debt problem, do we treat international debt as if it were an isolated aberration?

The actual structure of Third World debt – which is quite simple – is discussed at a later point. But at this stage it is worth dispelling one of the great myths about Third World debt – that the poor nations 'owe money to', or are 'in debt to', the rich nations. This is categorically not the case. At least 90% of the $2.3 trillion owed by the poorer nations are *owed to commercial banks and lending institutions* – the World Bank, the IMF, and the commercial banks of the world. That is to say, although denominated in foreign currencies, the debts of developing nations are *not*, in the main, 'inter-national'; they are debts that record an obligation on the part of debtor nations to banks – not to other countries.

3 The IMF and World Bank

In the public discussions that have led to the 'current consensus', we are being persuaded that the massive backlog of Third World debt is primarily due to the economic incompetence, or corruption, of their governments.

This is a supposition of the most extraordinary arrogance! Are we saying that the governments of the entire Third World are either corrupt or incompetent? And what short memories we have. If we are going to introduce 'corruption' and 'incompetence' into the argument, we should keep the balance right and remind ourselves of the record of the IMF and World Bank.

As mentioned in the introduction, the debt suffered by developing nations has been the subject of considerable study. Understandably, the main focus of analysis has been on the efforts of debtor nations to manage their ongoing financial crises and the damaging effects of endemic debt on their social and economic development. However a significant proportion – perhaps even the majority – of the studies have been accompanied by a trenchant criticism of the principal lending agencies, the World Bank and the IMF.

Over the last twenty years, these agencies have acquired a track-record of the most munificent incompetence and interference in the developing world. There is a massive body of authoritative literature analysing, protesting and vilifying these powerful global institutions, who have been described as 'The Poverty Brokers'.[11]

The rigour of the studies is beyond question, the findings are consistent and the conclusions are uncompromising. Case by case studies are available, detailing the World Bank's failings and the arrogant impositions of the IMF – a catalogue of their unfair demands and their inappropriate projects. These include schemes that have failed abysmally, poor risk assessment, no market prediction, liberal lending policies – all coupled with loan conditions that have deeply disadvantaged debtor nations, whilst blatantly favoured the trading desires of wealthy nations and their powerful multinational corporations.

Many observers have concluded that the gross failings of these two institutions have been directly responsible for the economic ruination of large numbers of developing nations. A *Daily Telegraph* editorial, 'Blueprint for Survival fails to Save the World Bank', concluded bitterly in 1997, 'Should Mr Wolfensohn agree that 50 years is a quarter of a century too long for the Bank, and pledge to kill it off before the millennium, then $650 million would be a price well worth paying... We could name a dam after him'.

In the *Financial Times*, Jeffrey Sachs of the Harvard Institute for International Development, an international authority on Third World debt, accused the IMF of being a 'power unto itself' – secretive and incompetent, accountable to no-one, and with a record of blatant favouritism to wealthy corporations. Larry Eliot, economics editor of *The Guardian*, laced his attack on these institutions with cutting humour when he commented that the IMF and World Bank 'are to world development what Basil Fawlty is to the world of catering'.

The fact is that over the past thirty years, the Third World has developed under the guidance – and often under the demands – of the IMF and World Bank. They have set the trade agenda in detail, recommended many of the projects, imposed budget targets and forced governments to change rules and regulations in what amounts to a virtual take-over of developing nations. The result has been an economic, financial, social, environmental and cultural disaster – and the debtor nations are left with the legacy of debt.

There is no recourse to, or redress from, the World Bank and IMF. Despite acknowledging the failure of many projects that they have suggested, sponsored and vetted, the World Bank has never accepted 'co-responsibility' in the form of debt remission. As already stated, the IMF's structural adjustment policies have come in for the deepest criticism. But the debts are recorded in the name of Third World nations – so the Third World nations must pay. Never mind the historical facts. And any cancellation of debts is to be termed 'forgiveness'. Graham Bird asks rhetorically;

> Is it reasonable to ask debtor countries to shoulder the burden of adjustment if it may be demonstrated that it was, in substantial part, policies in the industrial countries which caused the debt problems in the first place?[12]

Despite a world wide campaign in 1995, entitled *Fifty Years is Enough*, seeking the closure of the World Bank, and the direct IMF involvement (admitted by the IMF themselves) in fuelling the Asian financial collapse, the public images of both the World Bank and IMF have been resurrected. How this has been achieved

remains a mystery. However, the image recovery has been sufficient for these institutions to place themselves in the forefront of discussions of debt 'forgiveness'
through the HIPC Initiative. This is all the more extraordinary when it is understood that the HIPC programme endorses many of the key structural adjustment
policies of the past fifteen years – the very policies that brought the Bretton Woods
institutions such deserved vilification.

Chapter 4 contains a more detailed survey of the many errors, failings and
damaging policies pursued by the World Bank and IMF, whilst the HIPC initiative is evaluated in Chapter 13. At this point, it is enough to stress that the verdict
of thirty years' exhaustive study and committed protest has been that the World
Bank and the IMF are thoroughly and irrevocably implicated in the indebtedness
of the developing nations. No fair evaluation of the causes of debtor nation
distress, the grounds for cancellation, or any programme for the future recovery
of these nations, can possibly ignore this recorded involvement.

4   Debt – what debt?

The persistent failure, in fiscal terms, of the development model; the unexplained global tendency to debt; the widely recorded culpability of the World
Bank and IMF – these are serious omissions from the current debate over Third
World debt. However, a fourth and even more important consideration is typically
ignored. For the developing nations to be in a position of 'inter-national debt' is
a glaring contradiction of history.

The total developing country international debt of $2.3 trillion implies a mone-
tary imbalance of trade. It suggests that the debtor nations owe $2.3 trillion to
other nations – revenues that they have failed, over the years, to gather by
exporting. In other words the fiscal balance of trade states that the developing
nations owe $2.3 trillion worth of goods to other nations of the world.

But any realistic assessment of the material trade between the developing
nations and the wealthy industrialised nations must conclude that the debtor
nations have exported far more 'of value' than they have ever enjoyed as
imports. For decades, the Third World has been transferring, annually, vast quantities of goods and services to the wealthy nations – primary commodities,
manufactured and semi-manufactured goods, a wide range of raw materials and
minerals. In recent years, land, valuable industries and public assets – in fact
whole sectors of their economies – have been purchased by wealthy corporations
based either in the industrialised nations or internationally.

Far more 'value' has been exported from the debtor nations – and therefore lost
to their economies – than they have ever imported, using the loans they received.
Far more 'value' has been transferred to Western consumers, or corporations based
in the wealthy nations, than Third World nations have ever enjoyed in return. In
other words, the fiscal balance of trade, which denotes the debtor nations as having
enjoyed a net gain, is the opposite of the observable *physical* balance of trade,

which emphasises that the debtor nations have suffered a heavy net material loss. It has often been remarked that, in terms of goods and services, the debtor nations have repaid their debts many times over. Susan George states categorically;

> The debt has already been largely or entirely paid. The North is, in fact, substantially in debt to the South since it has received, since 1982, the cheapest raw materials on record and the equivalent of the value of six Marshall Plans, net, from the indebted countries.[13]

This is a vital consideration, and represents yet *another* economic contradiction of the utmost importance. The nations of the Third World are in financial debt, yet in material terms they stand firmly in credit. There is thus a conflict between the financial accountancy, which emphasises that debtor nations 'owe' something, and the real, physical balance of trade which emphasises the opposite. Having suffered considerable net material loss over the years, debtor nations surely owe nothing additional in physical terms of goods and services to any nations or other economic interests beyond their borders. How can the developing nations be in debt and in credit simultaneously?

The contradiction stems from the fact that the aggregate of debt is indeed an accurate record of a series of financial transactions, but the obligation to repay these debts is not a true statement of a failure to export. The obligation to repay constitutes a demand for revenues that can only be *obtained* by exporting. But that should not be taken to mean that a considerable amount of exporting has not *already* taken place. The crucial issue is price. The contradiction between the fiscal and the material balance of trade highlights the key issue of terms of trade. In short, the price obtained for the large quantities of goods and services that the developing nations have exported over the years has been insufficient to enable them to repay the debts they have incurred. They thus remain in debt, whilst having repaid their debts many times over in real, material terms.

The reasons debtor nations find themselves in this position are discussed at length in Chapter 6, which discusses the free trade ethic. At this point it is worth observing that the widespread judgement that the Third World has suffered years of material loss through trade and development finds little support amongst orthodox economists. Occasionally a writer will highlight the problem. For example, A. P. Thirlwall remarks;

> It could be argued that, instead of focusing on financial flows between countries, analysis ought to be directed to the real counterpart, that is on the exchange of goods and services...[14]

The reason for the scarcity of such comments is that it is one of the sacred dogmas of orthodox economics to accept that 'the market' determines 'price' as an accurate statement of 'value'. This is essentially the nostrum 'the value of something is what you can get for it'. Thus, coffee beans with a value of cents per kilo miraculously become coffee beans with a value of dollars per jar, as ownership switches from a low-income farmer to a high-profit corporate multi-national.

The concept of 'unequal exchange', which accepts that free markets can establish wildly unjust terms of trade and prices, and explains how pricing is heavily influenced by monopolies and wage differentials, has passed out of favour. Unable to admit of a concept of 'real wealth' or 'just value', and with an *a priori* acceptance of market prices, conventional economics offers few insights into the reasons for permanent Third World debt, since this involves a persistent questioning of why 'the market' blatantly fails to give a 'just value' to the 'real wealth' that originates in the debtor nations.

Summary

We now have four separate lines of argument, each of which emphasises that the Third World is not, or ought not to be, in a position of 'inter-national' debt.

1   The persistent and cumulative failure of the theoretical model that encouraged developing nations to 'borrow/invest/export/repay' suggests the nature, terms and context of loans to the Third World have been such as to render these inherently unrepayable.

2   The extensive historical record of detailed involvement by the World Bank and IMF not only confirms the above conclusion, but argues a high degree of co-responsibility on the part of the multilateral institutions.

3   The developing nations do not carry an 'inter-national' debt, but are under a financial obligation to banks and international lending institutions. In addition, the prevalence of escalating totals of monetary debt in all economic sectors, in all nations, irrespective of the level of development achieved by those nations, raises fundamental questions regarding the economic cause, status and meaning of modern debt.

4   The financial accountancy that denotes the developing nations as being 'in debt' to other nations is blatantly incorrect as a statement of the balance of trade. Debtor nations are obliged to act as if they do indeed carry an 'inter-national' debt, seeking export revenues via a continued surplus of exports over imports, in defiance of the fact that their debts do not actually reflect an imbalance of trade.

It is not necessary, however, simply to claim that the Third World 'shouldn't be in debt'. There is a detailed record of events that explains exactly how the process of development has drawn them into this profoundly unjust position. This involves going back in time, first to the Bretton Woods Conference at the end of the Second World War. It is also important to appreciate the conduct of international trade in the years preceding Bretton Woods since this provided many warnings that were determinedly ignored at the conference. Chapter 5 examines the 'years of conditionality' between 1970 and 1990, when international debt first assumed crisis proportions. It was during this period that the World Bank and IMF developed beyond anything envisaged at Bretton Woods and gradually acquired the extensive power and influence they wield today.

Such an historical approach is warranted on three accounts. First, Third World debt is mathematical and cumulative. The mistakes of the past are written into the debt total to this day. Understanding and apportioning responsibility for any past errors and failings is thus highly material. Secondly, the historical record contains many valuable insights into the causes and origins of Third World debt. Finally, and by no means of least importance, the historical record emphasises that Third World debt has been an international and humanitarian scandal for decades.

Endnotes

1   *New Internationalist.* May. 1999.
2   Susan George and Fabrizio Sabelli. *Faith and Credit.* Penguin. 1994
3   Susan George, Fabrizio Sabelli. *Op cit.*
4   Cheryl Payer. *Lent and Lost.* Zed Books. 1991.
5   Bade Onimode (ed). *The IMF, The World Bank and African Debt.* Zed Books. 1989.
6   George Soros. *The Crisis of Global Capitalism.* Little, Brown and Co. 1998.
7   Michael Rowbotham. *The Grip of Death.* Jon Carpenter Publishing. 1997.
8   OECD. *Development Cooperation. 1972 – 1980.* The World Bank. *World Debt Tables.* OECD. Development Cooperation. 1972 – 1980.
9   *Bank of England Statistical Abstracts.* HMSO.1995, 1998.
10 Shlomo Maital. *Minds, Markets and Money.* New York Basic. 1982.
11 Latin American Bureau. *The Poverty Brokers. The IMF and Latin America.* Latin America Bureau. 1983.
12 Quoted in E. Wayne Nafziger. *The Debt Crisis in Africa.* The John Hopkins University Press. 1993.
13 Susan George. *The Debt Boomerang.* Pluto Press. 1992.
14 A. P. Thirlwall. *International Monetary Reform.* Macmillan Studies in Economics. Macmillan. 1976.

4

Warnings from the past

Today's debt crisis did not begin, as some economists unfamiliar with the history of development have suggested, with the OPEC price rise of the 1970s. Still less did it begin when the BBC 'discovered' mass starvation in Ethiopia in 1985.

There is abundant published material on the crisis of development sweeping Latin America and Africa during the 1950s and 1960s, in which debt is no less a prominent feature than today. For example, in 1956 Argentina was unable to make repayments on her outstanding debt of $500 million, which therefore had to be rescheduled, as was Turkey's debt of $440 in 1959. In 1961 Brazil's debt of $300m was rescheduled; in 1962 Argentina's debt was rescheduled for a second time in six years, as was Brazil's debt in 1964, after only three years. Then in 1965 the debts of Argentina, Turkey and Chile all had to be rescheduled. Every year since 1965 has seen more and more nations applying for various forms of debt relief.

Today's debt crisis began when a few dozen powerful men gathered in Bretton Woods, New Hampshire, towards the end of the Second World War. The express purpose was to devise the institutions and ground rules for post-war trade. Not only did they get it wrong, their failure to design a more equitable machinery for international trade and development was absolutely inexcusable in the light of a century of economic instability caused by aggressive trading.

This chapter examines the self-interested power-mongering that took place at Bretton Woods, the partial, arbitrary nature of the eventual agreement and the copious warnings that were ignored. First it is important to outline some of the events in the decades before Bretton Woods, which themselves warned of the danger of unrepayable international debt and the ease with which it can occur.

A familiar pattern

Although it is often perceived as a modern problem, the history of endemic international debt goes back several centuries. From the middle of the eighteenth century, vulnerable nations regularly found themselves under acute financial obligation to other more powerful nations, or financial interests outside their borders.

R. Robinson details the historical link between debt, economic slavery, and civil war, describing a sequence of events that is all but identical to many aspects of modern Third World debt;

> Tunis in the 1860s, Egypt and the Ottoman Empire in the 1870s, the Chinese Empire in the 1890s ... imported European manufactures and capital by mortgaging their revenues and natural resources, but failed to invest them in producing enough exports to pay their debts. As their balance of payments fell into chronic deficit they depended increasingly on foreign loans with political strings, bowed under the sway of European governments and became pawns in European power politics. Impotent to protect their subjects from foreign exploitation, these regimes were now subject to civil disaffections ... The vast Taiping and Boxer revolutions in China, the Arabian revolution in Egypt, the series of abortive coups by old and young Turks at Constantinople ... desperately endeavouring to raise more revenue from landlord and peasant to repay foreign creditors, the old regimes succeeded only in provoking rebellions...[1]

It is both illuminating and sobering to note the parallel with today's debt crisis, in the progression through capital imports, investment, export failure, chronic deficit, civil unrest and finally rebellion.

There was no pretence of international charitable intent during this, the Victorian mercantile era. Although Adam Smith's invisible hand was assumed to ensure a measure of 'trickle down', these loans were not considered as aid in any sense. The motive was two-fold; to obtain a substantial return on the investment and, by creating a longstanding financial obligation, to exercise power and control over distant lands and governments. This was the age of imperialism, and money proved a subtle and powerful agent. Debt could create dependency in lands where overt political control was not possible, and proved a useful tool in attempting to undermine other imperial powers.

In 1934 Thomas Johnston, former Lord Privy Seal in Scotland, wrote about the British foreign loan 'spree' of the eighteenth century.[2] He records the massive bank loans totalling £100 million advanced between 1800 and 1825 alone, to countries as diverse as Prussia, Spain, Naples, the Argentine, Colombia, Guatemala, Denmark and Russia.

Johnston emphasises the political overtones of many of these loans – such as the financing of coups in South America in the early part of the century. As with today's Third World debt, many were 'bonded' loans, involving money raised on European stock exchanges which, when default occurred, left numerous small, private investors with worthless paper. The banking houses involved in these 'hazardous ramps' thus defrayed their losses whilst they mobilised funds in the pursuit of political influence and a 'golden harvest'.

There was frequent defaulting on these debts, which served only to underline the motives behind the continuing loans. Argentine defaulted in 1832, Colombia and Guatemala 'paid nothing for years'; Mexico defaulted on a loan made in 1824; eight states of the US borrowed a combined total of £15 million and 'paid neither principal nor interest'. Similar defaults occurred with loans to Portugal (1832), Colombia (1826), Honduras (1827), Paraguay, Nicaragua, Ecuador, Guatemala and Greece. When Mexico again defaulted on her debts in 1861, Britain, France and Spain invaded the country. This affords an early demonstration of the power of commercial lenders to command government support, and of the link between debt and imperialism.

With the world-wide depression of the 1930s, all Latin American nations except for Argentina defaulted on their repayments of international loans. Most of these debts were to commercial lenders, who were subsequently forced to cancel the debts. During this period, 19 of the 20 Latin American nations also experienced a change of ruler, many by violent overthrow. Third World debt was one of the major international issues of the 1930s and was blamed by many for the spread and severity of the Great Depression, by prompting widespread protectionism.

Parallels have frequently been drawn between the debt crisis of the 1930s and that of the present day, and with good reason. Trade was very aggressive during the inter-war years, and continual trade imbalances had led to 'creditor' and 'debtor' countries. Freely fluctuating exchange rates had been experimented with, but currency levels had failed to find equilibrium in a climate of speculative international finance. Wage and price cutting had been attempted in an effort to stimulate exports, but this had only prompted similar actions by competitor countries. Liberal loan and credit arrangements had sustained the combination of debt and trade imbalance, but these had only succeeded in deepening the fiscal problems of debtor nations.

This, then, was the background to the Bretton Woods Conference. In his opening address, the Brazilian delegate referred to the chaos of pre-war trade.

> There are still in the memory of us all the drama of monetary chaos, of restrictions of all sorts of international trade, of blocked currencies, of economic isolationism, of competition instead of co-operation among central banks, and of general unemployment. The civilised world must not permit a repetition of this tragic situation.[3]

Bretton Woods

The 1944 Bretton Woods Conference gave rise to the two institutions that have dominated Third World development over the last 50 years. The World Bank was intended to aid post-war reconstruction, especially in poorer countries, by providing them with loans for development. The International Monetary Fund came into existence a year later, in 1945. Its purpose was to provide an international reserve of money – a financial pool – upon which all member countries could call, whether rich or poor, should they hit temporary payment difficulties due to a deficit in their trade account.

Many works on Third World debt rightly criticise the constitution and remit of the World Bank and IMF. Unfortunately, most fail to record that these institutions were subject to scathing criticism at the time of their constitution. At the conference itself, during the months building up to it and for many years after, there were profound disagreements over the financial architecture established at Bretton Woods. Some of the disputes were over relatively minor matters such as the size of each country's monetary quotas, ranking, voting rights and where the offices of the IMF and World Bank were to be situated. The deeper disagreements involved the actual structure of the new institutions, their purpose and powers, the future framework of monetary exchanges and lending – indeed the entire nature of international trade.

The most serious dispute and, with respect to Third World debt, by far the most salient, concerned the key issue of the balance of trade between nations. As discussed above, sustained trade imbalances leading to 'creditor' and 'debtor' countries had been recognised as a major cause of the inter-war trading/financial chaos. The issue of the balance of trade was highlighted by the contrast between the two main schemes under consideration at the conference.

In the months leading up to the conference, the two major world powers, America and Britain, each tabled proposals suggesting a framework for international trade. These proposals were fundamentally different in character. They were based upon different priorities and with totally opposing views of the purpose of international trade and how this purpose might best be fostered. The British prepared a proposal, largely the work of John Maynard Keynes, for a system of trade accountancy which Keynes called 'The International Clearing Union'. The American plan, drawn up by a number of US Treasury officials including Secretary Henry J. Morgenthau and championed by Harry Dexter White, was for an 'International Stabilisation Fund'. The American proposal, and the economic priorities that underpinned it, are reflected in the two institutions we have today – the World Bank and IMF. In short, the American delegation won the day.

A comparison of the two systems of accountancy for international trade and the reasons for rejecting Keynes' 'Currency', or 'Clearing Union', offers a startling insight into Third World debt.

Throughout the following discussion it should be borne in mine that Third World debt constitutes a financial imbalance of trade. The lending of money to a developing nation allows that nation to buy in foreign goods. That nation thereby sustains a trade deficit. The nation's subsequent efforts to export surplus goods are simply an attempt to redress this imbalance of trade. But this requires the other nation(s) that enjoyed an earlier trade surplus, by exporting development technology, to then sustain a trade deficit and accept debtor nation goods. The settlement of Third World debt thus involves the redress of trade imbalances. Today's international debt is therefore a measure of the extent that debtor nations have failed to gain money by exporting, and creditor nations failed to accept a trade deficit having initially enjoyed a trade surplus. The determination with which the American delegation at Bretton Woods refused to accept the Keynesian mechanism designed to foster trade balances – in fact refused even to accept the principle of redressing trade imbalances – is detailed below.

Keynes and the Clearing Union

Keynes was highly regarded on both sides of the Atlantic. His reflationary policies were generally credited with ending the depression, particularly in America, where they formed the theoretical basis of 'The New Deal'. Keynes had written many times on international trade. However, two years before the Bretton Woods Conference was even mooted, he had begun seriously considering a new system of trade accountancy and new international institutions, aware that trade would be a key post-war issue. In a comment that harked back to the currency speculation of the 1930s, and which is remarkably prescient of today's global market where destabilising, speculative monetary exchanges outweigh trading in goods and services by 20 to 1, Keynes stated;

> Let no-one suppose, however, that we for our part intend to return to the chaos of the old world. To do so would be to bankrupt us no less than the others … We intend to develop a system of international exchange in which the trading of goods and services will be the central feature. Financial and capital transactions will play their proper auxiliary role of facilitating trade.[3]

Fundamental to Keynes' thinking was the importance of fostering a balance of trade between nations and avoiding the scenario in which some nations become 'creditors' and others 'debtors' through their trade accounts. Creditor nations were those who had exported more than they imported and thereby ended up with surplus revenues from an imbalance of trade. Debtor nations were those whose imports had exceeded their exports, and so suffered a monetary loss through trading – a trade deficit.

Keynes was aware of the destabilising macro-economic effects of such imbalances of trade. Debtor nations found their domestic industry and agriculture seriously depressed, not only by the loss of home markets, but also by the drain of money abroad. These combined to produce a tendency towards recession and low investment. Meanwhile, creditor nations experienced both a boost in demand and a monetary influx. The growth and investment this promoted made them seek export markets with even greater vigour.

This meant that imbalances in trade tended to become self-perpetuating and compounding in effect. Debtor nations, who needed to export more to redress the imbalance of trade, were thrust into recession. Their output, competitiveness and exports tended to decline. Meanwhile, creditor nations – already exporting more than they imported – were stimulated towards growth and investment, producing a surplus that required even more exporting and foreign markets.

The trouble at root, Keynes observed, was that creditor nations, having gained surplus revenues from an excess of exports over imports, simply failed to spend this money back in debtor nation economies. This is an inherently difficult problem to address since trade is not actually conducted between nations, but between commerce and consumers in different nations. The status of 'debtor' or 'creditor' nation is thus the result of the aggregate of commercial activity over which a government has no direct control. Also, the surplus revenue held by a creditor nation is not held by that government, but accrues to (mostly private) commerce. Thus, private commerce and consumption had within its power the ability to upset the balance of international trade, creating major economic disturbances between national economies.

Keynes argued that it was fundamental to a constructive framework of international trade that there be a mechanism to ensure a balance of trade between nations – or more accurately, to ensure that imbalances were redressed. The tendency of trade imbalances to become permanent and compounding had to be countered. In his proposals, Keynes also acknowledged another consideration that is almost ignored today. The notion of a favourable balance of trade – i.e. a trade surplus – actually disguises a completely irrational situation.

A nation that exports more than it imports is actually losing out in material terms. A creditor nation is acting as a net supplier of wealth to other nations, working to supply other nations (those with a trade deficit) with its excess goods and services. All that the creditor nation gains is money, an essentially worthless human artefact that is only of use when it is spent. One of the most articulate opponents of the Bretton Woods agreement, Sir Edward Holloway, criticised the term 'favourable balance of trade', and also drew attention to the danger of debt resulting from an aggressive trade policy;

> Now the only sound reason for a nation to export is to enable it to pay for necessary imports. The idea that a favourable balance of trade consists of exporting more than you import is obviously wrong, when you consider the situation in terms of real wealth, i.e. goods and services… [Before the war] nations strove for a so-called favourable balance and got those countries with the unfavourable balance into unpayable debt.[4]

Keynes viewed the aggression with which trade had been pursued in the pre-war years, the actions of commercial creditors in holding surplus revenues, the drift of the world economy into 'rentier' divisions, with creditor nations able to hold increasing sway over debtor economies, as a scenario wholly to be avoided. It had lead to governments promoting subsidy, tariff and quota regimes in which trade was becoming a form of economic warfare. There were also panic changes in currency valuations, which were not only destabilising, but compounded the status of debtor nations by devaluing goods and services whilst earning less in export revenues. Such a trading climate resulted finally in the protectionism of the Depression, in which all nations, their commerce and citizens were the clear losers. Keynes pointed out that such protectionism was understandable, given such aggressive, non-mutual trading;

> Laissez-faire had broken down before the war and had been a source of all those clumsy hindrances to trade which suffering communities had devised in their perplexity as being better than nothing in protecting them from the intolerable burdens flowing from currency disorders.[3]

Keynes 'Clearing Union' was an attempt to construct a machinery that took account of all the potential disturbances and difficulties of international trade. Acknowledging the need for a system of multilateral trade rather than bilateral nation-by-nation accountancy, the Clearing Union sought to foster trade balances by a range of fiscal mechanisms.

Keynes proposed a new, neutral unit of international currency – the 'Bancor' – and a new institution – the International Clearing or Currency Union (I.C.U.). All international trade would be measured in Bancors. Exporting would accrue Bancors, importing would expend Bancors. Nations were expected to maintain, within a small percentage, a zero account with the I.C.U. This would indicate that they had an overall equivalence of imports and exports. Each nation's Bancor account would also be related to its currency through a fixed, but adjustable, exchange rate.

The key feature of Keynes proposal was that it placed an equal obligation on creditor and debtor nations to maintain a balance of trade. In the words of Geoffrey Crowther, former editor of *The Economist*, 'debtor and creditor should be treated almost alike as disturbers of equilibrium'.[5]

Nations that imported more than they exported – debtor nations – would pay a small interest charge to the Clearing Union on their overdrawn account. This would encourage those nations to promote exports by a range of domestic policies as well as marginal currency devaluation. Equally, nations that ran an aggressive trade policy and exported more than they imported would also be charged by the Clearing Union for their surplus account. This would encourage those nations to find ways to spend their excess Bancors back in debtor nations – or gradually lose that surplus.

The efforts of debtor nations to promote exports was intended to coincide with the efforts of creditor nations to expend their otherwise worthless Bancor surplus. These charges were intended not so much as a deterrent or punishment, but as a benign 'feedback' mechanism, ensuring that, over time, trade remained in balance.

The basic concept underlying the Clearing Union was simple: to apply between countries the essential principle of banking as it existed within each country. 'This principle is the necessary equality of credits and debits, of assets and liabilities'... Member (countries) would have to pay a charge on their balances existing with the Union, *whether credit or debit*, and these charges would be progressively higher. Members would thus attempt to keep their balances as close to equilibrium as possible, using adjustments to the value of the currency.[3]

Keynes' proposal, although simple in essence, was the result of years of reflection on the difficulties of international trade accountancy, in acknowledgement of the tendency of unregulated trade toward conflict and imbalance, and full awareness of the potential of this to impact negatively on national economies, since these are very sensitive to monetary disturbances. The Clearing Union and its charge structure was thus set up to allow trade to be completely free and open, but to ensure that the aggregate of each nation's commercial activity was such as to promote a fiscal balance of trade.

Keynes took advice from a number of eminent British economists; Professor Lionel Robbins, Professor Dennis Robertson, James Mead, Roy Harrod and Sir Hubert Henderson. Lord Cato and Sir David Whaley also submitted comments, as did numerous Treasury officials. The Clearing Union was then refined for presentation to the United States. Lord Robbins later commented;

> ...it would be difficult to exaggerate the electrifying effect on thought throughout the whole relevant apparatus of government of the production of this document... Nothing so imaginative and so ambitious had ever before been discussed as a possibility of responsible government policy...[3]

Keynes' Clearing Union also carried, at its heart, a profoundly democratic ideal. Not only should the advantage of powerful commercial interest not be allowed to distort the balance of trade, but the citizens of a successful commercial nation should not see the results of their efforts constantly exported and removed from them. On a national scale, whilst a relatively few wealthy people involved at the commercial level might profit from accumulating and investing foreign revenues, the great majority of citizens in a creditor nation are effectively working to become net suppliers of wealth abroad. The pressure on nations with a creditor account to accept imports equivalent to their surplus exports was thus a pressure to allow the citizens of that nation to enjoy what they had worked for.

The benefit to the citizens of nations with a temporary trade deficit was equally apparent. With trade conducted in a neutral unit of international account – the Bancor – there is no monetary loss or disturbance to the domestic economy or pricing, or lack of demand affecting the 'clearance of domestic markets'. Instead of a being pushed towards a slump, the economy would be stimulated to greater production and exporting to redress the balance of trade.

The American position

The American team of economists, with Harry Dexter White as spokesman, did not have the same broad over-view of trade as did Keynes. This was born of a clear conflict of interest. America was a creditor nation, exporting more than she imported, with all this implies from the discussion above. The interest of the American economy was perceived in terms of her continued trading success. The notion that America might be under an obligation to expend her surplus trade revenues back into other economies was deemed completely unacceptable. Indeed, the main concern of the American delegation was to ensure a continuing 'favourable balance of trade' for the USA.

When the US team started negotiations in the months before Bretton Woods, her politicians had one over-riding pre-occupation – the likely effect of the end of the war on the American economy.

The Americans deeply feared that peace would precipitate another major recession. The US economy had grown rapidly during the days of the New Deal and production had then soared with the war effort. With the end of the war, not only would export levels have to be maintained, but output would have to increase. As the military effort was scaled down and her troops returned, the American delegation saw expanding trade as the only alternative to an economic crisis. Old markets would have to be kept and new markets would have to be found.

One of the US delegates, Harry Hawkins, Chief of the Division of Commercial Treaties and Agreements, commented;

> Given the largely expanded productive capacity of the United States during the War, and the fact that at some stage in the immediate post-war period we are likely to find ourselves in another acute depression... it might easily happen that British policy, under the influence of Mr Keynes and others, will be permitted to drift in a direction wholly opposed to ours unless we take pains to make our position clear on every suitable occasion.[3]

In short, America was faced with the problem that all modern economies have so far been unable to address – the problem of their own success, or how to mature into a productive but stable economy. Keynes' forward-looking framework and his philosophy of benign, mutual trading was totally alien and unacceptable to the American delegation.

It might not seem that unusual for a nation to perceive a problem in the light of its own immediate interests. But what is extraordinary is the extent to which the American national interest was pursued and finally secured at Bretton Woods, through their proposals for an International Stabilisation Fund.

Trouble at the conference

The argument at the Bretton Woods conference was intense. Van Dormael both presents the background and chronicles the discussions in fascinating detail.[3] Paraphrasing Keynes, Van Dormael remarks;

As a creditor nation with a large export surplus, refusing to take full payment in goods and accumulating gold the United States 'had made any general international system unworkable… the only hope of the future is to maintain economies in balance without great excesses of either exports or imports'.

Ironically, Harry Hawkins from the US delegation at one time reluctantly conceded this point;

It may also be true that, in the longer run, unless we can bring our import policy into line with our creditor position, no system for the multilateral settling of international accounts can be worked out.[3]

However, the official proposal carried to Bretton Woods by Harry Dexter White was for international trade to be conducted as a completely free market. Trading was to be conducted and accounted, as before, in national currencies. Nations were to be placed under no obligation to expend a trade surplus back into debtor nation economies. In this extract, Van Dormael includes a series of telling quotes by Dexter White, which demonstrate the isolated position adopted by the US;

The other countries had suggested that pressure should be put on creditor countries, and by that they meant mainly the United States… so they wanted these creditor countries to adopt a policy which would put less pressure on the exchange of the debtor countries and 'enable them to sell more goods here'. 'We have been perfectly adamant on that point. We have taken the position of absolutely "No" on that'. The debtor countries, on the other hand, would have to pay deterrent charges. And the more they borrowed from the Fund, the higher the charges would be, so that they would be under pressure to put their balance of payments in order.[3]

The fact that debtor nations were, by definition, already failing to achieve sufficient exports, and that the 'deterrent charges' might compound this difficulty, was brushed aside by Dexter White;

To the objection of one delegate that deterrent charges might accelerate the indebtedness of a country, instead of reducing it, White answered that these charges were low, but that it was necessary to create an inducement for the country to restore equilibrium.[3]

Despite the clear unease felt by other national delegates at the American proposal, the US delegation held both a decisive number of votes and great political influence. Keynes' Clearing Union had been rejected shortly before the conference, although Van Dormael's assessment of the proposal was that 'the aims were much broader and more comprehensive than those finally embodied in the Bretton Woods agreements'. With the Clearing Union abandoned, the US proposal was given full consideration at the conference, which Keynes agreed to chair in the hope of being able to improve the American scheme.

The Americans proposed that a 'Stabilisation Fund' be set up. All nations would contribute to this according to the size and strength of their economies. The fund would thus hold reserves of all national currencies. Any nation that found, as a result of a continuing trade deficit, that its domestic economy was suffering, could borrow from the fund. Thus the IMF was born, as a pool of funds intended to tide debtor nations over temporary difficulties in their trading account.

A second institution would also be set up – an international 'bank' with the purpose of lending money of the required denominations to underdeveloped nations, or those needing to borrow to rebuild their shattered economies after the war. Thus was born the International Bank for Reconstruction and Development – the World Bank.

Under the American plan, creditor nations would be allowed to accrue surplus trading revenues and, if they wished, exchange these for gold held by debtor nations. Dexter White claimed that by selecting gold as the unit by which surplus currencies could be exchanged, this established the accountancy of world trade in terms of a neutral currency;

> ... There are deemed to be some national prestige values and possibly slight economic gains in trade and financial transactions that accrue to a country having a currency that is widely used as an international unit of account. For that reason a unit belonging to no country would be more welcome to most countries than the unit of any selected country.[3]

Officially then, gold was to be the international currency. However America had been actively stockpiling gold since the depression and at this point held at least 70% of the world's entire total gold reserves. Also, the Americans insisted that gold was to be valued in dollars and all other currencies to be fixed in value against the dollar. Therefore, by choosing gold, *the dollar was effectively made the international unit of account*, a position greatly confirmed when gold convertibility was unilaterally ended by the United States in 1973.

There was a major dispute over the siting of the headquarters of the IMF and World Bank. Despite pressure from other nations, both institutions were established in Washington, where they have been accessible to extensive American political and commercial influence, as the following chapters detail.

At the final discussions at Bretton Woods, when discussing capital movements, which the United States saw as the basis of future lending to trade-debtor nations, Keynes again stressed that in the long run there had to be for every country a balance between exports and imports. If the United States went on exporting more than it imported, there was no remedy. 'The fund can't solve continuing problems of this sort'. If he wished to criticise the Fund he could make 'quite a good job of it'.[3]

Ongoing warnings and dissent

Returning to England after the conference, Keynes had to 'sell' the American agreement to parliament, or acknowledge that all his efforts had come to nothing. In an extraordinary series of letters, Keynes was questioned by a number of commentators in *The Times* letters column. Keynes' reply to one letter deeply critical of the Bretton Woods proposals was quoted in Chapter 2. In this, Keynes acknowledged that the agreement could indeed turn out to be 'destructive of international trade'.

In Britain there was a great deal of informed dissent from the Bretton Woods agreement. But parliament had been informed that a condition of the latest US war loan to Britain was acceptance of the conference proposal, and this was duly carried. The dissent, however, continued. In 1947, in a BBC radio broadcast entitled *We Beg to Differ*, Edward Holloway predicted unpayable debt as the consequence of the Bretton Woods agreement;

> ... There is no point in the continuation of a system which automatically leads to unpayable indebtedness between nations. The choice to be made in this matter of international financial machinery is crucial. It is a choice between peace and prosperity on the one hand, and on the other, bitter trade war between nations ... the international monetary fund does nothing to bring pressure to bear on nations to balance their accounts with the world in terms of goods and services... In our memorandum we pointed out our reasons for believing that the Bretton Woods Agreement would not work – and we particularly stressed the obligation of creditor nations enabling debtor nations to discharge their indebtedness by accepting a surplus of imports over exports. ... the Bretton Woods agreement ignores this obligation – and actually strengthens the position of creditor nations whilst imposing penalties on debtor nations... These proposals, we argued, would inevitably lead to a desperate competition for world markets ... default ... was certain to be the unfortunate fate of one or more of the nations concerned.[4]

The following comment by Geoffrey Crowther, written in 1948, carries a frightening final remark. Crowther was, after Keynes, perhaps the foremost economist in the UK between 1935 and 1950, one-time editor of *The Economist*, and author of *A History of Money*.

The two governing principles of the Keynes Plan were thus that the problem of settling outstanding balances should be solved by 'creating' additional 'international money', and that 'debtor' and 'creditor' should be treated almost alike as disturbers of equilibrium. It was these two principles that failed to find favour in the United States... It is the belief of the present author that Lord Keynes was right, and that the world will bitterly regret the fact that his arguments were rejected.[5]

Not even the American delegation were in agreement with the structure set up at the conference. Wilbert Ward, Vice-President of the National City Bank of New Orleans, remarked; 'If you are going to set up a bank you should set up an organisation to finance transactions that will in the end liquidate themselves. Otherwise it is not a bank... Where can we loan thirty to fifty billion around the world with any prospect of its being repaid?'

The Guaranty Survey in August 1945 commented that the IMF constituted 'an attempt to enforce exchange stability without striking at the causes of instability' and the prediction was made that if the project were established and then failed 'it could easily throw international currency relationships into chaos from which the entire world might suffer for years to come'.[6]

During the post-war years, continuing doubts were expressed on the activities of the Bank and Fund, and their tendency to generate debt that was unrepayable. The following statement by the United Nations Sub-Commission on Economic Development contains the strongest possible warning from an impartial and authoritative international body surveying the activity and role of the World Bank;

> The Sub-Commission is of the opinion that the terms on which finance would be available under the policy established by the Bank limit the effectiveness of this finance for underdeveloped countries. There are fields and types of investment required for economic development which can neither satisfy the preconditions required by the Bank nor carry the interest charges involved nor be liquidated within the period required.[7]

Summary

It is staggering to reflect that the world was warned of the dangers of Third World debt over half a century ago, and that these warnings were ignored. What is also so astonishing is the degree to which American interests were favoured, and their determined refusal to accept the lessons of the pre-war experience. During those years, Van Dormael points out that all the alternative 'false approaches' to the solution had been explored, including;

1   the idea that a freely fluctuating exchange would discover for itself a position of equilibrium.

2   liberal credit and loan arrangements between the debtor and the creditor countries flowing from the mere fact of an unbalanced (trade) creditor position, on the false analogy of superficially similar nineteenth-century transactions between old established and newly developing countries where the loans were self-liquidating because they themselves created new sources of payment.

3   The use of deflation, and still worse, competitive deflations, to force an adjustment of wage and price levels which would force or attract trade into new channels.[3]

These alternative false approaches have also been features of the recent decades during which the Third World has developed into debt.

The balance of trade and Third World debt

Institutions designed to redress trade imbalances, which would have supported the Third World in its efforts to escape from debt, were deliberately omitted at Bretton Woods. Instead, free trade was given the highest priority. Both the IMF and World Bank had, written into their charter, the requirement that they promote the free trade of goods and services throughout the world and, through their activities, endeavour to remove all restrictions to trade. Countries were placed under no obligation to maintain a balance of trade with other nations, but were permitted to seek a persistent trade surplus. The balance of international trade was left to 'free market commercial forces'.

By refusing to institute a mechanism designed to foster trade imbalances, allowing nations to seek a perpetual trade surplus, and giving the World Bank/IMF the task of promoting a free trade ethic, two destinies were sealed by the American delegation. First, America's economic supremacy would be permanently compounded. Second, the fate of the Third World was determined before a single loan was issued. This becomes even clearer in the later Chapter 5.

It is a source of great annoyance to students of Keynes that his name has become almost synonymous with the Bretton Woods agreement. In fact, Keynes' tried to ensure that the crudity of the American proposal was to some degree ameliorated, after his own infinitely superior scheme had been thrown out. Hans Singer and Soumitra Sharma conclude;

It is obvious from past experience that the institutions created at Bretton Woods have fallen short of the intentions of their architect [sic], J. M. Keynes, once more, repeating the experience after a span of 30 years... The debt situation as it stands now, and the way these institutions have handled it, has seriously endangered international economic stability – for which he relentlessly strove and argued.[8]

After all these years, it is immaterial to wonder whether Keynes' Clearing

Union would have worked, what its flaws were, or how it might have been improved. But one is certainly entitled to doubt whether it could have been any greater a failure than the combination of the World Bank, IMF and other free market conventions, such as floating exchange rates.

One is also entitled to point out that there was far more for the American people in the Keynesian proposals – but the American people were not at the conference. It was US politicians and powerful commercial interests who insisted upon institutions and a trading framework that have persistently secured their commercial and political advantage, and which have been open to their ongoing influence. One is also entitled to note that the American delegation won the day by virtue of debt, by making its war- loan conditional on acceptance by the British parliament of the Bretton Woods agreement.

However, leaving aside such afterthoughts, it is actually of far more importance to appreciate that the Keynesian proposal was predicated on an entirely different philosophy of trade. This is the concept of trade for mutual benefit. However it is applied in terms of institutions, this is a trading philosophy that the world clearly needs, and with even greater urgency today.

Endnotes

1   R. Robinson. *Developing The Third World. The Experience of the 1960s.* Cambridge University Press. 1971.
2   Thomas Johnston. *The Financiers and the Nation.* Methuen. 1934.
3   Armand Van Dormael. *Bretton Woods – The Birth of an International Monetary System.* Macmillan Press. 1978.
4   Edward Holloway. *Money Matters.* The Sherwood Press. 1986.
5   G. Crowther. *An Outline of Money.* Thomas Nelson and Sons Ltd. 1950.
6   *The Guaranty Survey.* 29 Aug 1945.
7   United Nations Sub-Committee on Economic Development Doc E/ CN.1/65.
8   Hans Singer and Soumitra Sharma. *Economic Development and World Debt.* Macmillan Press. 1989.

5

The years of conditionality

Rarely can two institutions have come in for extended criticism of the type that has been levelled at the World Bank and International Monetary Fund, and yet survived. This chapter records the failings of both institutions since Bretton Woods. There are two reasons for doing this. First, many echoes of the dispute at the conference over the proper framework for trade are echoed in the repeated criticism of the Bank and Fund. Secondly, the track record of the Bank and Fund are very relevant to the debate over debt, since their failings are written into the accumulating debt burden of the developing nations.

A number of earlier errors, major and minor, have been openly or tacitly admitted in Bank or Fund pronouncements. But whilst they may have 'reviewed their priorities', and certain failings have been 'acknowledged', this has not amounted to any assumption of co-responsibility for the current aggregate of Third World debt. Until such an acceptance is forthcoming, with a corresponding writing-down of debts, the record of World Bank/IMF mismanagement remains deeply relevant. In effect, the Bank and the Fund have an 'unpaid debt' to those developing nations that have suffered under their maladministration. The historical record is also important since it enables us to evaluate current Bank/IMF policy against their past policy, and against their track record of success or failure.

Such has been the range and scale of their documented failure, and so ruthless have their policy demands often been, that it is sometimes easy to forget that both the Bank and Fund harbour a generally benign intent, certainly so far as the two institutions' employees are concerned. As Susan George and Fabrizio Sabelli emphasise in their excellent study, *Faith and Credit*, World Bank staff undergo rigorous training, are strongly motivated and are deeply committed to the purpose of aiding the development of poorer nations. Unfortunately, this exacting training and level of commitment have actually proved to be part of the problem. Both institutions adhere to a narrow perspective of economics; non-conformity is 'trained out' of incoming staff, and the Bank/Fund view of 'sound economics' is firmly instilled. The desire to 'do good' translates into an almost religious zeal for the current set of priorities, whatever these might be. Meanwhile, the sense of conviction leads to a perpetual blind spot when it comes to considering weaknesses, alternative economic programmes and priorities, or accepting that certain fundamental errors continue.

Both the World Bank and, to a lesser extent, the IMF claim to have modified their policies in recent years. There has indeed been a verbal shift to advocating 'poverty alleviation', 'sustainable development' and 'environmental protection'. But whilst they may have reviewed some of their proclaimed development goals, they have not succeeded in reviewing their basic economic assumptions, which are still grounded upon neo-classical orthodoxy. The importation of financial capital, the pursuit of export revenues for debt service, internal 'adjustment' via demand management, an unquestioning acceptance of free trade – all these are still unchallenged dogmas in the catechism of Bank/Fund 'sound economics'.

It might seem cavalier to package two distinct institutions and criticise them simultaneously. But this approach is justified on at least two counts.

First, there is a high level of cooperation and integration at the policy level, which includes a combined approach in their dealings within debtor nations.

...While an IMF team looks into the balance of payments and exchange problems of a debtor country, a World Bank team discusses export promotion, industrial policies and appropriate tariff structure... In this way, cross-conditionality is imposed by the Fund and the Bank on the same country.[1]

The Bank will often only advance its development loans provided that an IMF-endorsed adjustment policy is in place and 'on track'. Meanwhile, returning the compliment, the Fund may only release its bail-out funds if World Bank criteria, as well as its own, are being embraced.

The second reason for coupling the two institutions is that it is the intention of this book to consider the broad issues involved in the debt crisis. It is true that the roles of the two institutions have changed and their importance fluctuated over the years. But the respects in which the Bank or Fund have been 'more' or 'less' to blame for specific failings are already well documented. The aim here is to evaluate their combined impact over the years. The Bank and the Fund are indeed 'twin-pack institutions', exchanging information and expertise, publishing a joint monthly magazine, sharing virtually the same address as well as giving each other powerful, mutual support for the neoclassical free market ideology they both embrace.

It might also appear questionable to direct such attention to the World Bank and IMF when the bulk of foreign debt owed by the developing nations is commercial. Only about 30% of the current total of Third World debt represents money loaned by the Bank and Fund, a proportion that has varied over the years. However the influence of these two official lenders has always been seen as far exceeding their monetary input. For several related reasons substantial commercial loans are rarely made to a developing nation that is not also being supported by the Bank and/or the Fund.

First, support is viewed by the commercial world as a seal of approval, the benchmark of 'sound economics'. Commercial finance therefore tends to follow, and be dependant upon, acceptance of Bank/Fund economic programmes. Second, one of the main Bank/Fund ideologies has always been the desirability of promoting the inflow of commercial lending and investment. Bank/Fund loan conditions are therefore deliberately tailored to attracting such foreign revenues, and lending implies that the borrowing country is undertaking those policy 'adjustments' that are conducive to foreign capital. Third, in recent years, loans to developing nations have been increasingly arranged as 'packages' involving the Bank and Fund in direct conjunction with commercial lenders. Therefore, as numerous critics have pointed out, the importance of the World Bank and IMF far exceeds their nominal monetary input, and can be said to influence the bulk of debtor nation borrowing.

Surveying the literature

It is important to do justice to the work of those who have analysed the activities of the World Bank and IMF and their involvement in the development/debt crisis. Criticism has flowed from professional and academic quarters; from recognised experts and from unrecognised (but often very astute) protest groups and lay critics. Politicians, eminent economists, development studies academics, observers with specialist knowledge of specific countries, food scientists, agriculturalists, environmentalists, even businessmen – representatives from all these have echoed the protest of similar groups in the affected developing nations. Between them, they have over the last four decades generated a library of books and papers so extensive that it is impossible to assimilate in its entirety. Criticism of the Bank and the Fund, and the development model and economic priorities they have adopted, include countless country-by-country studies, regional surveys, historical, trade and statistical evaluations, mathematical models, theoretical analyses and programmes for change.

The following section surveys the catalogue of policy failures that have, over the years, been most consistently nailed to the doors of the World Bank and IMF. As with all categorisation, there is a degree of overlap, not least in the fact that the principal effect has been to foster economic disorganisation and engender poverty.

Key issues

Export led growth

There can be few critics who have not drawn critical attention to the export-led growth model that has underpinned Bank/Fund thinking since the late 1950s. The direct, easy manner with which a loan is made contrasts markedly with the obligation to repay that loan by obtaining a surplus of exports over imports. To repay loans through a surplus of exports over imports involves a struggle in the competitive global market, where the difficulty of maintaining a trade balance, let alone achieving a trade surplus, is legendary. Loans also have to be repaid in scarce foreign currency.

Objections to the export-led growth model have been both empirical and theoretical. At the empirical level, there is the simple observation that debtor nations have blatantly failed, in aggregate, to achieve the level of trade surpluses required for loan repayment. A minority of individual nations have, over short periods, managed to reduce marginally their debt totals by successful exporting, but have not managed to sustain this.

For example, between 1946 and 1985 Latin American countries overall had an annual average GDP increase of 4.6%, but despite a rate of growth that constantly outpaced that of the richer nations, and 40 years during which an ever-increasing proportion of their economies were devoted to earning export revenues and repaying their creditors, these nations became ever more deeply indebted. Brazil increased its GDP four-fold between 1960 and 1980, but despite this effort, in 1960 30% of Brazil's export revenues went on debt repayments and by 1980 this had risen to 78%. Many developing nations have found that their entire export revenues have been insufficient to repay the interest on their debts. By 1990, Brazil had reached this position. The country exported $31.4 billion worth of goods and imported $22.5 billion worth, but her debt repayments were so massive that they took all her gain from exports, and still left her showing a huge loss.

At the theoretical level, the export-led growth model has been faulted on many counts. It has been pointed out that not only were the majority of developing nations (due to their indebtedness) placed in a position of needing a trade surplus, but that the wealthy industrialised nations also strive to secure trade surpluses where possible.

This raises one of the most fundamental issues of the debt crisis, a fact known by all students of basic economics, yet seemingly ignored by the Bank and Fund. Trade may increase, the volume of goods flowing round the world may increase, but trade surpluses for one nation imply trade deficits for another nation(s). In mathematical, monetary terms, *trade is a zero sum game* – and debts have to be repaid in the mathematics of money. In words that have been repeated a thousand times; 'It is clearly impossible for all countries to increase exports and reduce imports at the same time'.[2]

A situation has been created in which it is logically impossible for debtor nations to repay their debts, other than by the industrialised countries accepting a trade deficit. Surpluses for some countries imply deficits for others. Creditors cannot have it both ways – they cannot both export more to the debtors and receive higher interest payments from them. If they want the interest payments, then they must first accept the debtors' exports.

It is not being suggested that the Bank and Fund do not recognise this elementary economic law. The weakness of their economic model actually lies in the assumption that debtor nations can, or ought to be able to, obtain the necessary trade surpluses by net exports to 'creditor' nations. But in trying to increase their exports, the debtor nations immediately confront the strong capitalist countries, which are attempting to do exactly the same. The latter have many advantages. They produce on a very large scale, sell to a huge home market, have established markets abroad, enjoy highly trained workforces and sophisticated research facilities and possess a monopoly over many areas of technology and skills. In this light, the possibility of competing with them on equal terms is almost negligible.[3]

The inappropriate free trade agenda

The developmental imbalance between the wealthy industrialised nations and developing nations highlights the issue of free trade. As was discussed in Chapter 4, the promotion of free trade is written into the Articles of Agreement of both the IMF and the World Bank. In basing their policies on a free trade ideology, these institutions fail to reflect one of the most profound and, in terms of Third World debt, most relevant debates within economics. *Does free trade work?* Or more precisely, *is free trade equitable?*

Free trade sounds a perfectly reasonable and 'fair' basis on which to conduct international trade. It can certainly lay claim to being the dominant ethic in neo-classical economics. At a press conference in 1990, the former World Bank President, Barber Conable, said; 'If I were to characterise the past decade, the most remarkable thing was the generation of a global consensus that market forces and economic efficiency were the best way to achieve the kind of growth which is the best antidote to poverty'.

In fact, no such consensus exists. Much literature on Third World debt explicitly singles out the unquestioning promotion of free trade as a key factor in the causation of endemic Third World debt. There is also a considerable dissent from the free trade ethic within the field of academic, theoretical economics. Gunnar Myrdal states that free trade

... operates with [a] fundamental bias in favour of the richer and progressive regions against the other regions. The freeing and widening of the markets will often confer such competitive advantages on the industries in already established centres of expansion ... that even the handicrafts and industries existing earlier in the other regions are thwarted.[4]

The weakness of the free trade policy is so central to understanding Third World debt that the next chapter is devoted to analysis of this issue. It is an area of discussion that embraces falling commodity prices and factor prices, deteriorating terms of trade, the distinction between price and value, extractive foreign investment, and the critical importance of a nation's overall strength in terms of the world economic hierarchy. For now, it is worth recalling the resounding dismissal of deregulated trade by Keynes;

To suppose that there exists some smoothly functioning automatic mechanism of adjustment which preserves equilibrium if only we trust to methods
of laissez-faire is a doctrinaire delusion which disregards the lessons of
historical experience, without having behind it the support of sound
theory.[5]

Change the bad (old) advice for the good (new) advice.

The Bank and Fund have constantly been accused of 'shifting the goal posts'
and changing their advice to developing nations. For example, it was never
intended that the World Bank or IMF should act as the development engines for
the poorer nations. From the outset, the Bank was seen as a catalyst, funding only
those sectors that were unattractive to commercial investors. The main source of
capital was expected to be private finance, either as foreign direct investment or
commercial loans.

In line with this expectation, during the 1950s the World Bank deliberately
steered its funds towards 'non-economic projects' involving investment in transport, communications, power, education and health. Such investment was
expected to produce indirect, long-term returns, the loans being repaid out of
overall economic improvement of the economy. In 1948, the Bank commented;

> This is the type of development that is most appropriate to require assis-
> tance from the Bank, either in the form of direct loans or of guarantees.
> [The purpose is] to ensure well-balanced economic growth and a necessary
> prerequisite for the investment of private foreign capital.[6]

But only two years later, the United Nations Sub-Committee on Economic
Development delivered its warning, quoted in the previous chapter, that such
investment could not be expected to generate repayments at the rate being
demanded by the Bank. This was the strongest warning, from an official international agency of the highest standing, that debt problems were already being
created for the future. The Sub-Committee recommended that loans of this
nature, which could generate returns only indirectly by improving health, education and the general economic infrastructure, should have at least a fifty-year
payback period. However, World Bank loans continued to be issued under far
shorter term maturities.

By 1960, with the build-up of unpaid debts, some observers were classifying
such welfare and infrastructure development as 'luxuries', or 'social and unpro-
ductive development';

> Naturally governments like to be popular and genuinely want to make their
> peoples healthier, wealthier, wiser; and it is easy to justify too much luxury
> spending on these objects by saying that in general and in the end it is essen-
> tial to the progress of the economy.[7]

It is sobering to note that some developing nations, who were accepting the developmental advice and fiscal terms and spending such revenues in purposefully benign and populist social measures, were yet being blamed for the failure of that development paradigm. This is a historical fact that presents a stark contrast with the recent attribution of the debt crisis to 'corrupt, self-seeking, ruthless dictatorships'.

Not only was the Bank's 'catalyst funding' starting to create a mounting burden of debt, but other development advice was altering too. The developing nations had initially been advised to undertake agricultural improvements, which would be followed by the growth of an industrial sector. This followed the traditional economic theory that an agricultural surplus is the true basis for industrialisation. But commercial investment in agriculture, whilst it had spectacularly raised output and export volumes, had failed to produce financial returns for developing nations. With the build-up of unpaid infrastructure and welfare loans, the development model and the advice both changed.

Rapid industrialisation came to be seen as the route by which the emergent nations would develop. This was seen as the 'short cut to prosperity'. In addition, agriculture was perceived as needing additional input, requiring the support not just of private commerce, but agencies such as the World Bank. The United Nations Food and Agriculture Organisation (FAO) urged more capital for the Bretton Woods institutions, claiming that 'many projects are so productive they could repay such charges'. R. Robinson explains the thinking;

> 3 dollars of additional imports may permit the production of 10 dollars of additional GNP from domestic resources that would otherwise remain unused (a marginal productivity of 3.3 per dollar – attractive to anyone's thinking).[8]

With the persistent decline in commodity prices, the actual returns on such loans were spectacularly 'unattractive to everyone's thinking'. The significant change in this period was that the World Bank began to involve itself in loans for projects with an anticipated commercial return. Unfortunately, the loan-criteria applied by the Bank fell markedly below those typically employed by commercial investors, with a failure to evaluate projects fully, a failure to consider world market trends and poor country risk analysis.

The deteriorating economic and social conditions within the poorer nations was known, at this time, as the 'development problem', and theory changed constantly. For example, having been advised to undertake 'import substitution' during the 1950s, the developing nations were then advised to stop trying to produce their own versions of goods manufactured elsewhere, and eschew import substitution as an economic inefficiency.

Despite such constantly changing advice, the World Bank and other development agencies accepted no responsibility for the build-up of debt at this time, nor did they recognise any institutional failings on their part. This was the first phase of the cycle, to be repeated many times over the following decades, of 'give plenty of advice, wash your hands, blame it on the debtors and give more advice'.

Blame it on the borrowers

Blame it on the borrowers, or 'the debt stands…', has been the constant position of Western development agencies throughout the decades since Bretton Woods. The first phase, discussed above, involved basic theoretical models that were changed as they failed either to produce balanced development or halt the slide into debt. The second phase involved the years of 'project aid'. Loans were advanced for specific projects – dams, agricultural programmes, irrigation schemes, manufacturing industries, etc. The bulk of these were vetted by the World Bank or endorsed by other Western development agencies, and many were actually suggested by those agencies.

The literature discussing the failure of these grandiose schemes is extensive and includes many howling disasters. An appreciable number were ill-conceived from the start, often the brain-child of a simplistic planning mentality that lacked either the imagination or the diligence to consider environmental impacts, human displacement or the wide range of additional socio-economic knock-on effects that 'mega-projects' always involve. Such scandalous projects as the Narmada Dam were still being promoted into the 1990s. After a review in 1989, World Bank staff were unable to point to a single Bank-funded project in which the displaced people had been relocated and rehabilitated to a standard of living comparable to that which they enjoyed before displacement.[9]

Never has the World Bank, IMF or any other Western development agency accepted any level of co-responsibility for the projects that failed. Nor has there been any recognition that, even when these projects were not an outright disaster, few actually generated the financial returns that were predicted. All such projects were initially validated and endorsed on a financial basis, and the persistent failure to produce returns consonant with their financial investment has contributed to the gathering backlog of debt.

Structural adjustment

The ultimate example of 'blame it on the borrowers' involves structural adjustment, the package of socio-economic policies prescribed by the World Bank and IMF which, with slight modifications, is deemed universally applicable to all nations experiencing difficulties with their international debts. Since the early 1980s, the Bank and Fund have made their loans conditional upon following these sweeping reform programmes.

Structural adjustment is based on the assumption that the cause of each nation's debt crisis lies entirely within its *own* economy. The economy must therefore 'adjust' to the wider world economy.

Structural adjustment has seen teams of World Bank and IMF economists virtually taking over the economies of debtor nations in an attempt to 'turn them around'. Exchange rates, government spending, labour laws, domestic deficits, taxation, welfare programmes, land tenure, environmental regulations, wage cuts and public service cuts – all these have been subject to detailed requirement and constant scrutiny. Bade Onimode describes structural adjustment;

A typical conditionality package includes massive retrenchment of workers, trade liberalisation, cumulative devaluation, privatisation of public enterprises, free entry for multinational corporations, abolition of exchange, price and wage controls, withdrawal of subsidies across the board, a credit squeeze, budget cuts and general deflation of the economy. These preconditions and conditions are imposed on virtually all borrowers from the Third World, regardless of the particular conditions of their economies.[10]

The failure throughout the world of structural adjustment is legendary. An entire book could not contain the 'quotable quotes' available denouncing its theory and effect. The Latin America Bureau commented that throughout South America, it was hard to find a single country in which IMF programmes of adjustment had halted the economic decline. Analysing events in Chile, the Bureau stated;

The total collapse by 1981 of the monetarist experiment in Chile is a salutary lesson in the failure of IMF prescriptions, even when applied in their most rigorous form and by a government totally committed to their success.[11]

The proceedings of a conference in poverty-stricken Yugoslavia in 1989, held to draw attention to the status of that country as a 'European Third World nation', state;

In the last ten years, the whole IMF policy [for Yugoslavia] has been nothing but a failure. All its prognoses were proved wrong, and its policies and measures had an opposite effect from what had been expected ... the 'case' of Yugoslavia is clear evidence of another IMF policy failure, as well as of the failure of internal policy based upon the strategy of the IMF.[12]

The first World Bank structural adjustment programmes (SAPs) were in Kenya, Turkey and the Philippines in 1980. None is a success today and the United Nations Economic Commission for Africa in 1993 found fifteen African countries clearly worse off after structural adjustment than before. A 1988 World Bank study using nine key 'indicators' (indicators that were chosen by the Bank itself) found 'SAPped' countries in Africa made better economic progress than 'non-sapped' countries less than 50% of the time.[13]

Such was the impact in Africa that the 1987 Conference of the Institute for

African Alternatives (IFAA), called for the winding up of the World Bank and the IMF and a complete end to the dominance of the Bretton Woods international monetary system. The conference noted that;

> ...in virtually all cases, the impact of these [IMF and World Bank] projects has been basically negative. They have resulted in massive unemployment, falling real incomes, pernicious inflation, increased imports with persistent trade deficits, net outflow of capital, mounting external debts, denial of basic needs, severe hardship and de-industrialisation. Even the so-called success stories in Ghana and the Ivory Coast have turned out to offer no more than temporary relief which had collapsed by the mid 1980s. The similarity of these effects in different countries is underscored by their disregard of national peculiarities....The sectors that have been worst hit are agriculture, manufacturing and the social services, while the burden of adjustment has fallen regressively on the poor and weak social groups.'[14]

Michel Chossudovsky describes how SAPs are backed up by Bank/Fund 'advisors' lodged in relevant government ministries – the Treasury, agriculture, taxation, social services etc – to ensure adherence to the Programme. Bail-out loans are released in 'tranches', and failure to stay 'on track' leads to a block on the release of the next cheque. Chossudovsky comments on the far-reaching consequences of these programmes; 'Entire countries have been destabilised as a consequence of the collapse of national currencies, often resulting in the outbreak of social strife, ethnic conflicts and civil war.'[15]

The 1980 Arusha Initiative, signed in 1980 by a number of developing country representatives, claimed that the performance tests and analysis used by the IMF 'lack scientific basis' and that the policies intended to achieve economic stabilisation had in fact 'contributed to destabilisation and to the limitation of the democratic process.'

However, the Bank/IMF have been unrepentant as always. As late as 1994, the World Bank commented; 'Africa's disappointing economic performance in the aggregate represents a failure to adjust [rather than] a failure of adjustment... Adjustment is the necessary first step on the road to sustainable poverty reduction.'[16] This is a comment typical of many. However in a stunning admission the IMF stated in 1990;

> Although there have been any number of studies on the subject over the past decade, one cannot say with certainty whether [structural adjustment] programs have 'worked' or not...[17]

In 1989, the United Nations Economic Commission for Africa (ECA) published an *Alternative African Framework to Structural Adjustment*. This advocated a completely different approach to debt relief and development, involving measures such as land reform, heavy investment in agriculture for food self-sufficiency, closer links between agriculture and industry and more development of industry for domestic needs. This report was ignored by the Bank and Fund.

The Bank and Fund have accepted no responsibility for the economic, social and environmental consequences of structural adjustment, despite the repeated failure of the programmes, and regardless of the fact that these have been imposed upon debtor nations.

Failure to act on external causes of debt

Hand in hand with imposing structural adjustment, the IMF and World Bank have constantly been accused of failing to consider the flaws in the global economy. The cause of endemic debt is defined by the Bank/Fund as internal, therefore the only factors they address are internal. All 'external factors' – the ways in which the wider world economy impinges upon each developing nation – are ignored by structural adjustment, as they have been since Bretton Woods.

Yet external factors, such as commodity prices, aggressive exporting, protectionism by more powerful nations, monopoly powers of multinationals; all these are acknowledged to have played a key factor in the debt/development crisis. The FAO concluded that, during the 1980s, external factors such as deteriorating terms of trade, rising protectionism, historically high interest rates, declining markets due to recession in the developed countries, and other events beyond a government's control were such that 'external factors alone are enough to push the adjustment process completely off course'.[18]

This statement, and the call to act so as to remedy these external factors, was ignored by the Bank and Fund, as was the earlier call from the OECD for a New International Economic Order (NIEO) and trading framework.

Creating poverty for majority

The failure of Bank/Fund policies, just as with the debt crisis itself, impacts first and hardest upon the poor majority in debtor nations. A typical SAP involves cutting spending on hospitals, clinics, education, credit and welfare. The decline in investment in domestic agriculture, industry, research and infrastructure such as roads and power all trigger unemployment, which is swelled by the displacement of indigenous peoples from land diverted to export crops. The removal of subsidies and devaluation of currencies leads to a rapid rise in the price of staple foodstuffs.

The net result has invariably been a rapid and catastrophic decline in the standard of living amongst the poor majority, who already endure the harshest livelihoods.

Between 1980 and 1989 some thirty three African countries received 241 Structural Adjustment loans. During that same period, average GDP per capita in those countries fell 1.1% per year, whilst per-capita food production also experienced steady decline. The real value of the minimum wage dropped by over 25%, government expenditure on education fell from $11 billion to $7 billion and primary school enrolments dropped from 80% in 1980 to 69% in 1990. The number of poor people in these countries rose from 184 million in 1985 to 216 million in 1990, an increase of 17%.[19]

Generally formulated in obscure jargon, the complex Bank and Fund requirements to 'adjust' come down to three principles; 'export more, spend less, pay up'. Or as one cartoon caption put it; 'Stop Eating…' Structural adjustment has lead to such destitution in a number of countries that the phrases 'IMF riots' and 'IMF deaths' are now an accepted part of development jargon. A UNICEF study criticising SAPs showed that child mortality, child death, malnutrition, dropout from school, school provision, illiteracy and non-immunisation all increased between 1980 and 1985.[20] The study also noted an alarming re-emergence of diseases virtually eliminated during the 1950s. Meanwhile, the ECA noted that Africa would probably begin the millennium with a greater proportion of its population illiterate and unskilled than at the beginning of the post-independence era in the 1960s.

David Korten records that in Brazil between 1960 and 1980, the conversion of agriculture from smallholders producing food for domestic consumption, to capital intensive production for export, displaced 28.4 million people. Similarly, in India, large-scale development projects displaced 20 million people over a forty-year period. In 1989, ongoing World Bank projects were displacing 1.5 million people, whilst projects in preparation threatened to displace another 1.5 million.[21]

No conditionality for reducing poverty

Another major criticism of Bank/Fund lending has been the refusal to make loans conditional upon redistributive policies directed at poverty reduction, such as the redistribution of land, resources and wealth in an effort to reverse growing inequalities.

In response, the Bank has commented that it is not their proper role to interfere in issues of internal policy. But the entire basis of structural adjustment is just such interference, carried to a high degree of detail. Since the Bank and Fund have no qualms over dictating wage cuts, wide-ranging welfare cuts and diverting the economy away from the production of basic goods and services for domestic consumption, towards exportable goods – all policies which impact negatively against the poor majority – the claim to operate with a 'neutral social agenda' is clearly invalid.

No structural adjustment for creditors

The fact that the wealthy, industrialised nations are also drifting ever-deeper into unrepayable debt, yet are not subjected to policies such as structural adjustment, has not gone unnoticed by critics of Bank Fund policy. Yet the IMF Charter requires surveillance of all countries alike; and the Group of 24 (developing nations) has long since asked the IMF for equal treatment of all deficit countries.[22]

There is also much complaint over the fact that the more powerful nations operate many trade restrictions using tariffs and quotas, whilst the Bank/Fund/OECD/WTO demand that all such devices be dropped by debtor nations as a condition of the continuing stream of loans on which they are now utterly dependent.

The strong political representation of the wealthy nations within these multilateral agencies has often been seen as the cause of grave political bias.[23] Such export impediments on debtor nations have a critical effect on their ability to obtain interest payments. The position adopted by the wealthy nations is, in pure trade terms, highly contradictory since, to insist on debt interest payments is to insist on successful exporting, whilst to resist imports from the debtor nations is to hinder that exporting!

Management weaknesses

The management and organisation of both the Bank and the Fund have come in for the severest criticism by many observers. Often, these projects have been unsuited to the location, have had a severe environmental impact, have displaced indigenous populations, and have created economic refugees that have poured to cities and shanty towns.

But as Susan George and Fabrizio Sabelli point out, 'By the time the results of a given project become manifest, managers can expect to be working on something else, somewhere else'.[24] George and Sabelli cite as a typical example the case of the World Bank official most responsible for pushing the notorious Narmada Dam project in India, the funding for which was withdrawn after worldwide protest in 1992. This man was immediately promoted to a high position in the Russian department. Before working in the Bank's India section, he had been involved with another of the Bank's schemes decried for its appalling environmental impact – the Polonoreste project in Brazil.

George and Sabelli detail the many managerial weaknesses within the Bank. These include lack of adequate loan risk-analysis, lack of consultation with affected peoples, poor project approval procedures and hopeless lack of social/economic programmes to provide for displaced peoples. The 'drive to lend' was so unquestioning during the Robert Macnamara years that promotion within the Bank was at times entirely based upon the volume of loans an officer might succeed in 'pushing out the door'.

Failure to predict aggregate effect of general policy

One of the most serious management failings of the Bank/Fund strategy, deserving of a mention in its own right, has been its failure to coordinate and predict the consequences of their involvement in different countries. Encouraging a number of nations to increase production and export of identical commodities, and failing to anticipate that this would lead to surpluses and falling prices is a truly schoolboy error. Susan George remarks scathingly;

> Although it may seem barely credible, to the best of our knowledge the Bank's army of economists has never thought it relevant or useful to make a general assessment of the impact of the bank's own structural adjustment policies on market prices for commodities… Yet the first and most universal feature of any structural adjustment package is the re-orientation of the economy towards maximum production for export. Since dozens of countries are now subject to such packages, and since many of them export the same commodities, it does not take a Ph.D. in economics to foresee gluts and declining prices for everyone.[25]

Trying to cure debt with more debt

The overall perception of the debt crisis by the World Bank and IMF has come in for much criticism. In particular their financial response to the financial problem of debt has been repeatedly condemned. Tackling the problem of debt by issuing further loans that create more debt and raise interest payments certainly begs the most basic question. Herman Daly comments;

> The 'solution' to the debt crisis offered by the orthodox economist has been a further dose of growth. The way to grow is to invest, and the way to invest is to borrow. The solution to the debt is to increase the debt! Just why it is believed that this new debt will be used so much more productively than the older debt is never explained.[26]

Thirty years of responding to the debt crisis by issuing more debt cannot lay any claim to success. The gross total of debt owed by all developing nations in all regions throughout the world economy has increased without showing any sign of reversal. The increase has not been in simple numerical terms. For the vast majority of developing nations, and for the debtor nations as an entire group, the total has increased by most of the 'inflation-proof' standards commonly used by economists. Gross Third World debt has increased relative to GNP, relative to the current values of debtor nations' assets, relative to total exports and relative to the rate of inflowing loans and foreign investment. Similarly, the demand for interest repayment absorbs a greater proportion of export revenues and represents a growing proportion of GNP. *The Economist* remarked;

> Whatever in fact happens to interest rates or to Latin American trade, the debt is now so huge that it devours all improvement, requiring still bigger improvements the following year. The debt is a black hole, growing large on the money it absorbs. Far from being the main symptom of the Latin American malaise, the debt has become the malaise itself.[27]

The remorseless upward trend in debt has been disguised and confused in more recent assessments of the data, particularly since the late 1980s. For example, whilst the monetary aggregate of Third World debt has continued to rise, the GNP of debtor nations has risen more rapidly. As a result, the ratio of debt to GNP has marginally fallen for a number of debtor nations. This has prompted many economists to proclaim that the debt crisis has been solved, or is entering a more 'sustainable' phase.

In fact, the status of debtor nations has continued to deteriorate. The apparent improvement of debt/GNP ratio is due to the convention of accounting foreign owned enterprises as still part of a national economy. Many nations have attempted to control the growth of their debts by debt-equity swaps, by deregulating and privatising in line with Bank/Fund advice, and by accepting foreign buy-outs of their most valuable productive assets. But to account such enterprises and assets, now foreign-owned, as part of a national economy hardly constitutes a valid assessment of the status of a debtor nation that has, in one way or another, lost the ownership and control of its most productive assets.

Production of these enterprises is generally orientated towards exports, or to secure profits from within the domestic economy – profits which are then repatriated out of the developing country. Such enterprises, their productivity and capital value, cannot properly be viewed as constituting the assets of a debtor nation. When such foreign ownership – particularly by powerful multinationals – is taken into account, the relentless upward trend of debt/interest and the deteriorating economic status of developing nations is all too apparent. It also becomes clear how it can be that dynamic economic growth can continue to leave a nation's citizens in desperate poverty, and its government financially powerless to undertake much-needed domestic development. This issue is given more consideration below, in the discussions on debt-equity swaps and Foreign Direct Investment.

Susan George points out that it was not until the 1990s that the World Bank finally accepted that the debt crisis was not a crisis of liquidity, requiring a short-term injection of more cash, but of overall insolvency, with a backlog of debt that would have caused any commercial venture to be declared hopelessly bankrupt. In 1992, Bank President Larry Summers acknowledged the failure of feeding the flames of debt with yet more debt;

> This lesson is well learned now, but the cost of delay has been to put development on hold for a decade in many of these countries. A lesson for the future is the importance of acknowledging reality sooner.[28]

Susan George remarks scathingly on the Bank's easy remorse and failure to accept any degree of financial responsibility for its culpability; 'Right. We're the world's top development institution but we're a bit slow acknowledging reality, so we may have put the development of a few dozen countries on hold for a decade… but we're sorry and we accept our mistake'.[29] Thus, the World Bank knows how to say 'sorry', but doesn't match this with any reduction in debts caused by its own admitted error.

Debt-for equity swaps – another failure

During the 1980s, developing nations experiencing a debt repayment crisis were encouraged by the Bank and Fund to undertake debt-equity swaps. Indeed, for many years this was heralded as a potential solution to the crisis. In fact it constituted another failure of advice that once again left debtor nations in a fundamentally worse position. André Gunder Frank lists limitations and drawbacks of debt-equity swaps …

> The hills of equity in existence in Third World debtor countries are insufficient to be swapped for more than a small part of the 1000 billion dollar mountain of Third World debt, or even for any significant portion of it owed to private banks. Second, potential investors are primarily interested, not in the most heavily indebted countries but in areas they deem to have growth potential. Third, the procedure does not contribute to any new capital production, but transfers resources and enterprises to new, foreign owners. Fourth, debt-equity swaps alienate enterprises and resources, often publicly owned, at forced sale bargain prices.[30]

Susan George points out that debt-equity swaps may bring no change in the debtor's financial condition at all if one considers the long term. Profits on all these ventures can presumably be repatriated by the foreign purchasers later on. To the nation as a whole, it doesn't much matter whether the cash outflow takes place in the form of interest payments or repatriated profits. For example, Bankers Trust, an early swapper, in 1986 made a $60 million debt-equity investment in Chile's largest pension fund. In 1990 Bankers Trust collected nearly $50 million in profits on this investment.[31]

In their 1990 paper, *Can Swaps Solve the Debt Crisis?*, Felipe Larrain and André Velasco evaluate the overall economic impact of debt-equity swaps on developing nations. For example, between 1985 and 1988 Chile implemented the largest debt-swap programme, relative to size, of any developing country, involving $6.2 billion of formal (official) and informal (private) exchanges. Their study found that the debt-swap programme had reduced the debt total by less than $1 billion, from $19.7 billion to $19.0 billion. Although $6.2 billion debt reduction had been achieved, additional loans continued to mount and drove the debt total up almost as fast as the swaps reduced it. The authors ask;

> Does the relatively large debt-reduction achieved by Chile ($6.2 billion raised) mean that the country's debt problem is essentially solved? Can the Chilean experience be translated into a policy recipe for the other highly indebted countries? … This paper answers negatively on both accounts.[32]

After the three-year period, Chile had virtually no tradable or desirable assets left, state or private. Any income these might have generated was now lost in perpetuity as profits would be subject to repatriation rather than used to produce revenue, whilst the debt total was little changed. The country was clearly in a worse economic position with regard to tackling its debt.

Foreign Direct Investment – another failure

Foreign Direct Investment (FDI), particularly through the privatisation programmes imposed as part of structural adjustment, has been similarly criticised as another flawed paradigm. Instead of leading to new development via investment, as argued by the Bank, the Fund and a number of development economists, FDI has frequently provided yet another cloak for overseas buyouts of valuable developing nation assets. As an early example, Barnet and Muller found that of the 717 new manufacturing subsidiaries established in Latin America between 1958 and 1967 by the top 187 US based global corporations, 46% were established by buying out existing enterprises. As Barnet and Muller point out, such activity can hardly be described as new development and deprives developing nations of income and control in perpetuity.[33]

The theory underpinning FDI is similar to the borrow/export/invest/repay model. It is expected that the host nation receiving the inward investment will benefit from the development that takes place, through value added, through general stimulation of the economy and through the mobilisation of otherwise idle or inefficiently-used resources. In fact, the purchase of debtor nation assets at critically low values, the swallowing up of these revenues by the 'black hole' of debt and the emphasis on exports and loss of potential future revenues to foreign corporations mean that FDI has failed to improve overall living standards in debtor nations and the flow of capital is now from South to North.

Just as a World Bank loan requires more to be repaid than was borrowed, so inward investment eventually means there will be a net outflow of money from a country. FDI has become, in the words of Michel Chossudovsky, 'a new means of extracting surplus from developing countries'.[34]

Environmental damage

The environmental impact within developing nations of their struggle against debt has been extensively documented. Such has been the fiscal pressure on debtor nations that their own domestic industrialisation has often been underfunded and crudely extractive, with no thought for long term-husbanding of non-renewable resources or the aggregate consequences of pollution. The World Resources Institute concluded that the government policies responsible for so much rainforest destruction throughout Latin America were the direct knock-on effect of debt.

Many development economics books have described the way export crops take priority in debtor nations and monopolise the best land. Sometimes governments displace smallholders or they are bought out or forcibly evicted by wealthy land-owners. The indigenous populations then move into teeming cities, or may try to cultivate nutrient-poor forest soils, or move to hillsides that are easily eroded. As they try to eke out a living, the fragile ecology is upset and it is a mere matter of time before food supplies collapse.

In their efforts to compete for foreign investment, debtor nations have been obliged to allow foreign corporations the same leeway to extract and pollute as was granted to their domestic companies. This is despite the fact that such multi-national corporations possess both the technology and capital to undertake more sophisticated, environmentally sensitive development. The recent upsurge of environmental legislation in the wealthy industrialised nations has lead many industries to shift to less developed nations, for the reduction in costs this involves. Polluting American industry has often been re-sited in the Mexican Maliquarodas; European industry has shifted east to the impoverished nations of the former Soviet bloc; Japanese industry has relocated into the poorer Far East nations.

The World Bank has been extensively criticised for failing to make its loans conditional upon tough environmental standards. The first serious environmental programme was not introduced until 1989, and only then were projects subjected to screening for their probable environmental impact. However, the criteria and evaluation procedures were still vague, and Susan George described the process as 'tacking environmental tails on some quite nasty dogs', as the Bank 'attempt(s) to make up for lost time and count themselves satisfied when and if they can prevent some of the more predictable ecological disasters from occurring'.[35]

Favouring ruling elites in the Third World

The failure to attach conditions to loans to protect the poor majority was noted above. In fact, Bank/Fund policy has often been accused of actively favouring ruling elites, and showing a clear preference for creditors over debtors. New loans may be made merely to supply the foreign exchange to enable debtor countries to make repayments on old loans.[36]

Many writers have pointed out that the demand by the Bank and the IMF that commercial loans be converted to government debts in developing nations, as a condition of rescheduling, was a travesty of justice that bordered on outright illegality. Such commercial debts ought to have been subject to the normal private risk that attends commercial activity, and the failure of these debts should have been borne by the investors.

Not only foreign corporations, but the wealthy elites in Third World nations, have been protected and favoured by structural adjustment policies, the main impact of which has been upon the poor majority. Meanwhile, the demand to deregulate finance has permitted the wealthy minority a channel for unrestricted capital outflows. In addition, the induced recessions of structural adjustment have both encouraged this capital flight, and allowed the wealthy elites to take part in the 'cherry-picking' of collapsing small and medium-sized enterprises and to acquire large amounts of state property under privatisation programmes.

Fostering conditions favouring multinational commerce

The gains made by foreign commerce as a result of debt-equity swaps and FDI have already been noted. This is part of a general advantage accruing to foreign big business as a result of developing nations being in a state of perpetual fiscal dependence and exposure to permanent, inescapable debt. The opportunity for foreign commerce reaches its zenith during a Bank/Fund-induced recession following structural adjustment.

IMF adjustment programmes invariably result in the takeover of domestically owned businesses by their foreign competitors. The stabilisation programme squeezes domestic capitalists by cutting domestic demand and reducing their sales. Devaluation raises the costs of all the imports needed for their business, as well as all the unpaid debts from past imports. They lose the protected markets they had enjoyed before as imports are liberalised. The same liberalisation of imports often benefits foreign owned firms, which utilise foreign inputs – raw materials, machinery and spare parts – imported from a branch of the same multinational corporation. In the IMF induced recession, the locally owned firms may go bankrupt, curtail operations and fire employees and are highly vulnerable to take-over by a foreign firm. Foreign businesses, backed up by parent companies, may effect the take-over without bringing in foreign money, preferring to borrow from the domestic banking system. Even if new money is brought in from abroad, this type of 'investment' clearly does not represent the creation of new means of production, but simply transfers resources within the poor countries to foreign ownership.

The state of permanent debt offers many opportunities to foreign commerce, including a wide range of resources 'up for grabs', devalued assets, pitifully low labour rates, competitive reductions in corporate taxation, environmental deregulation and access to markets 'opened up' by the Bank/Fund free trade agenda.

The creation of a new global economic order

Jonathan Cahn comments on the way that the World Bank exercises a detailed degree of governance over debtor nations;

> The World Bank must be regarded as a governance institution, exercising power through its financial leverage to legislate entire legal regimens and even to alter the constitutional structure of borrowing nations. Bank-approved consultants often re-write a country's trade policy, fiscal policies, civil service requirements, labour laws, health care arrangements, environmental regulations, energy policy, resettlement requirements, procurement rules and budgetary policy.[37]

Criticisms of Bank/Fund policies have not been restricted to their impact on individual nations. The aggregate effect of 'identikit' deregulatory, free-market policies applied to over one hundred debtor nations has been so pervasive and powerful that it has contributed substantially to the creation of a new global economic environment. A single macroeconomic policy has been internationalised under the control of the World Bank/IMF.

It has often been noted that much aid is designed to subsidise the donor's exports or serve diplomatic, strategic or military purposes abroad. Thus lending to the Third World, debt and the encouragement to borrow often reflect political aspirations and the concerns of major powers to secure influence and control in key regions.

Over the years, the reliance of developing nations on a continuous stream of new loans has led to some very dubious involvement by the Bank and Fund in destabilising regimes whose policies differed from their perceived economic wisdom. For example, President Garcia's government in Peru and Salvador Allende's government in Chile attempted to follow their own economic programmes to find a route out of their debt crises. This included the nationalisation of some foreign-owned enterprises, and restrictions on debt repayments to a portion of export revenues that they deemed manageable. The Allende government was cut off from further loans from the World Bank and from commercial capital, despite the fact that this was a democratically elected, populist government. Later, under General Pinochet's military junta, Chile enjoyed abundant support from the Bank as it embraced its austerity and adjustment policies, regardless of the severe impact on the Chilean population.

While Bank/Fund policies are increasingly invasive and detailed, they lack the sanction of democracy. The multilateral lending institutions are therefore weakening the power of the state and the authority of government in their client countries. They are subject to no corpus of law. What is of concern is not just the lack of accountability, but the suspicion that interests other than those of the debtor nations are being favoured. Many commentators have concluded that the Bank and Fund, whether or not this is conscious, possess a 'hidden agenda' to serve the interests of the more powerful nations and, more particularly, international commercial and capital interests. Certainly structural adjustment programmes systematically undermine all categories of economic activity, whether urban or rural, that do not directly serve, or conform to, the interests of the global market system.

Debt therefore represents a powerful political instrument for subjecting debtor countries to international economic control and making them specialise at the level of production. As Bade Onimode puts it, 'Debt and the fluctuations in the prices of raw materials represent two of the most powerful political and economic instruments in the strategy of the Western industrialised powers to dominate the countries of Africa'.[38]

Summary

The issues outlined above are recurrent themes in the debt and development literature of the past four decades. They cast considerable doubt on the competence of the World Bank and IMF, and raise serious doubts over the allegiance, and perhaps even the motives, of the two organisations that have been at the heart of international development since the second world war.

Even if the thorny question of intent is laid to one side, the scale of criticism, its recurrence and the degree of agreement amongst observers over the key Bank/Fund failings suggest that the Bank and Fund bear at the very least a high degree of co-responsibility for the current financial position of debtor nations.

Although it might appear that the question of World Bank/IMF motivation is the 'Big Issue', it is arguably of far greater importance to assume their benign and equitable intent, and try to establish the reasons for the gross and repeated failings of their economic policies. Motivation is anyway notoriously difficult to establish. It is important to recognise that the policies have been legitimised by liberal, neo-classical economics, which is today's economic orthodoxy. At the heart of any notional Bank/Fund culpability lie the merits and demerits of the economic agenda that underpins their policies.

For example, the borrow/invest/export/repay model sounds rational. The free trade agenda sounds fair and equitable. The theory that capital should naturally flow from wealthy to under-developed nations to stimulate investment and growth appears logical. The paradox of development, and the debate over Third World debt, lies in the contrast between a collection of economic theories that are supposed to work, and massive documentary evidence that shows that they do not. The next chapter analyses what is arguably the key theoretical component of Bank/Fund ideology – the policy of free trade.

Endnotes

1   Conference of Institute for African Alternatives. Bade Onimode (ed). *The IMF, The World Bank and African Debt*. Zed Books. 1989.

2   Latin America Bureau. *The Poverty Brokers. The IMF and Latin America*. Latin America Bureau. 1983.

3   Latin America Bureau. *Op. cit.*

4   Gunnar Myrdal. *Economic Theory and Underdeveloped Regions*. Duckworth and Company. 1957

5   Van Dormael. *Bretton Woods – The Birth of an International Monetary System*. Macmillan Press. 1978.

6   *Memorandum on Financing Economic Development*. International Bank for Reconstruction and Development. Doc E / CN.1/50 1948

7   R. Robinson. *Developing the Third World. The Experience of the 1960s*. Cambridge University Press 1971.

8   R. Robinson. *Op. cit.*

9   David Korten. *When Corporations Rule the World*. Earthscan. 1995.

10   Conference of Institute for African Alternatives. Bade Onimode (ed). *Op cit.*

11   Latin American Bureau. *The Poverty Brokers. The IMF and Latin America*. Latin American

Bureau. 1983.

12 Jakov Sirotkovic in Hans Singer, Soumitra Sharma (eds). *Economic Development and World Debt*. Macmillan. 1989.

13 J. Cavanagh, D. Wysham and M. Arruda (eds). *Beyond Bretton Woods – Alternatives to the Global Economic Order.* Pluto Press. 1994.

14 Conference of Institute for African Alternatives. Bade Onimode (ed). Op cit

15 Michel Chossudovsky. *The Globalisation of Poverty.* Zed Books. 1997.

16 The World Bank. *Adjustment in Africa.* Oxford University Press. 1994.

17 Mohsin Khan. *The Macroeconomic Effects of Fund Supported Adjustment Programs*. IMF Staff Papers, Vol 37, No 2, 1990.

18 E. Wayne Nafziger. *The Debt Crisis in Africa.* Johns Hopkins University Press. 1993.

19 Conference of Institute for African Alternatives. Bade Onimode (ed). *Op. cit.*

20 E. Wayne Nafziger. *Op cit.*

21 David Korten. *Op. cit.*

22 André Gunder Frank. in Hans Singer, Soumitra Sharma. *Op. cit.*

23 Mary Sutton, Jennifer Sharpley, Tony Killick. *The IMF and Stabilisation – Developing Country Experiences.* Heinemann Educational Books. 1984.

24 Susan George, Fabrizio Sabelli. *Op. cit.*

25 Susan George, Fabrizio Sabelli. *Op cit.*

26 Herman Daly. *For the Common Good.* Green Print. 1989.

27 *The Economist.* April. 1983.

28 Quoted in Susan George, Fabrizio Sabelli. *Op. cit.*

29 Susan George, Fabrizio Sabelli. *Op. cit.*

30 André Gunder Frank, in Hans Singer and Sumitra Sharma. *Op. cit.*

31 Susan George. *The Debt Boomerang.* Pluto Press. 1992.

32 Felipe Larrain and André Velasco. *Can Swaps Solve the Debt Crisis?* Princeton Studies in International Finance. No.69. November 1990.

33 Barnet and Muller. *Global Reach; The Power of the Multinational Corporation.* Simon and Schuster. 1974.

34 Michel Chossudovsky. *The Globalisation of Poverty.* Zed Books. 1997.

35 Susan George, Fabrizio Sabelli. *Op. cit.*

36 Herman Daly. *Op. cit.*

37 Jonathan Cahn. 'Challenging the New Imperial Authority'. *Harvard Human Rights Journal* 6. 1993.

38 Conference of Institute for African Alternatives. Bade Onimode (ed). *Op cit.*

6

The free trade rip-off

One of the fundamental reasons for the failure of developing nations to obtain the revenues required for debt repayment has been that since Bretton Woods the rules and institutions governing international trade have been increasingly based on a 'free trade' or 'deregulated trade' ideology. International trade and the terms under which trade is carried out are bound to have a profound impact on developing nations. If trade is in any way persistently disadvantageous to them, this will clearly affect their financial position. When it is remembered that the borrow/invest/export/repay model relies absolutely upon successful exporting by debtor nations, trade conditions are clearly of critical importance.

In June 1999, with the Jubilee 2000 campaign gathering momentum, a delegation of Indian farmers toured Europe with the slogan 'Fair trade, not free trade'. The leader of the 500-strong group, Professor Najundaswamy, explained the reason for their demonstrations outside the headquarters of NATO, the WTO and bio-tech companies such as Monsanto; 'The global economic system is crippling the poorest'. 'Many farmers in the state have committed suicide', added Rajah Reddy, a cotton farmer from Pradesh in central India. 'We cannot compete. The poor are worst hit by liberalisation... everyone here is in debt. We are coming to Europe because the G8 countries must understand what is happening because of their policies'. The media followed their unsuccessful lobbying trail through Europe's capitals with the usual penchant for the quaint and curious, tinged with sympathy for a David up against a mighty Goliath, but with little depth of discussion.

There was no recognition that free trade ideology is a pivotal issue in the debate over Third World debt. There was no acknowledgement that the farmers' implicit claim, that free trade is unfair, is backed up by a powerful body of economic analysis and theory. In fact, the farmers eventually returned to India leaving the general public still not appreciating any clear distinction between 'fair trade' and 'free trade'.

A free trade ethic appears by definition an equitable or 'fair' basis upon which world trade should be conducted. The very word 'free' implies that the alternative is 'unfree'; in some sense oppressive and restrictive. However, there is far more to the free trade agenda than the notion of economic openness and the unrestricted exchange of goods and services. The theory of free trade is underpinned by a number of important expectations and conditions. Before examining why free trade is, or can be, grossly unfair, it is important to understand the major elements of the theory, which make the ideology so compelling to economists.

Free trade – the theory

At the most immediate level, the idea that nations might produce, or be capable of producing, goods and services of value to other nations, yet prevented in some artificial way from exporting or importing such products, is clearly intolerable. The potential for mutual benefit from trading in surplus goods is so obvious that the unhindered exchange of goods and services requires little justification. Free trade thus has at its heart a profoundly democratic ideal – that producers and consumers across the world have a right to be of mutual service to each other.

Free trade theory also points out that the barriers to trade that nations have often erected are expensive and disguise considerable economic inefficiencies. Government subsidies on domestic goods and services, and the bureaucratic machinery of quotas, restrictions and tariffs, all involve taxpayers' money. This means that consumers are paying more for products than they realise because of the taxation. Tariffs on foreign goods, whilst raising some public money to offset the bureaucratic administration involved, also raises prices for consumers.

In addition to the actual costs involved, the implication for economists is that inefficient producers are being subsidised and efficient producers penalised, to the overall detriment of consumers and commerce everywhere. Free trade theory argues that if consumers are presented with prices based on true costs, they will prefer and support the most efficient producers. Free trade is thereby intended to eliminate inefficient economic activity and promote the best use of resources.

Underpinning the concept of free trade promoting the efficient use of resources is the theory of 'comparative advantage'. This theory argues that in a condition of perfect global competition, every country would produce only those goods it makes most efficiently, and then trade them for everything else it needed. The result is that there would be more goods for everybody because the available resources – land, labour and capital – will have been used most efficiently.

Free trade is thus intended to promote the diversification and integration of national economies to their mutual benefit, since there will be more productive global economic activity *in toto*. Greater consumer demand in an efficient international economy with an open world market will confirm and direct the increasingly productive use of the world's resources. It is therefore claimed that, overall, free trade promotes total global economic activity and wealth creation.

Allowing 'the market' to establish the price of goods by competition between producers is a central tenet of free trade theory. Without interference by agencies 'external' to the pure economic process (such as governments), wage demands, factor costs, capital returns etc. will all adjust, as a result of competition, to produce 'the right price' for goods. Price will determine the success, or otherwise, of goods in the market. This in turn will confirm the most efficient producers and eradicate the less efficient producers and their networks.

The free flow of capital is deemed important by modern supporters of free trade, although as we shall see, such capital movement is specifically precluded in pure free trade theory. Modern free traders theorise that investment capital will tend to flow automatically from developed to underdeveloped nations. The rationale behind this is that investors seek out the maximum returns for their capital, and underdeveloped nations provide these greater opportunities, since resources will otherwise be either idle or inefficiently employed.

Following on from this, a further important expectation of free trade is that it will lead to a decrease in the inequalities between people, and between nations. This is sometimes known as the 'doctrine of convergence'. The free and open competition between commerce, labour, investors and all other agents involved in the economic process is seen as a levelling pressure tending to promote ever-greater equality between the various economic agents – including nations and regions. The doctrine of convergence argues that, for example, labour forces in poorer nations will undercut the wage demands of workers in the affluent West, creating prosperity for themselves whilst reducing the perceived 'surplus' prosperity in the richer countries.

Similarly, the doctrine argues that investors will compete with each other for the gains available from developing nations, to the point where their competition drives down the level of profit, adding to the advantage gained by the developing nations. Therefore the poorer economies will develop, eventually catching up with the richer nations, whilst the progressively efficient use of all resources – land, labour and capital – will ensure that there is more, ultimately, for everyone.

In summary, free trade is advocated under the persistent claim that it is a neutral arrangement, freeing the endeavours of humanity and promoting the use of resources in a way that will bring increased benefit to all.

Free trade – the caveats

Unfortunately, while these are the positive aspects of free trade theory, they do not by any means tell the whole story. From the days of David Ricardo, economists have warned that there are certain essential provisos if free trade is to produce the efficiencies, mutuality and progressive equalisation described above. Ricardo argued that free trade requires four essential conditions if it is to prove fair and mutually beneficial to the nations taking part;

- Capital should not be allowed to cross borders from a high wage to a low wage country.
- There must be a balance of trade between participating countries.
- There should be full employment within participating nations.
- There should be perfect competition, with no monopolies or oligopolies (i.e. near-monopolies).

In other words, the actual theory specifically warns that mutual benefit will *not* proceed from free trade between nations, in cases where those nations suffer any significant degree of unemployment, where permanent trade imbalances exist, where there are monopolies, and where net capital flows between developed and underdeveloped nations are permitted. Since this precisely describes the world we live in, it is hardly surprising that a free trade policy has proved, and is proving, less than mutual. History repeatedly demonstrates that under a free trade ethic, international trade rapidly becomes a game through which the most powerful nations constantly gain at the expense of less developed nations.

The observation that economically powerful nations have the capacity to maintain and increase their supremacy over less developed nations is an established aspect of trade theory. Although currently out of favour, the theory of unequal exchange contains a detailed analysis of how the existence of monopolies, capital power and wage differentials can invalidate the doctrine of convergence and lead to a cumulative process towards the impoverishment and stagnation of underdeveloped nations.[1]

The history of Third World debt since Bretton Woods provides abundant evidence of the tendency of free trade to prove exploitative. When we consider the many 'external factors' acknowledged as major contributors to the backlog of Third World debt, it becomes clear that these constitute a blatant failure, or misapplication, of the free trade agenda. The following sections deal with some of these key external factors, which present a salutary confirmation of the ignored caveats of free trade theory.

Commodity prices – or how to get more for less

There is no question that the developing nations have been exporting successfully in physical terms. Output has risen; export volumes have increased year on year; their economies have become increasingly devoted to export effort, to the plain detriment of domestic development, consumption and welfare.

For example, between 1958 and 1965, the production of the Third World increased by 97%, whilst that of the industrialised nations increased by only 19%.[2] Total export volumes from Third World nations to the industrialised nations more than doubled within this period alone.[3] Similarly, by 1980 the eighteen major debtor countries of the developing world were exporting in excess of 25% of their GDP, after twenty years during which their annual growth rate had been 4%, almost double that of the wealthy industrialised nations.[4] Why then, if they were producing and exporting so successfully, did the Third World emerge from this period even deeper in debt?

The key issue is price. Just as there can be no dispute that Third World nations have been successfully exporting in terms of the quantity of goods and services, it is equally clear that they have failed to obtain the monetary returns for their economic efforts. Since the 1950s, remorseless falls in world prices have robbed developing nations of the reward their efforts deserved and left them with an increasing debt burden. As far back as the 1960s, observers were able to remark that 'in the last ten years, developing countries have lost far more in the fall of prices of raw materials ... than they have received in aid from all the contributing countries.'[5]

If free trade theory advocates that price should be determined by pure competition, it also warns that the market will not necessarily establish a fair price if international conditions are not equitable. To apply free trade ideology and expect market forces to determine the price of goods traded between developed and underdeveloped nations is to disregard the most glaring discrepancies between free trade theory and the real world.

The wealthy nations possessed advanced buying, transport, wholesale and marketing networks, all dominated by large businesses that formed cartels, oligopolies and strategic monopolies. The underdeveloped nations were economically weak, produced many primary commodities, and competed with each other under acute financial pressure to supply these commodities to wealthy nations.

The result was completely predictable: the big monopolies have been able to persistently bid down the price they offer, leading to a steady fall in commodity prices. This has in turn led to a steady decline in total export revenues gained by debtor nations, leaving them quite unable to meet the obligations to their creditors.

The power of multinational commerce is reinforced by the indebtedness of the Third World. The backlog of debt actually represents a breach of two of the Ricardian conditions essential for trade to prove mutually beneficial. Lending to the Third World debt constitutes a long-term capital outflow from high-wage to low-wage countries. Also, when debt becomes permanent, it represents an enduring imbalance in trade between nations. As a result, developing nations are under a standing obligation to secure a surplus of exports over imports.

This places the debtor nations at a severe competitive disadvantage in their trade negotiations. The monopoly power and 'imperfect competition' between Third World producers and corporate monopoly buyers is reinforced by the exposed position of debtor nations, since they have to sell substantially into the world market.

The ubiquity of debt throughout the developing nations presents yet a further advantage to multinational corporate commerce. There is intense competition throughout the Third World to supply those commodities sought by the wealthy nations, who alone can pay with the hard currencies required for debt repayment. This competition has resulted in a surplus of most of the primary commodities, raw materials, foodstuffs, minerals and manufactured goods produced by the community of developing nations. Such surpluses allow the corporate buyers and monopoly interests within the wealthy nations to fix a price that takes advantage of gluts and oversupply. So acute has been the financial pressure of debt that the developing nations find themselves frequently bidding down the price of their own goods, in an effort to remain competitive and secure at least some return for their output.

As mentioned in the previous chapter, the World Bank is deeply implicated in the persistent falls in commodity prices. Many similar export projects in different countries were recommended and vetted by the Bank, on the basis of projected returns that omitted the fact that surpluses were effectively being organised, and price falls were therefore both predictable and unavoidable. The World Bank failed utterly to evaluate the aggregate effect of its own policies.

The dramatic impact of declining commodity prices on debtor nations has been widely acknowledged in the literature on Third World debt. Price indices have been compiled of major export commodities, including foodstuffs, minerals, raw materials and semi-manufactured goods. The studies show that these prices have either declined or persistently failed to keep pace with general world price rises. The net effect has been that for the past four decades, developing nations under pressure to secure surplus export revenues have seen the returns for their products drop remorselessly, year after year. The 'Kennedy Round' of GATT negotiations, conducted between 1963 and 1967, noted;

> There is a need to devise measures designed to attain stable, equitable and remunerative prices, thus permitting ... a dynamic and steady growth of the real export earnings of [less-developed] countries.[6]

However, subsequent to this round of GATT, prices continued to be largely determined by open competition.

Terms of trade

In addition to the decline in commodity prices and export revenues, the prices of goods *imported* from wealthy industrialised nations have steadily increased. This has left debtor nations trapped by ever-worsening 'terms of trade'. Still dependent upon essential imports from the industrialised nations, the prices of which rise inexorably, and yet seeing a steady fall in the prices of their own exports, the growth of debt is fed by both declining export revenues and the escalating cost of imports. On average, the price of manufactures bought by developing countries rose 14% over the period 1954-1966 and the price of goods sold by the developing countries fell by 10%. This represents a deterioration in terms of trade of 24%. Studies of Sub-Saharan African countries showed that their terms of trade deteriorated by at least 34% between 1980 and 1987 alone.[7] As the returns on their exports decline, progressively greater quantities of goods and services have to be exported in an effort to achieve the desired trade surplus. The result is 'a negative transfer of economic resources between debtor and creditor countries.'[8]

The decline in commodity prices is a perfect example of the Ricardian warning concerning free trade. Allowing the free market to determine the price of surplus goods, offered to corporate monopoly buyers based in powerful industrial nations, produced by underdeveloped nations, carrying massive debts, under pressure to export – this is bound to lead to low prices. In economists' jargon, instead of being a process involving mutual gain and 'equal exchange', there is 'unequal exchange' with the benefits accruing principally to commerce based in the wealthy nations.

Foreign investment – or 'how to buy a country'

Exactly the same disastrous failure of free market pricing, due to the gross economic imbalance between the developing and the industrial nations, occurs in another crucial area. Foreign investment, involving the purchase of assets and the payment of wages by large corporate businesses based in the industrialised nations, has again resulted in profound devaluation and poor returns for debtor nations.

This is referred to by economists as poor 'factor' terms of trade. It is best illustrated by comparison with the reasonably equitable foreign investment market that exists between the wealthy nations. For example, no British company can expect to buy or contract significant Dutch land holdings without paying a price that reflects the ability of Dutch agricultural companies to enter the competitive fray. Within Western Europe therefore, foreign and domestic companies are able to compete on a reasonably equal footing and governments are able to regulate where necessary.

In the Third World, by contrast, giant multinationals with their powerful financial base in the wealthy nations face little domestic competition. As for national governments – the corporations have these politicians over a barrel. Many corporations are so big that they totally dwarf nation states. Under acute financial pressure and desperate for foreign money, so long as the words 'debt', 'IMF' and 'World Bank' are not involved, Third World governments are once again at a huge negotiating disadvantage. Multinational corporations have been able to buy up land, mining rights, public and private companies – in fact, entire sectors of debtor nation economies – all at rock-bottom prices. The money this has brought in has had hardly any impact on improving the finances of debtor nations, whilst many of their most valuable assets are now owned and controlled by business interests in the wealthy nations. Debt-equity swaps fall within the same category, involving the transfer of valuable resources and assets at rock-bottom prices. Meanwhile, labour rates are similarly depressed. Multinationals are notorious for the low wages and poor conditions they offer in the Third World, effectively using these nations as cheap manufacturing outposts.

Such deregulated free trade – in this case the trade in assets and investment – runs counter to all the Ricardian caveats. Permanent capital flows between high wage and low wage countries – which is precisely what such foreign investment involves – are specifically warned against. Significant levels of unemployment, against a background of acute poverty, depress labour values to a minimum. The existence of long-term international debt constitutes an enduring imbalance of trade, creating the pressure to 'sell off the family silver'.

Foreign investment in debtor nations, long advocated as a sound development model, shows all the signs of another failed paradigm, akin to the failure of the borrow/invest/export/repay loan model. The initial pricing of factors is disgracefully low, output is directed principally to supplying overseas customers, corporate taxation is competed down to a minimum and profits are subject to repatriation. In economists' terms, the 'added value' of much foreign investment accrues not to the developing nation, but to the company concerned and its shareholders.

The Asian crisis – or 'how to pick up a bargain'

In the Asian financial crisis, we have witnessed yet another failure of the free trade myth, and a very significant new phase in the impoverishment of the developing world. It is one of the central claims of advocates of free trade that market forces will 'level up' the Third World and 'level down' the wealthy nations, gradually leading to the equalisation of wages, prices and values. Free market economists seem unable to appreciate that such disparities in value can be self-perpetuating, in fact reinforcing, rather than competitively reduced. But the 1997 Asian financial crisis demolished overnight the free trade 'doctrine of convergence' and demonstrated *par excellence* the extractive power of foreign investment.

The Asian crisis involved;

1   The mass withdrawal of capital from the Tiger economies.
2   This caused huge falls, both in their currencies and in values on their stock markets.
3   This capital was placed back into the industrialised nations by investors, strengthening their stock markets and commerce, and affording a huge fiscal boost to these economies.
4   The Tiger economies were forced to seek massive loans from the IMF, who insisted that they sell off publicly owned companies and deregulate as a condition of these 'bail-outs'.
5   Investors and commerce in Europe and America were able to move back in and acquire the most valuable industrial assets in these stricken nations, purchasing these at a fraction of their earlier market value.
6   Returns on these investments now provide an ongoing fiscal subsidy to the West.

The free market in investment and speculation wiped out almost overnight any slight narrowing of the income gap between the Asian Tiger economies and the West that had occurred during the previous two decades. This sudden mass transfer of wealth from the Far East to the industrialised West completely destroys the notion that free trade promotes equalisation between nations. Instead, free trade allows the wealthy nations to use their greater power – in this instance the greater strength of European and American capital, its mobility, and its aggression – to perpetually re-establish the income/wealth gap. The peripheral stock markets have become 'a new means of extracting surplus from developing countries'.[9]

The prospect facing the former Tiger economies of Asia is bleak. Their stock markets will recover – but the profits and future dividends will accrue to foreign investors and corporations. Their currencies will recover, but the overhang of additional debt will simply channel interest and debt repayments abroad. For the foreseeable future, the indebted Tiger economies will provide a fiscal subsidy to Europe and America through dividends paid on Asian assets and interest paid on IMF loans. The whole future has been rewritten for these nations, and Koreans will find that the $56 billion bail-out loan their government accepted will take a long, long time to repay.

It is no coincidence that the collapse of the Tiger economies followed a period during which they were either obliged, or enticed, to deregulate their capital controls and permit free trade in investment. Despite admitting that the Asian crisis involved an 'overcorrection' of the market, and that currencies and stock markets crashed to ridiculously low levels, conventional economists have not crit- icised the unjustified transfer of wealth out of Asia that occurred during this 'overcorrection'.

The bitter irony for the Tiger economies is that they have been blamed for the crash, whilst trying to play the Western economic game by the letter. They accepted the institutions, conventions and goals of industrialisation and export- led growth, for years struggling to work their way up the economic ladder. To be pushed to the bottom again and saddled with a debt burden that will make it all the harder to ascend a second time is an intolerable injustice. After decades of effort to improve their standard of living the events in South East Asia amount to an outrageous international crime.

There is an unwillingness to face up to the truth of what has happened in Asia. This was theft – an international commercial robbery carried out under the cover of 'free trade' and 'sound economics'. As a result of the free trade ideology applied to financial structures, the economic geography of the world has been suddenly altered beyond all recognition, counter to all justice, and with long- lasting if not permanent effect. It is a violation as serious as any military invasion.

With the increasingly mobile but erratic behaviour of international finance and the tendency of investors to create self-fulfilling prophecies by mass investment and mass withdrawal, a new pattern is clearly emerging. Instead of involving a progressive decline, Third World debt can now strike out of the blue. Nations that appear to be stable and enjoying a degree of prosperity can find themselves on the list of Heavily Indebted Poor Countries in a space of weeks.

Floating exchange rates – or 'how to lose on the swings and roundabouts'

The decision by the West to promote 'floating exchange rates' is another free market convention that has proved catastrophic for debtor nations. Not only trade and investment but also the actual values of their national currencies were to be left to the free market. It is worth remembering that floating exchange rates were experimented with during the 1930s debt crisis, widely condemned as a failure at that time, and deliberately avoided at Bretton Woods. They were gradually instituted after 1973, willingly by most industrialised nations, but often imposed on debtor nations by the World Bank or IMF as a loan-condition. The history of currency values since 1973 and the catastrophic effect these can have on national accounts shows the drawbacks of this volatile mechanism.

The theory of floating exchange rates is quite rational and its purpose perfectly benign. Indeed, the theory claims to address the problem of indebtedness and unbalanced trading by registering surpluses and shortages of foreign currencies. But the theory does not work.

The theory is that a nation that is a 'net importer' will be passing an excess of its currency into the broader world economy. Meanwhile, a nation that is a 'net exporter' will tend to retain its currency, which will therefore be in short supply. The international money markets will reflect these currency surpluses and shortages. The surplus currency of the 'net importer' nation will fall in value, making its goods and services cheaper overseas, promoting more exports. The currency of the 'net exporter' will increase in value, making its goods and services comparatively more expensive abroad. Thus trade imbalances and currency surpluses and shortages are intended to alter the price of goods to buyers in different countries in such a way that a balance of trade is perpetually fostered.

Unfortunately, like so much free market theory, this series of neat expectations is not a complete version of events. Nor does the empirical evidence support this reliance upon currency values to adjust the balance of trade. Despite the use of floating exchange rates, many nations have run persistent and substantial trade deficits or surpluses for years, clearly demonstrating the functional impotence of this mechanism.

There is a host of factors working to undermine the effectiveness of the floating exchange rate mechanism. To begin with, the loans advanced to the Third World have not been in their own currencies, but in dollars, pounds or yen – the 'hard currencies'. The floating exchange rate mechanism is completely compromised by this. A mechanism that relies upon surplus currencies to redress an imbalance of trade is hardly going to function if a nation runs up a trade deficit by expending another nation's currency!

More fundamentally still, relying upon exchange rate alterations to redress trade imbalances is rather a matter of wishful thinking in which half the relevant factors are ignored. There is the obvious, but frequently ignored point that, whilst lowering the value of a currency may promote exports, it will also raise the cost of imports. This of course is intended to deter imports. But if the demand for imports is 'inelastic', reflecting essential goods and services, contracts and preferences, then the net cost of imports may not fall, and may actually rise. Also, whilst the volume of exports may rise, appearing to promise greater earnings, the financial return per unit of exports will fall. So if the volume of exports does not rise significantly – if world demand is 'inelastic' – then a nation with a falling currency will see little improvement in export earnings. Time and time again, nations devaluing their currencies have seen volumes of exports and imports alter slightly, but with little overall impact on the financial balance of trade.

There are several additional 'facts from the real world' which undermine the effectiveness of the floating exchange rate mechanism. To rely upon surpluses to adjust currency values assumes that all currencies are equal, or 'neutral', in their value, and relate only to what they can buy in domestic markets. In fact, there can never be neutrality in currencies, and the world economy is dominated by a spectrum of hard and weak currencies, with political influence and overall economic strength lending colossal advantage, yet again, to the major players. This advantage is enshrined in the US dollar. Although present in the money markets in vast quantities that ought to lead to significant devaluation, the dollar retains its value by functioning as the *de facto* international currency. This is of particular relevance to Third World debt, since a considerable proportion of that debt is actually denominated in US dollars. Thus the 'demand for dollars' to repay debt actually helps maintain the value of the US dollar. The same is true, to a lesser extent, of the pound, the deutschmark and other hard currencies.

Another factor undermining the exchange rate mechanism is that foreign currency is not used primarily for purposes of simple trade. Since there is no obligation to 'spend back' revenues gained from trading into other countries, foreign currencies tend to be held as official currency reserves, or held by large financial institutions and employed for speculative purposes on the international exchanges. There has been a massive accumulation of such capital on the international money markets in recent years. Turnover on the foreign exchanges now exceeds $1 trillion per day.

The effectiveness of floating exchange rates in compensating for trade imbalances is thus heavily compromised. Export/import trade now accounts for less than 5% of international currency flows. Any shortages or surpluses of currencies due to the recent balance of trade are completely dwarfed by the total of foreign currencies traded for speculation. The values of currencies, instead of reflecting any recent imbalance of trade, reflect a range of other fiscal, economic and political considerations, involving revenues traded for speculative gain. This is a use of foreign exchange that, as the record shows, does as much to confirm as to redress previous trade imbalances.

Falling currencies – or 'how to extract more per dollar of debt'

In the context of Third World debt, there is one further, highly damaging effect of adopting flexible or floating exchange rates. The loans advanced to the Third World are denominated in the hard currencies, so instead of a nation's debt being related to the goods and services produced by its own economy, the debt is tied to the currency, goods and services of the wealthy nations. This is can only be described as a recipe for permanent international debt-slavery. If the value of a debtor nation's currency falls, vastly greater quantities of goods and services have to be exported to obtain the dollars needed for debt settlement. With debts gathering, the currencies of debtor nations have indeed perpetually fallen in value, so their exports earned fewer dollars. As the export revenues declined, so the debts mounted higher and the currencies fell ever further. The brief summary of this is that, as with so many other factors, Third World debt has been perpetually multiplied in material terms.

In the final analysis, the use of currency devaluation to promote exports by debtor nations is a catastrophic and glaring error. In connection with trading, the dominant factor in Third World debt is that the goods and services of the developing nations have, for decades, been sold vastly under value. To devalue a currency is to reinforce and compound this already gross under-valuation of goods and services, and lead to them being sold at ever lower prices, realising even lower returns.

Permanent capital flows – or 'how to depress the opposition'

Free trade theory is only expected to operate satisfactorily if there is an overall equal balance of trade. This is because, as Keynes noted, trade imbalances create major disturbances in the financial conditions within nations. A nation with a trade surplus experiences a monetary influx, with a consequent boost in demand, stimulus for growth and liquidity for investment. A nation that is a net exporter is therefore stimulated to sustain or even increase its level of exports, and finds it receives the monetary input to invest, cut costs and improve its competitiveness.

By contrast, the nation with a trade deficit experiences a monetary efflux, or loss, with a consequent fall in demand for domestic goods and services, and a decline in growth and investment. A nation that is a net importer therefore finds itself pushed towards recession with a drop in demand for domestic goods and services, and experiences a monetary loss that adversely affects growth and investment. It therefore tends to become a less competitive exporter.

Lower costs, cheaper goods and more aggressive exporting by nations with a recent trade surplus coincide with higher costs and prices and declining export competitiveness for nations that have suffered a trade deficit. This has two effects. First, deficits and surpluses continually reinforce each other and a restoration of the trade balance becomes ever more difficult. Second, the lack of competitiveness and liquidity within a debtor nation exposes its commerce to predatory take-over by commerce based in creditor nations. This further secures the advantage of creditor nations. Gunar Myrdal points out that the long-term result is that free trade promotes a 'circularity', rather like a game of Monopoly where a small initial advantage is developed and multiplied until the 'winner takes all'.[10]

Opening borders to promote (an imbalance of) trade

The continual insistence that nations borrowing from the World Bank/IMF should open their domestic markets to competition from abroad is usually portrayed as inherently justified; a sort of *quid pro quo*. The developing nations want something from the wealthy nations – their money in the form of loans – therefore the developing nations should give something in return. They should open up their economies to competition. In fact, the issue of loans coupled with a demand for greater access to debtor nation economies is, in fiscal terms, quite without logical basis.

As we have seen, the lending of money to developing nations institutes an initial imbalance of trade in favour of creditor nations. By the expenditure of these loans, debtor nations have sustained a trade deficit and the wealthy, industrialised nations enjoy a trade surplus. It is therefore a very dubious policy to simultaneously require debtor nations to expose their domestic economies to a flow of further imports. Rather, there is every justification for asserting that debtor nations should not be expected to absorb further imports until the trade imbalance associated with the loan has been redressed. Gunar Myrdal makes this point, emphasising that, far from requiring debtor nations to 'open up' their economies, it would have been far more logical to require the creditor nations to open their economies, and sustain a sufficient trade deficit to restore monetary equilibrium.[11]

History confirms the error of the illogical coupling of loans with a demand for greater access to debtor nation economies. Wherever it has been imposed, dropping trade barriers that protect domestic agriculture and industry has resulted in more powerful nations taking over many domestic markets, leading to a rise in imports. Far from helping the debtor nations earn export revenues, this principal economic condition which the IMF and the World Bank have always imposed has, without exception, made the situation worse.

Free trade and structural adjustment

It is worth briefly analysing the structural adjustment policy of the World Bank in connection with the free trade agenda. Structural adjustment is based on two theories; standard monetarism and the positive aspects of free trade theory. Orthodox monetarist theory requires debtor nations to;

1   Reduce internal demand for consumer goods and services, allowing revenue to be diverted from consumption to debt repayment. This involves wage cuts or freezes coupled with increased taxation.

2   Reduce government expenditure as far as possible, again allowing revenue to be diverted towards debt repayment. This involves cutting government investment, heavy reductions in health, welfare and education services and personnel, and the elimination of subsidies. The elimination of subsidies not only saves revenue but ties in with free market ideology.

3   Restrict the money supply to cut domestic demand and avoid inflation. This involves further reductions in government spending.

Meanwhile, free trade theory requires that the country

1   Open its borders to all foreign trade in all sectors, where it will be forced to compete in, and receive goods from, the 'most efficient suppliers' in the global market.

2   Develop those economic sectors, and concentrate on those goods and services, in which it can best compete. Having discovered its true 'comparative advantage', it will maximise its revenues and be in the optimum position for making debt repayments.

3   Drop all tariffs, quotas, restrictions, subsidies and similar 'inefficient protective devices'.

4   Deregulate to allow free influx of foreign investment in all sectors, and drop controls on inflows and outflows of capital. Stock exchanges and property markets should also allow unrestricted access to foreign investors.

5   Make its currency fully convertible and either devalue it or, preferably, allow it to float freely on the international money markets.

The inherent weaknesses of monetarism and deregulated free trade theory are utterly ignored by Bank/Fund programmes. These are defined as economic orthodoxy and are applied to debtor nations ruthlessly, despite the fact that few Western industrial economies adopt or even subscribe to such thinking without reservation.

In addition, the contradictions between the monetarist and free trade elements of structural adjustment are ignored. Quite how a nation with an economy collapsing like a pack of cards due to monetarist policies, with zero or even negative investment, can be expected to develop a 'comparative advantage' in anything is hard to imagine. Quite how the impoverished Third World nations can be accused of 'over-consumption' and expected to endure demand-restriction policies is equally baffling, while enduring wage cuts, bankruptcies, rising food prices, skyrocketing unemployment, social unrest, declining export revenues from currency devaluation and general deflation. No less contradictory is the expectation that debtor governments will be able to gather surplus revenues for debt repayment after deregulation has permitted foreign competitors to buy up the bulk of a nation's valuable assets at a fraction of their worth; especially when the foreign firms concerned are legally permitted to freely repatriate the profits. Such logical incoherence beggars all reason and judgement, and the results of structural adjustment have been spectacularly and predictably disastrous.

As a typical example, Zambia agreed to a Bank- and Fund-supported plan to auction its currency to allow it to achieve market rates. The currency plummeted, food riots ensued, austerity measures were recommended by the Fund and the currency fell to 10% of its former value. Zambia halted the process and the Bank suspended funds to Zambia. All this took place within a single year; 1985. In Tanzania, the Minister of Planning pointed out that the 1984/5 adjustment programme had clearly failed. The entire economy was faltering, with fixed investment dropping from +38% in 1970 to –35% of domestic demand in the years following 1980.

Free trade – tigers and red herrings

The former rapid growth of the Asian Tiger economies is a pattern of development that many economists promote as a model for the developing nations generally to copy, and one that symbolises free trade. But such an opinion is just plain wrong. The comparison is historically inaccurate in every sense. The Tiger economies conducted their initial and successful development under a regime of tight protectionism, in which foreign imports and capital outflows were heavily curtailed. Cheryl Payer states;

> the demand for import and exchange liberalisation... was not an ingredient of Japan's or of South Korea's development recipe. Imports and capital controls were a striking feature of foreign economic policy as well as an inseparable component of the overall growth strategy in postwar Japan. Instead both countries followed a strategy of jealously protecting the home market and of surprisingly successful import substitution. Nor did either country adopt IMF style austerity policies to restrain domestic demand.[12]

William Greider comments;

> The awesome paradox of free market capitalism in this revolutionary era is that the poorer nations that have succeeded most spectacularly during the last three decades are ones that exercised stringent controls over capital.[13]

Another historical difference between the majority of today's indebted nations and the successful Asian nations is that all the Asian Tigers, with the exception of South Korea, started from a financial position in which their international debt was low. Hong Kong and Singapore began their development with virtually no foreign borrowing, Taiwan with minor debts, and Japan was given technology by the United States in the aftermath of the second world war which gave her a flying start in rebuilding her economy. The only Tiger country which actually developed from a position of debt was South Korea, which remained heavily in debt and continued to suffer from widespread poverty even during the years when her economy was booming. In other words, far from the Asian Tigers providing a model for free trade and an end to debt, the very opposite is the case. This historical lesson is underlined by the recent decline of the Asian Tigers, which has coincided with the opening of their borders to free trade.

Apart from the historical evidence, sheer logic and mathematics point out the inability of free trade to help the Third World. The fundamental reason why the large number of indebted nations cannot 'develop their way to success' through embracing free trade principles is that it is simply not possible for them all to export successfully enough to escape from their debt. It is hard enough to become a net exporting nation, but to export in sufficient quantity to repay the interest on their colossal debts is something that cannot be done by debtor nations *en masse*.

This is never appreciated in the case-by-case approach to the world development problem. It is perhaps rational to imagine any one nation succeeding in the export markets, but how can *all* debtor nations do this? From which countries are they to obtain export revenues? Not from each other, for that would mean some debtor nations improving their financial status at the cost of others moving even deeper into debt; besides, a debtor nation is, by definition, the last place another debtor nation is likely to be able to sell its goods. The only potential sources of revenue for broad-based Tiger-style recovery by the Third World are the richer developed countries – but these nations are also indebted and struggling to maximise exports. It is pretended that a country can overcome its problems by the policy of free trade, but not admitted that other countries must fail.

But when these 'lowest cost countries' have won the export battle, what sort of revenues will they be obtaining? By definition, these will be low, because this is how and why they can win the export battle. What possible help can this be in recovering from debt? The debt will remain, or even grow. Indeed this is exactly what happened in the past. In a very real sense, the indebted nations have already tried to become Tiger economies; they tried it for forty years between 1950 and 1990 with coffee, bananas, tea, fruit and cocoa; and when this didn't work, they switched to petrochemicals and minerals; and when this didn't work they switched to manufacturing. How is industrialisation in order to supply microchips and cola going to alter the intense financial competition which results in ever lower prices, as more and more countries compete to supply what the richer nations want, products which the richer nations are also trying to produce themselves?

In summary, the Tigers did not achieve success through free trade policies, and it is logically impossible for more than a few nations to work their way out of debt, especially when the richer nations are also conducting their trading programmes from a position of financial insolvency;

> The model (of Tiger development) does not match the reality of societies held up as examples, and even if the model were real, it is not generalisable because world surpluses and deficits are a zero sum game.[14]

Price and value – the key issue

Perhaps the key failure in free trade theory relates to price and value. It is one of the sacred dogmas of free market economics that the market determines 'price' as an accurate statement of 'value'. In a sense, the entire history of Third World debt amounts to a pure indictment of this shallow acceptance, since the market blatantly fails to give a just value to the wealth that originates in the debtor nations. Ricardo's warning rings out loud and clear. Free trade – whether it be in manufactured goods, primary commodities or capital investment – between nations with wildly differing financial and technological development, simply is not fair game.

The issue of 'price', and the additional factors discussed above, all contribute to an explanation of the great contradiction of Third World debt. This is the discrepancy between a fiscal balance of trade which denotes the Third World to be 'in debt', and the physical balance of trade which common sense would assess as placing the Third World firmly in credit. In short, the Third World has been exploited and expropriated by a wholly inappropriate free trade agenda, first built into international trade ideology at Bretton Woods, and since progressively imposed upon the developing world, causing untold suffering and 'expropriation by economics'.

The pittance paid to Third World nations for their exports and assets has been widely recognised as an international disgrace for decades, leading to countless calls for price protection, equitable trade and international agreements on commodity prices and factor prices. Unfortunately, free trade ideology has exerted such a grip on the minds of economists that the concept of 'unequal exchange' is widely ignored, even though it actually constitutes an established and important element of trade theory. Indeed, the free market advocate, Douglas Irwin, has admitted that

> ...of all the economic arguments against free trade, the terms of trade argument appears to be the most robust and least subject to qualification or exception, and it remains the most widely acknowledged and generally accepted restriction to free trade admitted by economic theory.[15]

Summary

The theory of free trade is almost a religion amongst economists. This description does not, however, do justice to the strong diversity of opinion over the merits of free trade. Indeed, John Hicks claimed as long ago as 1959 that free trade was no longer accepted by economists, even as an ideal, in the way that it once was.[16]

More recently, in 1997 Alan Freeman commented on the 'doctrine of convergence', stating emphatically;

> The most fundamental point to grasp is that free trade produces inequality.

The neo-classical doctrine of convergence predicts that in consequence of trade, the disparities between trading nations should disappear over time. The nearest adequate term for this idea is 'cretinous'. No serious known fact supports it.[17]

A misplaced free trade agenda is implicated in declining commodity prices, poor factor terms of trade, currency instability and the wholesale transfer of wealth out of the developing nations through the financial markets. If it does nothing else, this broad failure of the free trade ethic demolishes the derogatory claim, persistently made by conventional economists, that Third World debt is the product of economic incompetence, the mis-spending of loans and a failure to invest.

The failure of the doctrine of convergence is not difficult to appreciate. The caveats of free trade warn of the danger of circularity. Permanent capital flows, both through trade imbalances and debt remission, inevitably confer an increasing advantage on creditor nations whilst debtor nations find themselves progressively impoverished.

The deteriorating status of many debtor nations is disguised by two factors.

First, the continual issue of fresh loans and constant foreign investment buy-outs, and the acceptance that this is somehow a 'normal' state of affairs, allows free market economists to imagine that there will be a 'turn-around' at some imaginary point in the future.

Second, the massive transfer of wealth, in the form of assets, to foreign investors is not accounted as a loss to debtor nations. It is a convention to account foreign-owned assets and their output as part of the capital base of developing nations. This allows economists to regard as prosperous a heavily indebted nation, largely owned by foreign investors either directly or via stocks and shares, where output is heavily oriented to exports and where profits are repatriated out of the country. The same economists will continually scratch their heads as to why this wealth perpetually fails to improve the lot of the poor majority, whose numbers grow constantly, while the true domestic economy contracts as it is progressively sold off.

The culpability of the wealthy nations for the débâcle of imposing free trade on an indebted Third World takes the case for debt cancellation forward on two fronts.

First, there is the fact that these free market mechanisms have been imposed by the wealthy industrialised nations, and their corporate and political representatives.

Second, the Third World has clearly repaid its debts in real terms of material wealth. If no real debt exists, no financial debt should exist.

Endnotes

1   Gunar Myrdal. *Economic theory and Underdeveloped Regions.* Duckworth and Company. 1957.

2   Pierre Jalée. *The Pillage of the Third World.* Monthly Review Press. 1968.

3   Pierre Jalée. *Op. cit.*

4   Peter Nunnenkamp. *The International Debt Crisis of the Third World.* Harvester Wheatsheaf Press. 1986.

5   Arghiri Emmanuel. *Unequal Exchange.* Monthly Review Press. 1972.

6   Douglas A. Irwin. *Against the Tide; An Intellectual History of Free Trade.* Princeton University Press. 1996.

7   A. P. Thirlwall. *Financing Economic Development.* Macmillan Studies in Economics. Macmillan 1976.

8   Michel Chossudovsky. *The Globalisation of Poverty.* Zed Books. 1997.

9   Michel Chossudovsky. *Op. cit.*

10   Gunar Myrdal. *Op. cit.*

11   Gunar Myrdal. *Op. cit.*

12   Cheryl Payer. *Lent and Lost.* Zed Books. 1991.

13   William Greider. *One World Ready or Not.* The Penguin Press. 1997.

14   Cheryl Payer. *Op. cit.*

15   Douglas A. Irwin. *Op. cit.*

16   J. R. Hicks. 'Free Trade and Modern Economics'. In *Essays in World Economics.* Oxford: Clarendon Press. 1959.

17   Frances Hutchinson. *What Everyone Really Wants to Know About Money.* Jon Carpenter. 1997.

7

Monetary analysis of Third World debt

erhaps the gravest, and certainly the most astonishing, omission from the debate over Third World debt is the lack of any monetary analysis. Debt is measured in monetary units – millions or billions of pounds, dollars, francs or yen. Despite this, in the extensive literature on debt and development, no single book appears to exist that analyses Third World debt from a purely monetary perspective.

Modern debt is acknowledged to be a widespread and baffling problem. We have already seen how Third World debt fails to reflect the physical or 'real' balance of trade, which emphasises that the developing nations are not in a position of true debt. A similar judgement must surely be passed on that dynamo of achievement and symbol of prosperity, the United States. That the wealthiest and most powerful nation on earth carries a national debt of $5.5 trillion, mortgage debts in excess of $4.5 trillion and commercial debts of $4 trillion are facts that do not make immediate sense. If the debts of the wealthiest nation on the planet are mounting faster than those of any other nation, what hope have the developing nations of ever escaping the 'debt trap'?

The Americans are the most heavily indebted people of an astonishingly indebted age. Everywhere debt is escalating, flatly contradicting the common-sense assessment that ours is an age of progress, achievement and staggering productivity – another clash between the economic measurement of 'debt' and what is true in the real world. In discussing the Third World, the profound and unexplained indebtedness of the entire planet ought surely to direct our attention to an analysis of debt, if not out of suspicion for its validity, then in an effort to understand the nature of debt so as to address its consequences more effectively.

This chapter explores the nature of modern debt and money. It describes the money supply mechanism employed in modern economies and outlines the actual monetary structure of Third World debt. This offers a further explanation of why developing country debts have become a permanent feature of the global economy – a trap from which impoverished nations cannot escape, however hard their peoples may work or rapidly their economies may expand.

Money and debt

The reason for the global escalation of debt is simple. 'Debt' has been built into modern economies as the foundation of their monetary system. Throughout the world, national economies rely upon their banking system to create their medium of exchange. Banking has, over the years, switched from being a mechanism whereby money is lent between people, to being a mechanism for supplying money to the entire global economy. Typically, a staggering 95% of the money stock in the modern economy is now the product of bank lending – numerical money or 'credit' – created by the process of fractional reserve banking. In short, the process of 'going into debt' is relied upon to supply money to the economy as a whole.

There are two main sections in this chapter, focusing on the nature and role of money in the global economy. The first outlines the role of banking as the money supply mechanism within national economies. It lays particular emphasis on the status of economically advanced nations, since the intractability of Third World debt cannot be understood without an appreciation of the gross indebtedness of the wealthy nations, and it is their over-reliance upon banking that is the direct cause of this. The second section is an analysis of the precise monetary structure of the loans extended to developing nations.

1   The debt-based national money supply

The money stock within developed nations is almost entirely supplied by banking through a process that, regardless of the impact on Third World debt, raises serious questions of social justice and economic suitability. There are two aspects to this money supply, which are considered separately below. The first is private and commercial debt. The second is borrowing undertaken by government through the national debt.

(a) Private and commercial debt

In the UK, as in most developed nations, over 95% of the entire money stock currently consists of bank credit, created by the action of lending to private borrowers. The true function of banks and building societies in creating and supplying such a vast proportion of the nation's money stock is in stark contrast to the public perception of these institutions as 'lending other people's money'.

When a bank or building society advances any loan, this loan contributes to a direct increase in the total money stock; it is thus not just a loan, but a creation of additional money. This increase in the money stock then provides the banking system with the deposit base from which to advance further loans, which then also contribute directly to the money stock. Thus the money stock is almost entirely composed of a vast aggregate of outstanding loans, past and present, which provide the money stock against which further bank credit creation will take place. In effect, money is borrowed into existence and into circulation from banks and building societies. Andrew Crocket observes;

> Taking the banking system as a whole, the act of lending creates, as a direct consequence, deposits exactly equal to the amount of lending undertaken. Provided, therefore, banks all move forward in step, there appears to be no limit to the amount of bank money they can create. Even more than this, there would appear to be a basic instability in the banking system.[1]

By this method of money creation and supply, any increase in the money stock is directly paralleled by a pro-rata increase in the total of outstanding debt. It is this parallel between debt and the money stock, and the action of lending institutions in supplying the money stock on condition of future repayment, which has given rise to the descriptive term, the 'debt-based money system'.

It is worth dwelling on the actual process of credit creation by banks, since this will help us clarify the position of Third World debt at a later stage. Bank credit creation is essentially a circular, feedback mechanism. If a borrower is granted a loan of, for example, £5,000, the bank simply approves credit to this amount. None of the bank's depositors will find their deposit has been reduced, immobilised or in any way affected by this loan. When the £5,000 loan is spent, the credit will pass from the borrower to a recipient, who will then deposit the cheque or money order in their bank account. The banking system then receives the £5,000 cheque as a full deposit of new money. Banks and building societies, in accepting cheques, do not distinguish between credit that has just been created as a loan, and credit that is simply transferred from one account to another.

Although this sum was created as a loan, total deposits within the banking system will have increased by £5,000, with a corresponding and equivalent increase in the total of debt. The increase in deposits then provides the collateral against which further loans can be advanced, resulting in yet more deposits and then yet more lending. It is this circular 'feedback of deposits' mechanism, whereby loans create deposits, thus providing an increased deposit base for further loans, that provides the bulk of the money stock in a modern economy. Perhaps the best description of the situation to which this leads was provided by H. D. Macleod;

> When it is said that a great London joint stock bank has perhaps £50,000,000 of deposits, it is almost universally believed that it has £50,000,000 of actual money to 'lend out' as it is erroneously called... It is a complete and utter delusion. These deposits are not deposits in cash at all, they are nothing but an enormous superstructure of credit.[2]

This is the money supply mechanism underpinning the modern economy. It is a measure of the power of this mechanism that the stock of bank credit in the UK economy has increased from £11.1 billion to £655 billion pounds between 1963 and 1997. (See the table and graph on pages 93 and 94).

Banks and building societies

Modern banking is often described as 'fractional reserve banking' because of the nature of the legislation that governs the ability of banks to create credit. Under the Basle Accord of 1989, the legal requirement is that domestic commercial banks should hold reserves of at least 8% of their total outstanding loans. Banks should not make loans in excess of this figure. Because loans are accounted as assets of a bank, banks are not obliged to wait for their deposit base to increase, but can project and multiply their loans to the extent that these are still 'covered' by reserves of 8% of total loans. Of course, because of the perpetual escalation in the money stock and constant demand for more loans, banks must steadily increase their reserves. This they manage in part through the difference between the rates of interest paid to depositors and collected from borrowers, and in part through direct investments.

It is important to appreciate that building societies and 'savings and loans' societies now function as part of the banking sector, with the ability to create credit. For many years, these institutions were viewed as 'financial intermediaries', simply lending out money they held on deposit, and making no net contribution to the aggregate money stock. However, with the increasing duration of mortgages, the decreasing requirement that building society depositors leave their savings in 'time-deposits' and the proven contribution of building societies' mortgages to the growth of their own deposit base, the credit-creating ability of building societies and their functional similarity to banks has become apparent.

Building societies may not operate against a fractional reserve in quite the same way as banks, but this does not significantly hinder their credit-creating abilities. Their deposit base continually increases as a result of earlier lending, both by themselves and banks. Also, building societies are now legally permitted to act as borrowers in order to maintain their accounts. For this reason, no-one today will ever find that a building society refuses their request for a mortgage on the grounds that the society itself 'hasn't got enough money'. The contribution of building societies to the total money stock is apparent from the annual monetary statistics released by central financial authorities, such as the Bank of England or Federal Reserve.

The growth of the money stock

The annual statistics available from central banks give details of the net results of bank and building society lending, the creation and growth of the money stock (M4), and the corresponding growth of debt (M4 Lending Counterpart). Bank of England Statistical Releases detail the UK money supply and the table opposite shows the growth in the total money stock since 1963, and also the parallel growth in the total of outstanding debt carried by industry and individuals. The table also shows the declining proportion of money, in the form of notes and coins, supplied to the economy free from debt by the government. For purposes

Year	Total coins & notes (M0) £ billion	Total debt (M4 Lending Counterpart) £ billion	Total Money Stock (M4) £ billion	Percentage of Money Stock issued Debt-free (M0/M4)
1963	3.0	9.0	14.1	21%
1965	3.3	11.6	16.0	20%
1967	3.7	13.0	18.8	19%
1969	3.8	15.8	23	17%
1971	4.3	19.2	27	16%
1973	5.1	32	39	13%
1975	6.5	43	53	12%
1977	8.1	52	65	12%
1979	10.5	72	87	12%
1981	12.1	101	116	10.5%
1983	12.8	151	161	7.9%
1985	14.1	209	205	6.8%
1987	15.5	291	269	5.8%
1989	17.2	438	372	4.6%
1991	18.6	586	485	3.8%
1993	20.0	625	525	3.8%
1995	22.4	679	585	3.8%
1997	25.0	780	680	3.6%

Source; Bank of England Statistical Releases, 1995, 1997.[3]

of comparison, the final column shows the amount of government-created notes and coins as a percentage of the total money stock.

The data in the table above is reproduced in graph form on the next page.

Composition of the money stock

The table and graph show that there has been a marked change in the composition of the money stock over the last forty years. The role of coins and notes, and their proportion of the money stock, has fallen from over 20% to less than 4%. This is due entirely to lack of demand for this tangible, physical form of money, and an increasing use of credit and debit facilities in which monetary transactions are carried out by credit card and computer transfers. However, this apparently innocuous trend away from physical money towards 'number money' has had a profound consequence. Coins and notes are created '*ab initio*' and free from debt.

Graph of "Money Stock" (M4) and Domestic Debt 1963 - 1996

£ Billions

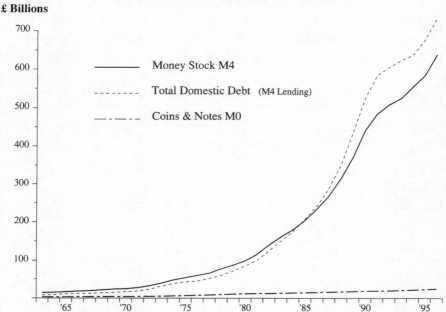

By a process of exchange with the banking system, the government, which creates the notes and coins of a nation's currency, spends this quantity of original money into the economy, *debt free*. By contrast, all numerical money, or credit, only comes into existence *in parallel with an equivalent amount of debt*. Thus the decline in use of notes and coins has had the vicarious effect of significantly decreasing the positive, debt-free basis of the UK money stock from 21% to 3.6%, and increasing the reliance of the economy upon debt-created money to the current level of 96%.

Of the £680 billion of private and commercial debt associated with the supply of the UK money stock in 1997, Bank of England statistics show that some £490 billion was borne by individuals, mostly as house mortgages, whilst the remainder was the backlog of debt carried by various forms of commerce. The massive increase in the money stock created and supported by mortgages offers a valuable insight into the fiscal pressures operating within developed nations. These pressures are of the greatest significance in evaluating the international monetary flows that impinge upon Third World debt.

Mortgages

Figures from the Council for Mortgage Lenders and the Building Societies' Association[4] show that in 1997 a total of £411 billion was outstanding on mortgages in the United Kingdom. This means that a total of £411 billion had been created and circulated through mortgages, representing approximately 60% of the total money stock. In America the 1997 total outstanding on mortgages stood at $4.2 trillion, representing over 80% of the money stock.[5] The startling decline in housing equity over recent years and the difficulty faced by people with high mortgages underlines the very questionable principle of relying upon housing debt to supply money to an economy.

The United Kingdom is heralded as a property-owning democracy, but the evidence does not support this – indeed the evidence points in the opposite direction. The number of owner-occupiers has risen substantially in the UK over the last 30 years, but this trend towards home-buying has disguised a dramatic decline in true home ownership and a massive upsurge in housing debt. Over the period from 1960 to 1996, the proportion of privately owned houses owned outright without a mortgage dropped from 51% of the housing stock in 1960 to 35% in 1996. This was despite 36 years during which these notional home-owners paid out increasing sums as mortgage payments. Meanwhile, the total number of mortgaged properties rose from 3.3 million to nearly 11 million, rising from less than 20% to nearly 50% of the housing stock. The marked increase in the total of properties under mortgage is compounded by the amounts owed on these 11 million mortgaged properties. In 1960, the average debt outstanding on a mortgaged house stood at £990, equivalent to approximately 1.1 times the average annual wage. By 1996, the average debt on a mortgaged house was over £38,000, equivalent to twice the average annual wage.

In summary, not only do citizens in the UK own outright a smaller proportion of houses than 30 years ago, and not only are there nearly four times as many mortgaged properties, but on those mortgaged properties people owe nearly twice as much in relation to their annual income. An equity analysis of the overall situation shows that, in 1960, 19% of the total value of the UK private housing stock was under mortgage. By 1996, 37% of the value of the nation's private houses were subject to mortgages.[6]

In the United States, the 1997 total of $4.2 trillion outstanding on mortgages represented 48% of all private housing equity. This has risen from 36% since 1967, despite no overall increase in the proportion of owner-occupied homes during that period.[7]

Commercial and industrial debt

Mortgages are not the only form of debt through which money is raised in the developing nations. Extensive debt is also carried by industry, agriculture and other forms of commerce. In the UK, commercial debt increased from 11% to 20% of GDP between 1963 and 1996, whilst debts outstanding to Other Financial Institutions grew from 4% to 18% of GDP over the same period.[8] The growth in all forms of internal debt – consumer, commercial and financial – highlights the severe monetary pressure under which businesses and citizens in the wealthy nations operate.

(b) The national debt

In outlining the financial status of developed nations and the basis of their money supply, we must examine the institution of the national debt, which acts as a vital part of the money supply to an economy. The mechanism of the national debt is relatively straightforward. It involves the assumption of debt by a national government in order to obtain the additional revenue needed to cover any annual shortfall of taxation.

There are two principal sources of revenue upon which governments can call for this; (1) commercial banks and building societies and (2) savings, insurance, pension and trust funds (the non-banking sector).

Governments draw up official treasury or federal bonds to fund the Public Sector Borrowing Requirement (PSBR), and these bonds are auctioned on the money markets. Depending upon whether the bonds are bought by the non-banking sector (e.g. pension and insurance funds) or the banking sector (all lending institutions), money is either recycled from savings in parallel with debt, or created by the act of bank lending, again in parallel with debt.

It is important to be clear about the nature of the contribution of the national debt to a nation's money stock. When government bonds are bought by the non-banking sector, funds held in various savings institutions (pension, life assurance and trust funds etc.) are brought back into everyday circulation, the sums being re-disbursed into the economy through public services and other spending. Thus, monies relied upon for future payments are recycled into the economy, in parallel with a debt undertaken by the government, and registered against the nation's assets. However, when government bonds are bought by the banking sector, additional money is created since the purchase is made against, or using, the bank's fractional reserve. Just as with private/commercial debt, additional bank credit is thus created and new deposits of bank credit result.

In summary, bonds bought by the non-banking sector recycle monies from savings into everyday circulation; bonds bought by the banking sector contribute to the total money stock. There is a parallel increase in debt in both cases.

It is very significant that, although national debts contribute to the total money supply, most developed nations currently register a money stock lower than that created by private/commercial debt alone. Meanwhile, that money created via the national debt is now completely absent from the money stock. The reason for this discrepancy is that over the last two decades, the majority of nations, including the UK and the United States, have suffered a considerable and sustained net loss of revenues to the international arena. This outflow is evident in the UK money stock: the table on page 93 shows how the total of debt began to exceed the money stock during 1985.

Closer examination of this data shows that, for example, in 1963 the level of private/commercial debt (£9 billion) was markedly less than the total money stock (£14.1 billion). Since coins and notes totalled £3 billion, the addition to the circulating money stock from the national debt was both significant and apparent. In the 1970s there was substantial financial deregulation of national economies, including Britain's, prompting substantial outflows of capital. The chart shows that by 1985, private/commercial debt had begun to exceed the money stock (M4 Lending Counterpart £209 billion; M4 £205 billion). This was despite coins and notes produced debt-free to the value of £14 million and a national debt of £155 billion (approximately 20% of which represented purchases by the banking sector, which had thereby created £31 billion). Therefore at least £35 billion of UK money had been lost to the international arena or to other nations. By 1996, the total money stock stood at £680 billion. The total of £780 billion of private/ commercial debt, £25 billion of coins and notes, plus national debt of £380 billion (approximately 20% of which represented purchases by the banking sector) indicates total money creation amounting to £881 billion. Comparing this with the actual money stock (M4) of £680 billion, the total loss of revenues thus stood at approximately £200 billion.

This position of negative financial equity is not peculiar to Britain. The United States, through the *de facto* use of the dollar as the international currency, has lost massive quantities of money created by private/commercial borrowers and the Federal deficit to the international arena. It should be stressed that these debts remain in spite of such monetary efflux. Borrowers throughout the economy are still liable for repayment and interest charges, even if all the money these debts have created has been lost from the domestic economy.

Wealthy nations and the pressure of debt

At the end of 1997, the UK national debt stood at approximately £400 billion, that of Canada $600 billion, Germany DM500 billion and America's national debt exceeded $5 trillion. The aggregate of national debts coupled with the private/commercial debt directly associated with the money supply places these nations in a position of permanent financial exposure.

The requirement to service and/or repay the gathering total of debt places a significant and growing burden on all sectors of developed nation economies. Over the last two decades, the requirement for mortgage interest and capital repayment has risen; standing interest charges and distress borrowing by commerce have risen, local authority debt and interest charges have risen, and so has central government debt. Nor have these increases been merely a reflection of monetary inflation, but they have increased in real terms, rising by comparison with GDP and against other indicators.

There is, as a result, acute financial pressure within the economies of the wealthy nations. Commerce finds itself perpetually under threat from over-exposure and increasingly vulnerable to the vagaries of the business cycle. The business cycle itself, which reflects the momentum of new borrowing and its effect on demand and investment, has proven increasingly volatile. Domestic borrowers, through their house mortgages and other forms of credit-buying, are now increasingly reliant upon maintaining their income, and vulnerable to interest rate increases and the penalties of default. Governments find an increasing proportion of their tax receipts are absorbed by the demands of interest payments on the national debt, and are obliged to perpetually increase this debt both to meet their public service obligations and to maintain liquidity and demand within the economy.

All governments find themselves in the position where they must monitor a wide range of financial data and base their fiscal policy decisions on the conflicting demands of taxation, maintaining consumer demand, balance of payments data, the annual deficit, inflationary and deflationary pressures, and so on.

It is notable that this increasing financial pressure bears no relation to the real wealth of these nations, but is a function of the money supply principle they have adopted. In physical, productive terms, nations such as America, Britain, Canada and Germany are extremely wealthy. However their economies are founded upon a financial system that registers a massive and constantly escalating total of debt, as a function of their money supply. As we shall see, this is of the greatest significance to Third World debtor nations.

2   The nature and composition of Third World debt

It might be wondered how it can be that the wealthy nations are able, from a position of such perpetual monetary shortage and insolvency, to lend money to the developing nations. The answer to this is that *they do not*. The money advanced to Third World nations is not money loaned from the wealthy nations. The sums advanced as loans to Third World nations consists almost entirely of additional monies that have been created by the commercial banking mechanism specifically for the purpose of the loan concerned. The loans are not loans of pre-existent money, but additional sums of money created by the process of fractional reserve banking. In other words, the same debt-based banking process used to supply money to national economies is also employed for the creation and supply of funds to debtor nations. Thus, these monies are not owed by debtor countries to the developed nations, but to private commercial banks.

Although earlier chapters have contained considerable discussion of the World Bank and IMF, the point has already been made that the bulk of developing country debt does not involve these institutions. Over 65% of Third World debt involves money loaned from commercial sources – i.e. commercial banks. We now examine the three major sources of loans to developing nations, starting with the dominant commercial banking sector before studying the contributions of the World Bank and IMF.

Commercial loans

Commercial banks employ precisely the same credit-creating mechanism in advancing loans to developing nations as they do in making loans within a domestic economy. Whether operating against a fractional reserve or simply by virtue of holding an excess of unloaned deposits, international commercial banks extend credit to both governments and private commerce in other countries.

None of a bank's depositors finds their deposits reduced or affected in any way by the act of lending to an overseas borrower, any more than if the money were loaned to a domestic borrower. Naturally, the bank cannot guarantee or assume that the credit it advances will return to it as a future deposit, nor to which country it will eventually return as an additional deposit. But the same constraint operates within a nation's domestic banking system. And just as a loan within a national economy must return as a deposit somewhere in the national banking system, so a loan to the Third World must create an additional deposit within the global financial system as a whole.

A number of factors operate to lend 'back-up' to commercial banks in the credit-creating process of Third World debt. First, loans to the Third World are not intended for expenditure within those national economies, but for foreign purchases. Such loans are advanced in the hard currencies of 'creditor' nations, and thus are more likely to find their way back to those nations. Also, much aid has been, and still is, in some degree 'tied' back to purchases from the economies advancing these loans. Finally, the majority of banks issuing such loans are in no sense themselves tied or restricted by national borders, but are international corporations with lending and depositing facilities world-wide. As a result, the fact that loans to the Third World are 'cross-border' does not in any way change their status as creations of credit, additions to the global money stock and back-up for further loans, whether national or international. The myth of 'recycled' petrodollars from the oil price rise in the early 1970s provides a perfect illustration of this;

> Far from the 1973 OPEC price rise leading to the 'recycling of surplus petrodollars', as is commonly portrayed, the supposed recycling was a creation by banks of additional money as a debt, equivalent to those deposits of petrodollars. What is more, through the increased price of oil, much of this additional money, advanced as credit to the Third World was spent back into the Arab countries, and their monetary deposits thereby increased, proving beyond doubt that money was being created, not lent. The 'recycling' period was a period of mass money creation by international banks, involving a massive increase in the global money supply, and massive additional debt for the Third World.[9]

The World Bank

The loans advanced by the World Bank also involve the creation of money as credit, and constitute additions to the global money stock. Holding only a nominal reserve contributed by the wealthy nations, the World Bank raises large quantities of money by drawing up bonds and selling these to commercial banks on the money markets of the world. Thus, the World Bank does not itself create the money it advances to Third World nations, but sells bonds to commercial banks which, in purchasing these bonds, create money for the purpose. The World Bank therefore functions rather along the lines of a country's national debt. Just as with the government bonds of a country's national debt, when a commercial bank makes a purchase of World Bank money-bonds, the commercial bank creates additional bank credit against the deposits held at that time. And just as with other forms of bank credit creation, this instantly creates additional monetary deposits.

In essence, the World Bank acts as broker for commercial banks, who are the actual money-creation agents and who hold World Bank bonds in lieu of monies they create in parallel with debts, these debts being registered against Third World nations. Although these loans may be denominated in pounds, dollars or francs, such loans advanced under the auspices of the World Bank have no necessary connection with respective national economies, and in no sense represent monies loaned by these nations, nor debts owed to them by developing nations. The debts are owed to private, commercial banks (through the World Bank) in respect of money they have created through the purchase of debt bonds.

The International Monetary Fund

The money-creating activities of the IMF are slightly more complex. The IMF presents itself as a financial pool – an international reserve of money built up with contributions (known as quotas) from subscribing nations, that is, most nations of the world. However, credit creation accompanies almost every aspect of IMF funding. It is best to analyse the basis of the IMF's lending ability, the money creation and the debt associated with it, into its component parts.

(a)   25% of each nation's IMF quota is paid in the form of gold, the remainder in the nation's own currency. The 25% gold quota is the only component of IMF lending capacity that does not, in some way, constitute additional money created in parallel with debt.

(b)   The 75% of a nation's quota payable in national currency is today invariably funded by the government concerned through the sale of bonds, thus adding to that nation's national debt. Therefore the IMF, whilst not itself creating credit, places monetary demands on member countries for quotas that can only be funded by increases in each country's deficit. This involves the sale of government bonds to commercial banks, leading to money creation by those banks. This source of revenue forms the main fund of IMF monies available to developing nations.

(c) The total funds of the IMF were substantially increased and its function and status as a money-creation agency clarified when, in 1979, the IMF instituted Special Drawing Rights (SDRs). These SDRs were avowedly created as, and intended to serve as, an additional international currency. Although they are 'credited' to each nation's account with the IMF, if a nation borrows these SDRs (defined in dollars) it must repay this amount, or pay interest on the loan. Whilst SDRs are described as amounts 'credited' to a nation, no money or credit of any kind is put into nations' accounts. SDRs are actually a credit facility, just like a bank overdraft – if they are borrowed, they must be repaid. Thus, the IMF is now creating and issuing money in the form of a new international currency, created in parallel with an equivalent debt, under a system essentially the same as that of a bank – the IMF 'reserve' being the original pool of quota funds.

(d) Since the monetary demands on the IMF are constantly increasing, due to rising demand for Third World loans, the quota demands by the IMF have reached the point where (so-called) creditor nations such as America and Britain are reluctant to undertake yet more bond issues and further national debt to supply these funds. Therefore, in recent years, the IMF has begun to circumvent the restrictions of its overall quota. By co-operating directly with commercial banks to organise more substantial loans than it can fund from its own quota resources, the IMF administers 'loan packages' made up in part from its own quotas and in part from commercial sources. For example, of the $56 billion loan advanced under the auspices of the IMF to South Korea in the wake of the Asian crisis, only $20 billion was actually contributed by the Fund itself, the remaining $36 billion being arranged by direct co-operation with international commercial banks who created money for the purpose.

Summary

In the modern global economy, the banking sector creates money as credit in parallel with an equivalent debt. Private, commercial and government borrowers all contribute to the creation of a money stock that only exists and continues to circulate so long as sufficient agents remain in debt to the banking system. Increases in the money stock require increases in the gross total of debt.

In 1998, $2,200 billion was outstanding as Third World, or international debt. The great majority of this sum represents money created as credit by commercial banks, in parallel with debt. In no sense do the loans advanced by the World Bank and IMF constitute monies owed to the notional 'creditor nations'. Third World nations are not 'in debt to' the industrialised nations; they are in debt to commercial and multilateral banks and lending institutions. This is reinforced by the fact that, in submitting quotas to the IMF, the creditor nations are themselves obliged to undertake debt, raising these quotas by recourse to their national debts. Thus, even if some of the money loaned to debtor nations can be traced back to the creditor nations, this money can be traced back further to the banking sector.

Whilst not in debt to the industrialised nations, to meet the obligation to repay their debts to the international banking sector developing nations must re-obtain the sums advanced to them by exporting goods and services to these nations. This represents a major economic anomaly. A debt towards one group of institutions (commercial and multilateral banks) finds expression as a debt towards another group of institutions (the industrialised nations), despite the fact that no such obligation truly exists.

The near-impossibility of achieving such export revenues from 'wealthy' nations, which are likewise deeply indebted, reinforces the conclusion that Third World debt is inherently lacking in validity. In order to appreciate this, it is necessary to discuss the effect of gross international debt on trading relations between countries. The following chapter therefore applies the above analysis of the structure of Third World debt, and the nature of modern money, to the economic problems faced by the developing nations. A full monetary analysis, coupled with the foregoing chapters on the defects in the accountancy of trade, confirms categorically that Third World debts do not deserve to be considered as true debts between countries. These debts are little more than a reflection of the current 'debt-based' financial system and inadequate trading conventions. The further conclusion is that this reliance upon banking and debt to create the medium of exchange creates a financial system that is grossly deficient, and provides insufficient support to national and international economies.

Endnotes

1   Andrew Crocket. *Money.* Nelson. 1997.
2   H. D. Macleod. *The Theory of Credit.* Longman Green. 1984.
3   Bank of England. *Annual Statistical Releases*, 1995, 1997. HMSO.
4   *A Compendium of Building Society Statistics* (Eighth Edition). The Building Societies Association. 1990. Steve Wilcox. *Housing Review 1996/7.* The Joseph Rowntree Foundation. 1997.
5   Patrick A. Simmons (ed). *Housing Statistics of the United States.* Bernan Press. 1997.
6   Statistics are a summary of data published by The Bank of England, Council for Mortgage Lenders, Building Societies Association, Department of the Environment Housing Construction Statistics.
7   Patrick A. Simmons (ed). *Op. cit.*
8   Michael Rowbotham. *The Grip of Death.* Jon Carpenter. 1997.
9   Michael Rowbotham. *Op. cit.*

8
Monetary reform and Third World debt

The previous chapter dealing with the mechanics of money creation contains little reference to the Third World or development literature. There are two reasons for this. First, the intention was to present a clear description of the little understood process by which money and debt are related in modern national and international economies. The process is at once simple yet, since it is essentially an abstract world of numerical accountancy, rather nebulous and hard to grasp. Comments from development literature on the damaging effects of debt would add little. The second reason for not including a battery of relevant extracts from Third World debt literature is that the quotes do not exist – or rather, they are extremely uncommon.

Rare observations

Statements showing an awareness of the link between debt and money, and suggesting that this might have a bearing on Third World debt are, as the saying goes, as rare as hens' teeth. There are a few, however. The following comment by Lord Lever and Christopher Huhne shows recognition of the role of banking in Third World debt, the creation of money that this involves, and a clear sense of unease;

> As the deposits rolled in, the banks hastened to lend. Later the lending itself created new deposits. This is to make no more than the well-known point that in every banking system, every loan creates a new deposit in the system as a whole... [In lending to the Third World] the advanced countries had thrown a single vulnerable section of their economies, the banking system, into a task which it could not bear without official support... debtors inevitably became vulnerable to the disintegration of market confidence.[1]

Benjamin Hopenhayn and Marcelo Dinenzon also mention the key role of banking in supplying money (or 'liquidity'), and draw attention to the risk and uncertainty this automatically creates;

> A central feature of the post-Bretton Woods regime(s) is the primary role of bank credit as a source of international liquidity... [via]...endogenous

monetary creation through a banking system. In view of the 'nervous' behaviour of private banking and its shifty perception of risk, the provision of international liquidity became associated to a high degree of uncertainty.[2]

Even straightforward comments making the link between Third World debt and the heavy indebtedness of the wealthy nations, such as the following, constitute a rarity;

> ... the largest debtors are still saddled with huge debts. To this one must add the fact that the richest countries of the world also have a huge debt which endangers their economic growth too, thereby leaving less room for further economic assistance abroad.[3]

By far the most perceptive comments on Third World debt and the financial system are to be found in the book by Lord Lever and the economist Christopher Huhne, *Debt and Danger*, from which the first of the above quotations is taken. Lever and Huhne also discuss the damaging effect of international debts being denominated in foreign, 'hard' currencies. They make astute observations concerning the position of complete dependency in which this places the developing nations, since these debts cannot be 'rolled over' automatically or by choice. Debtor nations must entreat the World Bank/IMF or the Paris Club for the luxury of debt-deferment – a process that the wealthy nations indulge in constantly with their escalating, unrepayable national debts denominated in their own currencies. Lever and Huhne comment;

> The truth is that neither conventional creditworthiness indicators nor the results of Third World policies suggest that the build-up of debt, at least to the end of the 1970s, was misplaced. What was unsustainable was the system and the nature of that debt.[4]

Apart from a few such references, Third World debt literature is largely devoid of monetary analysis and simply accepts the existence and validity of debt without questioning the monetary system of which it is a part. There is, however, a separate body of literature that is highly critical of banking and the debt/money relationship. This is the field known as 'monetary reform'.

Monetary reform

Monetary reform is a very contentious province of economics. Indeed, in a discipline noted for its range of opinion and conflicting schools of thought, monetary reform still remains firmly outside the boundaries of acceptability, and quite 'beyond the pale'. It has been said that the surest way to ruin a promising career in economics, whether professional or academic, is to venture into the 'cranks and crackpots' world of suggestions for reform of the financial system. The result is that, in public at least, economic commentators generally avoid completely the issue of money and debt, even when this is obviously a core issue.

For example, early in 1997, Malaysia was visited by Michel Camdessus, Director General of the IMF, who praised its sound economy and predicted a bright future for the nation. Within three months the entire Malaysian economy was a financial ruin as the Asian financial crisis struck. At the height of the crisis, as national economies tumbled like so many dominoes, there was much talk is about 'weak fundamentals'. A global recession affecting America and Europe was predicted by some economists – but it didn't happen. Malaysia was forecast as having a bright future, but collapsed. America was seen as doomed to fall – but was almost unaffected. Whatever else may be said about 'weak fundamentals', they are clearly a cocktail of monetary data so difficult to read, so full of variables and so delicately complex, that economic orthodoxy is useful to describe a crash after the event, but seems quite unable to predict it. Cynics might call this an intellectual evasion.

During the succession of national economic collapses, few mainstream commentators ventured to observe that modern economies suffer not so much from 'weak fundamentals' as a fundamental weakness – they are all rendered inherently unstable by a financial system based almost entirely upon lending and credit. A key ingredient in every currency and stock market crash was excessive debt and poor debt ratios – and yet no-one asked why modern economies are so exposed to debt!

No-one puzzled over the vulnerability of the mature, wealthy nations. No-one inquired into the contradictory fact that, the wealthier a nation becomes in material terms, the further its financial accounts seem to deteriorate, keeping it permanently 'on the edge'. No-one pointed out that modern debt is not truly a measure of borrowing between people, industries or nations, but a direct function of banks creating and supplying the national and international money stock. No-one questioned the dominance of banking and our astonishing reliance upon a 'credit' form of money. No-one urged that, if we almost exclusively create money as a function of debt, we can hardly be surprised if debt becomes a problem.

What is so surprising is not just that these fundamental issues were not raised. What is really astonishing is that the world has been here before, but we seem to have forgotten! Little more than half a century ago, monetary reform – the idea that the financial system was over-reliant upon banking, and that this needed an urgent review – was a vital and active area of debate. Up and down the country, indeed all around the world, economists, politicians, newspapers and discussion groups hotly debated the reformist ideas of Irving Fisher, Frederick Soddy, C. H. Douglas and the social credit movement. Today, it is as if these critics, astonishingly influential in their day, had never existed. Their powerful critique of the economic chaos of the depression years has been almost lost from public and political consciousness.

There is a very sensible dictum, 'don't bother to re-invent the wheel'. When a body of critical literature, especially one that is historically based, claims to address a contemporary problem, it often pays to listen to the past. Without wishing to make excessive claims for the proposals of past monetary reformers, their analysis of the problems caused by a debt-based economy offer many profound insights into today's Third World debt crisis.

The lost debate

At the time of the depression, critics of the monetary system claimed that an economy based upon banking found itself in a position of perpetual instability. It was inherently vulnerable to slumps and booms, driven or depressed by the rate of borrowing. It would surge, then crash as business and consumer confidence waxed and waned, and as banks' lending policy altered. However, the monetary reformers' arguments went far deeper than the issue of 'boom-slump-boom'. Monetary reformers mounted a wholesale attack on the adequacy of the financial system.

The most provocative and hotly contested claim by monetary reformers was that, with the use of bank credit as the dominant form of money, the economy was not self-liquidating. In other words, the economy suffered from a recurrent 'lack of effective demand' and was unable to sell all the goods it was capable of producing.

This was clearly a radical and disturbing concept. For an economy to be capable of producing goods and services, yet incapable of selling them to its consumers, would indeed be a bizarre circumstance. The monetary reformers pointed to the 'poverty amidst plenty' of the depression, when food was left to rot in the fields or burnt as fuel, whilst people starved and industry collapsed for want of sales to a population with no way to express its 'real demand' for the abundant goods and services of their own economy. The lack of effective demand, or 'lack of purchasing power', from which the economy suffered was blatant for all to see. But the criticisms of monetary reformers went yet further. They argued that even outside a recession, when the economy did appear to be functioning properly, this was only because of perpetual investment and growth. There was still an underlying 'lack of effective demand' from the established economy. This was only being compensated for by growth, since the investment injected essential fresh bank credit into the economy.

The underlying 'lack of effective demand' made the economy reliant upon this constant investment. Economic stability was impossible. Simply to continue functioning, the economy had become dependent upon constant development, constant borrowing, and constant growth involving the speculative production of additional goods. This pursuit of economic change was directed neither by genuine demand nor sensible purpose.

People were caught up in this pattern of growth, ever more firmly tied to full-time wage-earning by debt and lack of purchasing power. Those displaced from employment by new technology would find themselves recycled into new jobs, producing new goods which were not necessarily needed or wanted, but for which markets would have to be created. An age of perpetual growth, speculative production and reliance of the economy on 'marketing strategies' was prophesied. Work, employment and production were becoming an end in themselves, justified by little more than being a route for distributing incomes to a population increasingly wage-dependent as their debts grew.

The lack of effective demand and pointless over-production forced nations to search for overseas markets, both as outlets for their unsold goods, and in pursuit of revenues to bolster their illiquid economies. Since all nations were under such pressure, they became locked into an impossible and irreconcilable economic conflict – export warfare – where each nation attempted to become a net exporter. But since for every net exporter there must be a net importer, in aggregate, nations were searching for markets that didn't exist.

It was further argued that a bank-based money supply had a dramatic impact on government revenue and the nature of taxation. The perpetual scarcity of money in a debt economy led to a shortfall of taxation revenues and annual government borrowing. Meanwhile, the cumulative backlog of an interest-bearing national debt resulted in taxation becoming ever more predatory and oppressive.

There were micro-economic effects too. Monetary shortage not only drove people and businesses further into debt, but this gave a pronounced advantage to cheap, low-cost products. Thus, the financial system was accused of being responsible for the many 'jerry-built' products of the inter-war depression years.

So unbalanced was the financial system that banking – which ought to reflect economic activity rather than dominate it – had actually become a focus of policy, exerting growing centralised control over both the economy and individuals. Ultimately, this was because banks administered the debt bondage in which all were held, and banks were the source of fresh debt upon which the economy was becoming increasingly dependent.

In summary, the monetary reformers claimed that the monetary economy had come to dominate and distort the real, productive economy. Conflicts, pressures and a cycle of development were being fostered by a financial system that did not reflect reality. Banking had secured a 'monopoly of credit creation' and government, by refusing to create and circulate a sufficient medium of exchange free from debt, was neglecting its primary fiscal responsibility. Governments had thereby abandoned their peoples to perpetual economic slavery in a dysfunctional, out-of-control economy.

From these assertions, it is clear that this was not just an economic critique, but a highly charged socio-political debate. The significance of these arguments is further emphasised when they are placed in a broader historical context.

The historical thread

Monetary reform did not start with the Great Depression, but has an ancient pedigree. For centuries, disputes over 'money-lenders', 'the banking controversy', or the 'the currency question' rumbled on, usually in the background, but sometimes the forefront of politics and economics.

Money-lenders and goldsmiths were despised and persecuted for their deception in lending gold they did not have, and collecting both interest and the property of defaulting borrowers. The early banks were vilified for their ability to do the same – creating and circulating large quantities of promissory notes.

Bishop Berkeley asked as long ago as 1763 'whether or not it be a mighty privilege for a man to create a hundred pounds with the stroke of a pen?' He also alluded to the lack of effective demand. ('Whether we are not in fact the only people that may be said to starve in the midst of plenty?') as well as the export imperative: 'Whether the quantities of beef, butter, wool and leather exported from these islands can be reckoned the superfluities of a country, where there are so many natives naked and famished?'[5]

John Wheatley wrote of early commercial banks; 'I shall endeavour to prove that the paper of country banks must ever form an inefficient and dangerous medium of circulation, from its liability to sudden contraction in the period of alarm; and its tendency to as sudden an increase in the moment of security'.[6]

In 1793, Edward King spoke out against the creation of money by banks: 'The issuing out of any notes for general circulation ought to be as sacred to government ... as the issuing out of gold and silver coin is sacred to government; and to the mint at the Tower'.[7]

There was extensive pamphleteering of monetary issues during the appalling post-Waterloo depression. An anonymous tract, *The Gemini Letters*, blamed banks for the acute famine sweeping the country and advocated a new medium of exchange. 'It is idle to talk of overproduction when we have a population clothed in rags, and most sparingly supplied with the mere necessities of life'.[8]

In 1842, with the depression still recurrent and poverty widespread, John Grey presented proposals for an entirely new financial system. In words that echoed the militant monetary reformers of the Great Depression, he raged;

> There are millions of people in England, Scotland and Ireland, able and most anxious to be of mutual service to each other; who can be of none for want of a proper medium of exchange between them. When the question is asked whether store houses are empty or not, as the cause of such distress ... Full! Full! Full! is the one monotonous response to every enquiry of the kind. Houses, furniture, clothes and food, are all equally abundant; whilst a market! a market! is the everlasting cry of the myriads, who, to become a market to each other, have only to eschew the enormous error which pervades their system of exchange.[9]

Pouring scorn on the idea of overproduction, Grey wrote; 'It is the underproduction of money, added to a total want of any definite principle, either of increase or diminution thereof, which constitutes the real evil.'

In America, Abraham Lincoln claimed that a government had not only a right, but a solemn duty to create the nation's currency.[10] The 'money question' was both a public and prominent debate in America. There were few 'neutrals' – American presidents and congressmen were either at loggerheads with, or in league with, the commercial banks. The banks' expressed intention was to act as the money supply agencies to the US economy. The skulduggery employed by commercial banks in the form of bribery, corruption, insider dealing, bought legislation and deliberate recession has been extensively documented.[11]

Back in the UK, Robert Peel had already attempted, but failed, to secure for government the right of monetary issuance with his 1844 Bank Charter Act. His stated intention was clear; 'Our general rule is to draw a distinction between the privilege of issue, and the conduct of the ordinary banking business. We think they stand on an entirely different footing.'[12] In 1875 Gladstone commented;

> The state ought ultimately to get into its own hands the whole business of [money] issue, and that ... course should be taken upon the first favourable opportunity.[13]

Monetary reform between the wars

The years of the Great Depression highlighted the inadequacies of the financial system, and with modern productive capacity, the case was so obvious. The 1930s were the years when 'poverty amidst plenty' became a political slogan. Families throughout Europe and America were literally starving whilst farms and industries went bankrupt in droves. In Germany, bands of workers rummaged through the slag heaps of the Essen foundries in search of fuel, whilst mountains of unsold coal had built up in the Ruhr valley. In France, Spain, Italy, Scandinavia – everywhere the picture was the same. People wanted to work, but farms and factories could not afford to hire them because no-one was able to buy their products.

It is almost impossible to convey today the prominence of the debate over the monetary system in the inter-war period. The newspapers talked about monetary reform. The politicians discussed it. A Royal Commission – The Macmillan Committee – was set up 'to enquire into the workings of the financial system'. There were Social Credit study groups up and down the UK, whilst the founder of the movement, C. H. Douglas, was welcomed by enthusiastic supporters in America, Australia, Canada, Japan and numerous other countries. Frances Hutchinson writes of widespread interest in Douglas' ideas;

> [Douglas] was called upon to explain his theories to select committees and at public meetings in universities, town halls, trade union gatherings,

churches and on the radio. His travels included visits to Tokyo, Oslo and the USA. In 1933-34 a world tour took him once again to Canada, the USA, Australia and New Zealand, where he addressed meetings and broadcast on the radio to a popular audience. On 25 January 1934, Douglas addressed an audience of 12,000 in Sydney Stadium, five thousand being turned away. His address was relayed to an estimated radio audience of one million, factories being shut down to provide sufficient power for the event. His coast-to-coast broadcast in America was estimated to have reached ninety million, and he received an equally enthusiastic welcome in Canada. In each location his invitations to speak were organised by a network of study groups, often church-based, membership of which dated back to the early 1920s. Throughout the Dominions, disillusionment with the Bank of England was particularly strong, and active Social Credit supporters were estimated to be in their tens of thousands.[14]

Douglas was by no means the only critic of the financial system. In America, a public competition was run for the best monetary reform scheme, which received hundreds of entries. Roosevelt, Churchill and other prominent statesmen endorsed the issue – a number of Bank of England directors even made statements accepting the need for fundamental change. A former director of the Bank of England, Vincent Vickers, was one of those to become a convinced monetary reformer. In his foreword to Robert Eislers' book on monetary reform, Vickers wrote;

> The existing monetary standard is unworthy of our modern civilisation and a growing menace to the world... I am qualified to tell the public that in my view, it is entirely mistaken if it believes that the monetary system of this country is normally managed by 'recognised monetary experts' working in accordance with the most scientific and up-to-date methods known to modern economists... The Bank of England should no longer attempt to stifle the efforts of modern economists, nor persist in regarding all monetary reformers as impertinent busybodies trying to usurp her authority. When we see great sections of the community clamouring for monetary reform – then, surely, it is time for the government to seek advice elsewhere, and to encourage open discussion. .. It is not 'productive industry' with its new machinery which is the root cause of our unemployment and our uncertainty, but 'finance', with its antiquated mechanism, which has failed to adapt itself to modern requirements.[15]

This is akin to the present Governor of the Bank of England stating publicly that we ought to listen to the monetary views of the New Economics Foundation and Greenpeace. In one of his election speeches, Roosevelt referred to the growing pressure for monetary reform. Keynes described this speech, and the significance of the monetary reform debate as;

in substance a challenge to us to decide whether we propose to tread the old unfortunate ways or to explore new paths; paths new to statesmen and to bankers, but not new to thought. For they lead to the managed currency of the future, *the examination of which has been the prime topic of post-war economics.* [Italics added][16]

The monetary reform movement was world-wide. Robert Eisler, a well-known Austrian economist working with the League of Nations, made proposals for a scheme to expand production, by the increase of what he called 'stable money'. An American economist, Arthur Kitson, claimed that America was the hub of the monetary reform movement;

> Whereas in Great Britain the new economists, with the possible exception of the Douglas school, have been rather like isolated voices crying in the wilderness, in America they have now the ear of the nation. The spectacle of want and despair, with 13 million unemployed, in the richest of the nations, so familiar to us in the old world, has there, as we have always hoped and expected it would, brought instantly into the forefront the broad issue whether the machine is to be allowed to enslave or liberate humanity.[17]

Another noted American economist, Irving Fisher, advanced a scheme which he called '100% Money', which was essentially that the government should create sufficient currency to keep pace with the bank creation of credit, and oblige banks to restrict their operations to this 100% reserve of coins and notes. Although a highly regarded public and academic figure, Fisher's proposals were ignored.

The Swedish economist, Brynjolf Bjorset, records that in all over two thousand schemes for monetary reform were advanced during the period from 1925 to 1930.[18] All had a common theme in their repudiation of the level of industrial and government debt dominating the financial system.

Keynes – it's hard to let go

Why was such a prophetic and vital debate lost? In part, discussion was ended by the second world war, after which the issue of monetary reform was lost in the rubble and the rush to build a New Jerusalem. But undoubtedly the major factor ending the public debate was Keynesian theory, which was adopted as the solution to the depression and then proceeded to dominate post-war economic thought.

In choosing Keynesianism, the world chose debt. It was accepted by Keynes that there could be a lack of effective demand, but not accepted that this had anything to do with the fact that the financial system was based upon banking. Indeed, Keynes' remedy enshrined banking in the solution, since the government would support the economy's occasional 'lack of effective demand' by recourse to the national debt – the arrangement by which governments raise additional revenue by selling bonds to commercial banks, who create additional bank credit. It was argued and expected by Keynes that such a government deficit would be a cyclical phenomenon – that it would be run up during a slump and paid back during a boom.

Half a century of deficit financing, during which national debts around the globe have continually escalated, has shown the error of basic Keynesian monetary theory. National debts are not cyclical; they are unrepayable. Moreover, modern economies are utterly reliant upon their national debts and the additional credit they create. This has led to broad agreement that a national debt is most accurately considered as an aspect of the money supply. This raises a fundamental question. Why does a government, the one institution with the positional authority to create money *ab initio*, concede this privilege to the banking sector even to the extent of becoming a borrower and debtor itself?

The cost of half a century of applying Keynesian deficit financing is that nations now pay billions of dollars, pounds or francs annually as interest on their national debts – sums that eat deeply into the revenues needed for public spending and provide a handsome profit for the banking sector.

Clearly we ought to be re-addressing the fundamental monetary debate of the 1930s. Instead, whilst Keynes' monetary theory has been largely dismissed, his major monetary policy is still adhered to. The resort to deficit financing by governments whenever necessary, to support an economy faced with recession, is still standard practice. In other words, we have a key economic policy, acknowledged as essential to maintain the function of an economy, without any rationale whatsoever. We have a major economic policy that has proved wildly erroneous according to its original theoretical basis, which has deepened the debt and interest burden on national economies and which presents all governments with a complete imponderable – 'How big should the deficit be?'

The question cannot be answered simply because the very need for such a deficit has no theoretical basis. One week there can be no money – the next, Gordon Brown has £35 billion of additional revenue, which it has been 'decided' can be 'afforded' under the deficit that no-one can explain, no-one even pretends can be repaid, but which all countries are obliged to run. The gap in fiscal theory is truly a yawning chasm.

Plus ça change

Since the 1930s, monetary reformers have been increasingly dismissed as cranks and reactionaries and pushed into the economic underworld. Although many of the problems they addressed have re-surfaced and many of their warnings proved justified, the 'money question' has seldom appeared in the UK media, and there is little public awareness of the significance of the debate or of its former prominence. Before considering the relevance of these arguments to Third World debt, it is worth re-examining some of the claims made by monetary critics in the past.

Despite the best efforts of (presumably) the best economists, nations still endure the 'business cycle', which is now accepted as being as inevitable as the weather, although it is a bizarre and clearly unnecessary chain of self-perpetuating events.

As for the growth of debt, the previous chapter presented statistics showing the alarming increase in the numbers of mortgaged homes and indebted households. That this is the age of mindless growth and speculative production is beyond dispute. There is an unquestioning pursuit of production and employment, regardless of its merit, and we divert ever more effort to the design, production and marketing of the most vacuous and puerile products. An entire industry based on psychological manipulation – the marketing sector – is devoted to persuading the public that they 'need' a constant stream of goods they have never needed before. Today, advertising, image-creation and various marketing strategies represent a staggering 18% of the American economy. The global export battle in pursuit of foreign markets and revenues is so severe that at times it threatens international relations. As for control of the economy, no-one even pretends that the modern economy is responding to what people really want, nor that it is under any rational control. The only explanation, as we charge into the future like an express train, is that 'you can't stop progress'.

The declining durability of goods is now the subject of well-documented study. The bulk of modern furniture has no hope of enduring to another generation. Kettles that could once be relied upon for a decade or more need replacing after little more than eighteen months. The pursuit of cheapness has resulted in the nutritional value of many basic foodstuffs declining so markedly that there is deep concern at the long-term medical consequences.

Work, work, work. Studies in the UK and across Europe show that we are working longer hours and suffering more stress than for many decades. 'The overworked American' is legendary for his/her moonlighting to make ends meet, whilst average wages have declined in real terms within the US over the past decade. People used to discuss 'the coming age of leisure', but this kind of talk seems to have disappeared. The economy dictates that we must all work, strive for better performance and increase output – to compete with the Americans, Germans and Japanese who must also work, strive for better performance and increase output to compete with us. Even education is increasingly subordinate to the needs of the economy.

All the monetary reformers' claims have proved, to a greater or lesser extent, accurate and justified. Man *has* become a slave to his economy. Banking has become the focus of policy in the modern world. Alan Greenspan and the Federal Reserve debate quarter-points of interest rates and the world holds its breath. Why should this be, other than that debt and borrowing exert a crushing dominance over the economy? The IMF and World Bank exert quasi-imperial control over two-thirds of the globe via their structural adjustment programmes intended to resolve the problems of Third World debt, despite which that debt continues to mount. And the most powerful institution in the future Europe is to be the European Central Bank, answerable to no political process, which will apply its fiscal and economic policy to an entire continent.

History, paper and credit

When monetary reform is placed in its broader historical context, it becomes clear that we are still locked in a debate that has raged since the Middle Ages and that has been directly associated with the most appalling economic instability, deprivation and injustice.

Money-lenders and goldsmiths were despised and persecuted for their deception in lending gold they did not have, by creating and circulating large quantities of promissory notes. The trouble was, paper money was not considered to be true money – true money was gold and silver, the minting and seignorage of which belonged by ancient prerogative to the Crown. And since bank paper money and promissory notes were not regarded as proper money, it was acceptable for banks to issue their 'promises to pay'.

Modern fractional reserve banking is little more than an elaborate, institutionalised descendant of medieval money-lending. Today's banks enjoy the additional privilege of being allowed to receive their own 'promissory credit' as fresh deposits, account this as real money, and use this as the basis for additional credit creation, banking against the perpetual growth in deposits that the system creates.

The 1844 Bank Charter Act finally accepted that paper notes were indeed circulating as money, and attempted to regulate their creation and circulation. But by then, 'bank credit' was already a considerable component of the money stock and far exceeded paper notes in importance. Paper money has declined in importance in just the same way, and for precisely the same reason, as did gold in earlier times – convenience. Today we find it convenient to operate an almost entirely numerical money system. We pay, get paid, buy, sell and save almost exclusively using various money-transferring devices such as cheques, money orders, credit cards etc. It is this numerical money commonly called 'credit' that forms the dominating 96% element of the money stock, with only 4% of notes and coins. But although it is the dominant form of money, there is no true *supply* of numerical money – only that generated by banks and building societies as they lend and thus create bank credit. There is no money supply for credit. In effect, we are back with the banking controversy of the moneylenders and the nineteenth century, only this time the dispute is over credit, rather than paper money.

The provision of a money stock by bank lending impacts across the entire economy through debt, interest payments, costs, overheads, prices and incomes. Since modern debt is associated with the supply and circulation of money, the total of debt is absolutely un-repayable. For these debts ever to be repaid would involve the withdrawal from circulation of virtually the entire money stock. Any significant repayment of major institutional debts – such as national debts, total outstanding mortgages, commercial debts – is simply impossible and difficulties are bound to be faced over the repayment of individual debts. Indeed, the modern indebted economy constantly needs additional borrowers, involving a perpetual increase in both debt and the money stock.

There is an obvious tension involved in an economy where money is relied upon as a circulating medium of exchange, and yet at the same time the entire money stock is also being sought by debtors trying to pay back their debts! Somebody, somewhere is in pursuit of, and under an obligation to repay (or pay interest on), virtually every pound/dollar/franc/yen in circulation. To the extent that yesterday's borrowers succeed in paying back debt, there must be more borrowers today to compensate and support the circulation of money. It is clear that this is an arrangement with an enormous degree of built-in tension, instability and conflict. It is also obvious that this cannot be the only way to fund an economy. There must be other financial systems less reliant upon perpetual borrowing, and less exposed to debt.

Monetary reform

Although there have been a wide variety of monetary reform schemes, there is a common basic agenda. In the past, the monetary controversy has often centred around the right and privilege of the Crown, or the government, to enjoy the seignorage from the creation of money, rather than allow this to accrue to the banking sector. In fact, the matter has far less to do with the rights and privilege of government than with the *responsibility* of government, a point first noted by Lincoln. A government has a duty to provide the nation with a sufficient medium of exchange 'to satisfy the spending power of government and the buying power of consumers'. Vincent Vickers coined the phrase that the nation's money stock should be 'spent into the economy, not lent into the economy'.

This is the basic monetary reform agenda. Whatever institutions are involved, whether these be defined as representing 'The State', 'The Government' or 'The Crown', an economy should actually be supplied with a medium of exchange. This medium of exchange should be supplied, not on condition of debt, but circulating free from a background of debt. There should actually be a money supply, rather than a stream of credit created by the act of borrowing, which is in itself a statement of monetary inadequacy, and which results in ever-expanding volumes of credit-money with a countering debt demanding that money's repayment. Citizens have a right to be provided with a medium of exchange as a neutral, cost-free entity, circulating free from a background of debt, facilitating the exchange of goods and services.

It is generally accepted that there should be a relationship between the money stock and the quantity of available goods and services – it has yet to be established that the terms under which this money stock is supplied are of equal importance. Thus, economists constantly analyse the annual growth of the money stock, but pay virtually no analytical attention whatsoever to the mountain of debt accompanying and providing that money stock! Nor do they consider the option of an alternative financial system where a significant proportion of the money stock essential to an economy is actually provided to that economy, thereby automatically reducing the need and demand for borrowing, coupled with sensible restrictions on borrowers and lenders to prevent undue inflation of the money stock.

There is ample rationale for such a policy. Back in the 1950s and 1960s, over 20% of the money stock consisted of cash currency. The annual input of coins and notes was created by the government without a parallel debt, and spent into the economy through the public sector. Inflation was low, growth more stable, and mortgage and other debt levels far lower. The lower debt-uptake meant that the money supply was not prone to excessive annual growth, and interest rates, which were not used as a tool of monetary restraint, were generally below 4%. Clearly the modern economy does not need more cash currency, but it does urgently need a boost of liquidity. For the government to act to compensate for the dramatic decline in the use of cash by creating a debt-free input of numerical money – which is what a modern economy principally runs on – is a policy screaming out to be applied. Why should the decline in the use of cash mean that the difference is made up entirely by banking and debt?

The government issuance of money has always been dismissed as inflationary. But this need not be the case. If sensible restrictions were placed on banks and building societies, the government-issued money supply would be compensated for by curtailing the production of new bank credit. For instance, there could be a limit, and gradual reduction, in the number of times a person is allowed to multiply their annual income as the basis of a mortgage. Since house mortgages support over 60% of the money stock, this could make a dramatic contribution to preventing monetary inflation as well as putting a break on the relentless rise in house prices, which benefits no-one. It would also mean that, over the years, house buying would become a competition based on money people have got, rather than as at present, on money they haven't got.

In contrast, a government *deficit*, which creates money by using the banking mechanism, is indeed inflationary. Debt is created, the government must repay both capital and interest, and the demands of each year's deficit increases as a result.

An entirely new social agenda and radically different fiscal conditions would prevail in an economy where adequate liquidity was provided and where lending was moderated by regulations that allowed a constructive, distributed level of borrowing, but which prevented competitive inflation, both of the money supply and prices. Many monetary reformers have outlined such schemes and regulations, and a wide variety of models are available.

The rentier economy and the failure of economics

By refusing to criticise the financial system and its reliance upon debt, our economists have failed to notice that, when every pound or dollar in circulation involves an equivalent pound or dollar of debt, a 'rentier economy' is automatically established. A financial system is in place that leads to an enduring, profound and socially corrosive injustice.

Interest eats into incomes through mortgages and other consumer debts. Interest charges form part of the price of goods and services. Interest is charged against indebted local councils and added onto the council tax. The government pays interest from our taxes. We are paying interest on debts when we pay our electricity, water or phone bills or have our car repaired. Interest charges are everywhere.

These interest charges are then distributed to people with bank and building society deposits. When the entire money stock is on loan to the economy, there is a perpetual redistribution of money – and hence wealth – to the 'haves' from the 'have nots'. Debtors find it difficult to get out of debt, whilst depositors enjoy a perpetual un-earned gain.

This is a rentier economy and it constantly widens the gulf between rich and poor, enshrining injustice at the very heart of the financial system. It also subverts the free market completely. The 'market' may be 'free', but people are bound to it by their dependence on goods and services. People are tied to paying taxes and many essential goods and services. When these goods, services and taxes carry heavy interest charges, consumers are remitting a tribute, as part of every payment, to the better off. Dependence on a free market, coupled with a rentier economy, where the entire money stock is subject to debt and interest, is a recipe for endemic social injustice.

This is not to contest the charging of interest or criticise the relationship between creditor and debtor. But in an entirely debt-based financial system, where virtually none of the money stock circulates free from debt, the 'rentier effect' is magnified to the level where it creates a terrible and enduring division. No-one can save without there being another person in debt. No-one can even get a pay cheque without someone else being in debt. The wholesale charging of interest on the entire money stock constantly thrusts down those on a low income and in debt, keeping them permanently indentured to work.

Economic theory is completely stood on its head by the rentier economy. The textbook explanation of debt and interest is that debtors have borrowed money from creditors, and the creditors are entitled to the interest they receive. In a debt-based economy, the order of events is completely reversed – the only reason today's creditors have any money is because, in the past, other people have gone into debt. In a very real sense, creditors owe it to debtors that their money even exists! And far from the act of lending involving a loan of actual money and a degree of risk, forbearance and commitment on the part of the lender, the lender shoulders no risk and can withdraw his money at will. Meanwhile, banks create additional credit to advance to borrowers and the entire money stock is perpetually inflated at a cost to both debtor and creditor!

The fact is, people with deposits are not lending anything. It is banks who lend – they lend credit-money they have created out of nothing, using the convenient fact that they are trustees of monetary deposits to shield this. Depositors are actually *penalised*, for although they receive interest for leaving their deposits with the bank, the bank is simultaneously inflating the money supply and reducing the value of their savings! Regardless of the fact that interest is paid to depositors, over the last three decades money left in a bank or building society has actually fallen in overall purchasing power.

So who gains in a rentier economy? Ultimately, the financial gain from a debt-based economy accrues to the banking sector, since these institutions acquire a permanent 'lien' over the property and assets against which debts are secured. By creating and issuing money as a debt repayable to them, they lay tacit claim to assets equivalent to those debts. Thus, Britain's building societies now own 35% of the UK housing stock through the mortgages they have advanced.

The concept of a rentier economy is an important concept in understanding Third World debt, since an *international* rentier economy has been gradually established. This is discussed later.

The debt-based financial system and Third World debt

There is a great danger that introducing monetary reform arguments into a work on Third World debt could prove very counterproductive. The study of alternative financial systems is not currently accepted as a respectable province of economics, despite the fact that a number of authoritative economists have, over the years, urged that this was a crucial area of reform. As a result of decades of neglect and professional ostracism, monetary reform remains the province of amateurs, and suffers inevitably as a result.

Many of the proposed schemes for reform have flaws. Critically, they tend to lack both political and institutional awareness and the entire subject of monetary reform needs considerably more study. However, the criticisms that monetary reformers have directed at the debt-based financial system remain powerful, and it is these, rather than their programmes for reform, that are of main concern in this book. With this in mind, it is worth applying the monetary reform critique of a debt-based financial system to Third World debt.

Lack of purchasing power

With the removal of protectionist barriers, the world can increasingly be regarded as a single economic unit. There is a glutted world market with a recorded surplus of goods and services in virtually every economic sector – too many producers, not enough buyers and a cut-throat scramble for markets. Taken alongside widespread and increasing levels of poverty in all nations, and the 'real demand' for goods and services that this implies, there is a dramatic confirmation of the monetary reformers' thesis of a 'lack of effective demand'.

There is a pitiful and frustrating parallel between today's 'poverty amidst plenty' and that of the Great Depression. Just as the agricultural workers of the 1930s were cut off from and denied the produce of their own labours, only to see it rot in the fields, so countless citizens in the Third World today are denied the fruits of their own economy which are produced for export, swelling the saturated global market.

Constant lending and investment

That the global economy is completely reliant upon constant investment is widely recognised. However it has become increasingly clear that it is not so much additional production, but new loans that are critical. Starting with the Mexican peso crisis in 1982, the Third World, and with it the global financial economy, has only been sustained by continual bail-outs of additional credit. There has been little pretence that these loans were for investing in development; their purpose was avowedly to provide liquidity. The need was clearly for sufficient funds for debtor nations to keep up with their interest payments, continue functioning, and not precipitate a collapse of the global financial system. In effect, the Third World debt crisis has severed the link between loans and physical investment and demonstrated the reliance of the global economy on a perpetual stream of fresh bank credit.

Work and slavery

The Conference of the Institute for African Alternatives discussed in depth the subjugation of the African states to Western priorities, and the drift of debtor nations into a position of international debt-slavery, declaring;

> The evidence... leads to the conclusion that the importance of the debt of African countries to Western creditors is not measured mainly in financial and economic terms, i.e. in terms of what the debt brings to creditor agencies and countries, but the debt represents rather a powerful political instrument: an instrument for subjecting debtor countries to international specialisation at the level of production and exchange...[19]

Many Third World debt critics have pointed out the parallels between Third World debt and wage-slavery, or 'peonage'. In the words of Cheryl Payer;

> The system can be compared point by point with peonage on an individual scale. In the peonage, or debt-slavery system ... the aim of the employer/ creditor/merchant is neither to collect the debt once and for all, nor to starve the employee to death, but rather to keep the labourer permanently indentured through his debt to the employer... Precisely the same system

operates on the international level. Nominally independent countries find that their debts, and their constant inability to finance current needs out of exports, keep them tied by a tight leash to their creditors. The IMF orders them, in effect, to keep labouring on the plantation… It is debt slavery on an international scale. If they remain within the system, the debtor countries are doomed to perpetual underdevelopment or rather, to development of their exports at the service of multinational enterprises, at the expense of development for the needs of their own citizens.[20]

The position in which the debtor nations find themselves, in perpetual obligation to creditors who bail them out by issuing more debt, bears a striking similarity to the scenario outlined by C. H. Douglas, who warned of the dangers of perpetual wage slavery;

> The policy is to load us individually and collectively with debt so that we shall be the slaves of our debtors in perpetuity. It is impossible to obtain money to pay off the debt, owing to the fact that our debtors are at the same time in sole control of the power of creating the money which is required to pay off the debt.[21]

Export warfare

A monetary reform critique offers a penetrating insight into the trade warfare that dominates today's global economy. It also highlights the vulnerable position of Third World nations. For debtor nations to find themselves under pressure to export is logical. What is not logical is for so-called 'creditor' nations to be under a similar pressure. But the fact is, there are no true creditor nations. Because of their background of chronic debt, the entire community of nations – even the most wealthy – conduct their trade from a position of gross insolvency. However, trade offers all nations the opportunity to obtain revenues from beyond their borders and thereby alleviate their insolvency via a trade surplus.

A nation that is a net exporter is finding a market for its unsold surplus produce. It is also gaining revenue from abroad that can improve the solvency of its indebted economy. So whilst it makes no sense in real terms (of the physical, material balance of trade) for a nation to be a perpetual net-exporter, in a debt-based economy it makes perfect financial sense.

The 'export imperative' is driven at the commercial level as much as at the government level, with businesses constantly seeking additional overseas customers. The pressure on commerce to seek export outlets is fuelled in part by the lack of purchasing power inherent in a heavily indebted economy and the consequent need to seek a wider customer base, in part by surplus productive capacity, and in part by the fact that foreign-based businesses are similarly attempting to capture domestic markets in pursuit of their own additional sales.

It has often been pointed out that constructive international commerce cannot support such a generally aggressive policy, rooted as it is in economic conflict both at the national and commercial level. A constructive balance of trade, equating exports and imports, would require any nation with a trading surplus to spend the revenues it had thereby gained back in other countries that had sustained a trade deficit. However, no provision is made for holding or even defining the revenues gained by any excess of exports over imports as a surplus, and there is no intention to spend these revenues back in nations that have sustained a trade deficit. Instead, revenues gained by exporting are absorbed directly and permanently into a nation's economy.

Ultimately, the reason for this is that any surplus export revenues a nation might gain from trading do not actually constitute a surplus – a nation with billions of dollars of outstanding government, private and commercial debt does not experience export revenues as a surplus, but as a boost to industry's sales and liquidity, and a chance to reduce commercial borrowing or government debt. Any export revenues that are obtained by privately owned industries form part of those industries' income and are either disbursed as incomes to employees, expenditure and investment, or used to pay standing interest charges. Any export revenues that are obtained by publicly owned industries or via taxation of private commerce are either disbursed through government expenditure, or in settlement of maturing national debt bonds. Export revenues are thus rapidly absorbed, and such is the ubiquity and scale of debt within the wealthy nations that no surplus registers. The fact that export revenues may be obtained in foreign currency denominations is no barrier to these revenues becoming absorbed into the national economy since the foreign exchanges provide full convertibility of most currencies.

An explanation for the global 'export imperative' is clearly vital to understanding Third World debt. The desire of the wealthy nations to seek a trade surplus and resist imports has been one of the key ingredients of the debt crisis. Indeed, the entire edifice of lending by the World Bank and IMF has frequently been criticised from the standpoint that it involves a thinly disguised attempt to subsidise exports from the wealthy nations. Cheryl Payer comments;

> As developed countries began to tie foreign aid disbursements to purchases from their own countries' respective businesses, the distinction between aid and export promotion became blurred... The official capital flows ... financed an export surplus for the developed countries [and] an import surplus for the poor ones...[22]

The Bretton Woods Conference was dominated by the desire on the part of America to continue as a net exporting nation, regardless of the material loss to her citizens that this automatically involved. The desire of the wealthy nations to find new outlets for their products and maximise export revenues was backed up by the demand that loans to the Third World be conditional upon trade liberalisation. As pointed out earlier, this was a move that was certainly not warranted until the initial imbalance of trade involved in loans to developing nations had been redressed.

The Third World and the global money supply

The origin and flow of revenues involved in lending to the Third World are very revealing. As pointed out in the previous chapter, loans made to the Third World involve additions to the global money supply. Also, the existence of Third World debt is a record of a trade imbalance. Money loaned to the debtor nations was spent on buying in technology from the wealthy nations for development. This money the debtors have failed to regain, since it has become absorbed either into the wealthy nations or into the broader international economy. The debt, however, remains lodged against the developing nation.

All these considerations amount to one startling conclusion. By taking on unpayable debts and acting as export outlets for surpluses from the wealthy nations, the debtor nations are acting as part of the money supply to the wealthy nations and the international economy. The developing nations carry the debt associated with the creation and supply of the money required to purchase surpluses from the wealthy nations. The aggregate of $2.2 trillion dollars of Third World debt is thus a measure of money-creation; the debt is borne by the Third World, but the money has been absorbed like a sponge into the economies of the far more heavily indebted wealthy nations who have also found outlets for their unsold goods and services.

The power of banking

Monetary reformers claimed that the banks' monopoly of credit creation granted such power to the banking sector that an entire economy was placed under its control. Many modern observers have commented that the policies, the dominance and the bias of international institutions such as the World Bank and IMF constitute a form of neo-colonialism, or financial imperialism. The permanent indebtedness of the Third World has provided the basis upon which the World Bank and IMF have dictated economic and political policy to the great majority of developing nations, including the imposition of an inappropriate free trade agenda and ruthless structural adjustment. Martin Khor, Director of the Third World Network in Malaysia, stated;

> Structural Adjustment is also a policy to continue colonial trade and economic patterns ... which the Northern powers want to continue in the post-colonial period. Economically speaking, we are more dependent on the ex-colonial countries than ever we were. The World Bank and IMF are playing the role that our ex-colonial masters used to play.[23]

The Conference for African Alternatives was forthright in stating;

> We will conclude by suggesting that debt and the fluctuations in the prices of raw materials (be it the price of bauxite, tin, tea, cotton or cocoa)

portrayed by the leaders as external constraints to which external countries have to 'adjust' their domestic society, represent two of the most powerful political and economic instruments in the strategy of the Western industrialised powers to dominate the countries of Africa.[24]

In 1936, C. H. Douglas commented on the hidden agenda behind a debt-based financial system. In terms that apply equally to citizens in a debt-based national economy, and developing nations in a debt-based global economy, he warned of the loss of independence and how creating economic dependence can be used to gain political power;

What is being aimed at so far as you can put it into a few words, is a pyramidal slavery system by which people are kept in their places... If you can control economics, you can keep the business of getting a living the dominant factor of life, and so keep your control of politics just that long and no longer.[25]

The international rentier economy

There is now a firmly established international rentier economy. Debtor nations remit a perpetual tribute to the wealthy nations and their corporate interests, and are kept in a state of permanent monetary bondage as interest payments, profit repatriation and dividend payments syphon money from their economies. André Gunder Frank comments;

In the present crisis, this speculative financial mechanism is an important instrument to effect the neo-colonial drain of resources and capital from poor to rich, which is analogous to the colonial drains during past economic crises. However today's drain is a relative haemorrhage... Many Third World countries are now being drained of 5 and 6% of their GNP and 30 to 50% and more of their export earnings annually, through the resource transfer of their debt service.[26]

A Brazilian statesman famously stated;

The Third World War has already started. It is a silent war. Not for that reason any less sinister. The war is tearing down Brazil, Latin America and practically all of the Third World. Instead of soldiers dying there are children. It is a war over the Third World debt, one which has its main weapon, interest, a weapon more deadly than the atom bomb, more shattering than a laser beam.[27]

The international rentier economy operates not only through interest payments, but through stock markets which have 'become a new means of extracting surplus from developing countries'.[28] Wedded, however, to the free market religion, our economists keep expecting the developing nations to compete their way into the global economy – without noticing that an entire region that had worked for decades to build a degree of prosperity has just been plunged back into poverty and yet deeper debt. It is worth taking another look at the Asian crisis in an effort to unravel one last paradox – the great American escape.

In the months and years leading up to the Asian crisis, America's stock market was grossly over-valued, with price/earnings ratios at an all-time low. The dollar was strong against other currencies, making trade difficult for US manufacturers. Inflation was low, growth had been worryingly high for at least five years. Years of competitive investment had left US businesses with uncomfortable debt ratios and low yields on their stock. The US balance of trade was appalling, with net imports over the previous decade of billions of pounds, and the national debt was increasing like a balloon. Unemployment was so low that it was deemed both a constraint on continued growth and the basis of wage rises that were already exceeding growth in output. The bubble was ready to burst, many analysts judged.

By contrast, Malaysia's currency had proved stable and her current account was reasonable. Her balance of trade, output and growth were deemed not only sustainable, but gave the promise of further growth. Commercial debt ratios were good, although many of these debts were accounted in US dollars. There was a bias towards short-term debt, but this was itself an expression of commercial confidence that these debts were repayable within the terms of the contract. Hence, the IMF gave Malaysia a good 'progress report' whilst analysts were fixing worried looks at the world's powerhouse – the American economy.

But when the crash came, it was Malaysia and other economies from Asia, Latin America, Africa and East Europe that suffered a 'correction'. The American economy not only avoided the 'Asian flu', but within months was back on its star-blazing trail of growth and prosperity.

This requires some explanation. It is one thing for economists to make an error of judgement. But to predict a crash on the basis of a battery of data that screamed aloud 'weak fundamentals', only to see a re-doubling of US economic strength and prosperity, is not a misjudgement, it is to miss out totally on the nature of the game. There was far more to this than a matter of America being 'lucky' in avoiding the crash – this was the international rentier economy at work.

The sequence of events has already been outlined by which Western financial interests first withdrew from and speculated against the Far East, then returned to re-acquire the foreign stock, assets and currency they formerly owned (and considerable additional wealth under privatisation) at a fraction of their former price. Without suggesting that she was the only nation to benefit in this way, America's corporate and financial interests world-wide were very significant, and have become even more so. On top of buying 'more for less', US domestic investment and debt ratios were significantly improved by returning capital. Operating profits from the increased ownership of foreign assets are now accruing steadily to American corporate businesses, improving their global competitiveness and supporting their domestic operations.

In addition, America's massive financial sector – which is ultimately the key to her global economic dominance – has experienced a boom. As the Asian crisis deepened and spread, huge bail-out loans were rapidly put together for the Far East, Russia and Latin America. These were arranged through the IMF and commercial banks, with substantial business for the US commercial banking sector. Not only is the US banking system reaping handsome profits as a result, the loans advanced were almost exclusively denominated in dollars – since the foreign debts owed by the crisis-hit nations were dollar debts. The issuing of dollar loans to developing nations whose industrial infrastructure and other assets are increasingly foreign-owned – with substantial US representation – provides a direct channel for loan revenues to find their way back to the US economy.

Ultimately, the reason America avoided a crash was because so many other nations suffered a crash. America was able to capitalise in countless ways, consolidating her financial and corporate hegemony, subsidising her economy and enjoying a stream of incoming dollars from profit/interest repatriation, whilst the debt associated with the creation of this new global credit has been lodged against the stricken economies. Thus America, and to a lesser extent the European countries, have displaced both the debt and the inherent instability of a debt-based financial system onto other nations.

A perfect example can be found with the Republic of Korea. In 1998, Korea was offered a staggering $56 billion package, from the IMF and commercial banks, to recover from the Asian crisis. Her total external debt now stands at $154 billion. During the following year, 1999, her exports totalled $133, while her expenditure on imports was only $94 billion. This would appear to leave Korea with a trade surplus of $39 billion – surely a current account that would allow the country to reduce its debt significantly. However, the $154 billion debt is largely owed by the government, and such debts are not paid off by trade surpluses; trade revenues accrue largely to private commerce. International debts have to be paid off by government taxation, collected by the difference between tax receipts and expenditure. In 1999, the Korean government did not manage a tax surplus for any debt repayment, despite the massive $39 billion trade surplus. Why? Because the surplus accrued to private business and much was repatriated abroad, to America and Europe. The final element of the jigsaw is that American finances are so healthy, with a booming economy, that by early 2000 moves were being made to try to reduce the American national debt.

The American nation enjoys a perpetual un-earned income, both in the form of in-flowing money (conveniently denominated in its own currency) and in the form of real wealth, being able to purchase at will from a glutted world market desperate for dollars, whilst even some of this expenditure will eventually return as profits accruing to its extensive world corporate empire.

Just as a very wealthy man on a huge fixed income is protected from a depression, which impacts on the poor and middle classes, so America escaped the threat of collapse. And just as the depression actually provides the man with the opportunity to add to his wealth by buying up property, land or businesses at knock-down prices, America has consolidated her position as the great global property owner, financier and 'rentier nation' par excellence.

The status of Third World debts

What is the true status of Third World debts, in the light of the foregoing analysis? The economic as well as the popular perception of debt is of a transaction between a borrower and a lender. As a result, if one person, business or sector carries a debt, this is assumed to be a reflection of borrowing from another, representing deferred payment or comparative economic efficiency. However, when all money has to be borrowed into existence in the first place, debt reflects a range of completely different factors.

First, the aggregate of debt is no more than a measure of the aggregate demand for money. Second, any given debt is not necessarily an accurate expression of either economic performance or productive ability; nor, still less, does it represent debt involving a transaction between a borrower and a lender, a bank having created additional money as credit. Third, where all money has to be borrowed into existence, the distribution of debt is a measure and record of which individuals, businesses, sectors or nations have been forced into a position in which they become the money-creating/debt-undertaking agency. Fourth, when all money has to be borrowed into existence, debt is widespread, excessive and bears absolutely no relation to real wealth or productive ability. Finally, and most critically, when all money has to be borrowed into existence, and only continues to circulate on condition of continued debt, the total of debt is absolutely un-repayable.

The essentially un-repayable nature of Third World debt in the modern world is confirmed by comparison with other institutional and sectoral forms of debt. The graph opposite, of total Third World debt, bears a striking similarity to the escalating money stock shown in Chapter 7.

This graph shows that, like the debt associated with a national money stock, Third World debt never decreases, a fact that thereby supports the contention that Third World debt is also properly considered as an aspect of the global money supply – not a true borrower/lender transaction. The history of finance shows that escalation of debt and the money stock are built into the debt-based money supply process and Third World debt exhibits all the same characteristics. Mortgages provide another perfect illustration of the overall intractability and escalation of debt. The graph on page 128 shows the growth of UK mortgages since 1966.

There is a sharp conflict between the growth of mortgages and neo-classical economic rationale. Mortgages are viewed as debts owed by a borrower to a

Developing Country Debt

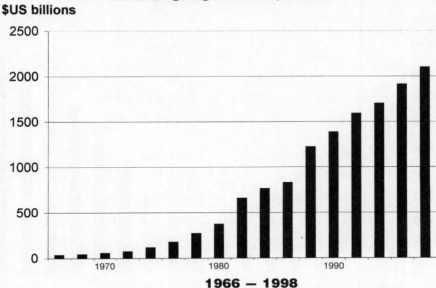

$US billions

1966 — 1998
Source: World Debt Tables; World Bank. 1972, 1978, 1990, 1998

lender and, as such, inherently and ultimately repayable. But this is not the status of modern mortgages. Although it is possible for any one person to pay off his or her mortgage, it is absolutely impossible for the community as a whole to buy its houses outright, since mortgages are heavily relied upon for money creation. Nor is this a stable situation, but a deteriorating one, with ever more dwellings subject to mortgage, ever more money raised against housing and mortgages of progressively longer duration. In terms of the status of these debts, mortgages do not reflect *borrowing from* – but borrowing money into existence.

Third World debt exhibits precisely the same features as modern mortgages. Although any individual sum of money advanced might be repaid, or any one nation might marginally reduce its debt from time to time, overall (and for most individual debtor nations) repayment proves impossible and total Third World debt inexorably increases.

This same escalating pattern attends national debts, which is why these too are properly considered as aspects of the money supply. The growth of the US and UK national debts are represented below.

Again we have a conflict with neo-classical economic rationale. Although contemporary theory of national deficits describes a mechanism designed to compensate for cyclical falls of demand and problems of temporary liquidity, national debts have mounted steadily since their inception and in absolute terms have proved to be quite un-repayable. The empirical evidence is that national debts are not cyclical phenomena, balancing out over a business cycle, but persist

UK Total Outstanding Mortgages

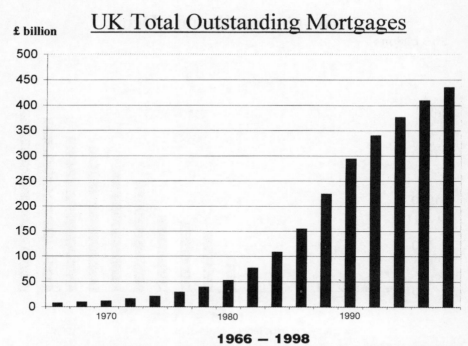

£ billion

1966 — 1998

Sources: Building Societies Association; Bank of England; Council for Mortgage Lenders.

and grow. Thus, they do not truly reflect borrowing according to any of the accepted economic criteria, but represent that part of the money supply where the debt is undertaken by governments.

Once again, the same status attends Third World debts. As with national debts, these have shown themselves to be quite un-repayable in aggregate. The comparison with national debts goes further, since Third World debt has a similar bond structure. Also, just as payments on maturing national debt bonds can generally only be managed at the same time as a government is issuing more bonds to raise revenue, so additional Third World debt is frequently required to pay the interest on past Third World debt – new, larger bond issues replacing and funding payments on the old as the World Bank and the IMF 're-schedule' and re-mortgage the Third World.

The growth of these debts – mortgages, national debts and Third World debts – cannot be dismissed as mere expressions of monetary inflation since they have risen in real terms. The average OECD national debt rose from 34% to 76% of GDP between 1976 and 1990, UK mortgages rose from 10% to 63% of GDP between 1960 and 1996, whilst Third World debt rose from 13% to 44% of debtor nation GDP between 1970 and 1996. This is no mere numerical inflation, but very significant debt growth in real terms.

Assembling all the relevant considerations, Third World debt should be considered as an aspect of the global money supply for the following reasons;

United States National Debt

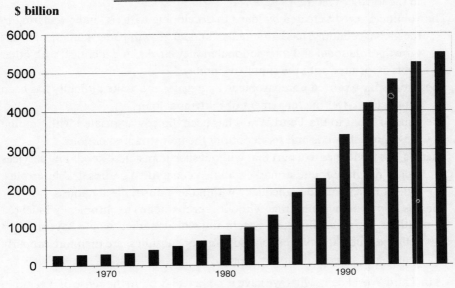

1966 — 1998

Sources: OECD; Federal Reserve.

United Kingdom National Debt

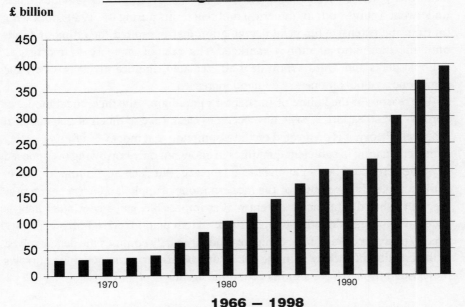

1966 — 1998

Sources: Bank of England Statistical Releases, 1990, 1995, 1998.

The bulk of loans to the Third World involve the creation of additional money in the form of credit.

The volume of credit created by loans to developing nations, and circulating in the global economy, has exhibited an annual growth pattern identical to the growth of national and international money stocks, and identical with other debts associated with the supply of money.

These loans have proved unrepayable in aggregate, and acute difficulty has been experienced over the repayment of individual loans.

The issue of loans to the Third World has been directly associated with funding the export of goods and services from the industrialised nations.

There is good evidence to assert that without such loans these goods and services would not have found a market, and so constituted an unsaleable surplus, indicating a demand inadequacy within the industrialised nations.

There is also good evidence that without repeated loans to chronically indebted nations, the global financial system and global markets would have suffered collapse. Such acts of financial support, or subsidies, are therefore properly considered aspects of money supply.

In Third World debt, what we have is not a real debt, in the sense of a genuine obligation between a lender and a borrower. Third World debt is a numerical phenomenon; a paper debt; an illegitimate debt with absolutely no economic meaning or validity, other than as a measure of money created in a global economy where all money is created as debt. In support of this judgement, it is noteworthy that all sectors and forms of debt analysed on the previous pages underwent a surge both in numerical and real terms during the 1980s, following on from the extensive financial deregulation that permitted the efflux of funds onto the international money markets. The rate of increase in mortgages, national debts and Third World debt all escalated significantly at precisely the same time as global monetary demand increased.

The reason for the failure of the debtor's paradigm – the theoretical model of borrow/invest/export/repay – now becomes clear. Like so much of neo-classical economic theory, it is predicated on the assumption that money is a freely existing entity, circulating in sufficient quantities to allow not only borrowing (as opposed to money creation) but repayment to take place. But such an assumption disregards completely the nature of the modern money supply; and net repayment is precisely what the financial system makes impossible, since continued debt is necessary to maintain the money stock in circulation. The borrow/invest/export/repay model assumes, compares and ultimately confuses the debt involved in the creation of money with the debt that a borrower incurs when he borrows pre-existent money from another economic agent.

Debt and development theory

The concept of Third World debts as an aspect of the global money supply is completely alien to development theory. Any number of quotes are available showing that loans to the Third World were advanced on the basis that these were not envisaged as forming a permanent burden, but inherently repayable and therefore temporary. For example, Jeffrey Sachs states; 'The standard assumption ... is that the borrower can attract any loan that can feasibly be paid back'.[29] The United Nations has commented;

If funds for long-term development could be committed on the basis that they would be repaid out of the resulting larger future earnings, many projects which do not now seem economically feasible might become profitable and self-liquidating.[30]

Employing more academic terminology, Vincent Crawford notes that even in the 1980s, the underlying framework of international debt/credit relationship was still being studied 'according to a two-period Fisherian model in which borrowing smoothes inter-temporal consumption'.[31] In other words, debt was viewed as involving deferred consumption, saving, investment and repayment.

The expectation was that Third World countries would pass through the development phase where capital had to be borrowed, and after repayment would eventually emerge as financially independent nations. In the words of R. Robinson, 'Virtually all recipients of aid are attempting to establish a process of growth which can continue in the future without further assistance.'[32]

A. P. Thirlwall lists the five theoretical stages through which a debtor country is expected to pass on its way to becoming a creditor nation. The final two stages ought to involve the net repayment and extinction of debt, but Thirlwall notes the clash between theory and empirical evidence;

There will come a stage when debt grows slower than the economy and debt as a proportion of the national income will fall. Finally there will come a stage when ... net indebtedness declines. The sequence from net debtor status to an ultimate creditor is a model sequence ... In the case of the developing countries in the mid 1970s, however, there is little evidence that they have the ability to pay off past indebtedness... If anything their indebtedness is mounting absolutely and as a proportion of national income.[33]

At some point during the late 1980s there was a subtle, almost subconscious mental adjustment to the permanent nature of Third World debt. It became acceptable to talk about 'rolling over' Third World debts, which were increasingly analysed by comparison with GDP or GNP, with the suggestion that there was an acceptable debt/GDP ratio. During the 1990s, the term 'sustainable debt' became fashionable.

The claim that it is acceptable to have any degree of permanent international debt, particularly one that is allowed to increase numerically, but diminished by an analysis that relates it to GDP, is quite false. International debt is unlike other categories of debt in that it relates to, and expresses, a trade imbalance, and can only be redeemed by rectification of that imbalance. A standing international debt means a standing obligation on debtor nations to remit excess goods and services to creditor nations. This involves the permanent subjugation of, and transfer of wealth from, the developing nations to the wealthy nations. The term 'sustainable' debt, if this is used to imply permanence, or any continuation of debt beyond the point at which the imbalance of trade in 'real wealth' has been redressed, is a wholly false economic concept.

Summary

Modern debt is not truly a measure of borrowing between people, industries or nations, but a direct function of banks creating and supplying the national and international money stock. This monetary understanding integrates and explains many of the various elements of established Third World debt analysis. In particular, it offers an explanation for the aggressive trading of 'creditor' nations and their unwillingness to sustain a trade deficit sufficient for debts to be repaid.

The immediate reason that the developing nations have been unable to repay their debts and correct the financial balance of trade, along with the material balance of trade, was that the terms and conventions of trade set up at Bretton Woods have resulted in them receiving a pittance for their exports. The ultimate reason is that national and international economies are founded on a debt-based financial system. Third World debt is part of the money supply to the global economy and, like all other large institutional debts, cannot actually be repaid.

In Third World debt, what we have is not a real debt, in the sense of a genuine obligation between a lender and a borrower. Third World debt is a numerical phenomenon; a paper debt; an illegitimate debt with absolutely no economic meaning or validity, other than as a measure of money created in a global economy where all money is created via debt.

Since the monetary demands of the global economy will certainly not decrease, repayment of Third World debt – so long as money is only created as a debt – requires that some other agency, institution or economic sector undertakes the debts currently born by debtor nations in order to maintain this $2,200 billion in circulation. Under debt finance, the only way the debtor nations can hope to see the gross total of their debt reduced is if the debt associated with the monies created is shifted to other nations.

Since the wealthy nations and their peoples are already massively indebted, and their debt is growing at the same time as Third World debt is also growing, there is little likelihood that the trading battle between nations will result in anything different from the established pattern of continued and growing debt for all nations. The only alternative is to 'break the chains' – to borrow the Jubilee 2000 phrase – the real chains – the unnecessary linkage between money and debt. This is the subject of the next chapter.

Endnotes

1   Harold Lever, Christopher Huhne. *Debt and Danger.* Penguin. 1985.
2   See chapter in; Hans Singer, Sumitra Sharma (eds). *Economic Development and World Debt.* Macmillan Press. 1989.
3   Hans Singer and Sumitra Sharma. *Economic Development and World Debt.* Macmillan Press. 1989.
4   Lord Lever, Christopher Huhne. *Op. cit.*
5   Bishop Berkeley. *Queries.* 1746.
6   Quoted in F. W. Fetter. *The Development of British Monetary Orthodoxy.* Harvard University Press. 1965.
7   Edward King. *Considerations on the Utility of the National Debt.* 1793.
8   Quoted in F. W. Fetter. *Op. cit.*
9   John Grey. *An Effective remedy for the Distress of Nations.* 1842.
10   Abraham Lincoln. *Monetary Policy.* Senate Document 23. 1865.
11   Bill Still, Patrick Carmack. *The Money Masters.* Royalty Production Co. 1998.
12   Quoted in F.W. Fetter. *Op. cit.*
13   William Gladstone. 3 *Hansard* CCXXII. 1985. March 17, 1875.
14   Frances Hutchinson. *What Everyone Really Wants to Know About Money.* Jon Carpenter. 1997.
15   Quoted in Brynjolf Bjorset. *Distribute or Destroy.* Stanley Nott. 1936.
16   Quoted in Richard Douthwaite. *The Growth Illusion.* Green Books. 1992.
17   Quoted in Brynjolf Bjorset. *Op. cit.*
18   Brynjolf Bjorset. *Op. cit.*
19   Conference of the Institute for African Alternatives. Bade Onimode (ed). *The IMF, The World Bank and African Debt.* Zed Books. 1989.
20   Cheryl Payer. *The Debt Trap.* Monthly Review Press. 1974.
21   C. H. Douglas. *Dictatorship by Taxation.* Institute of Economic Democracy. 1936.
22   Cheryl Payer. Conference of Institute for African Alternatives. *Op.cit.*
23   Quoted in; Jackie Roddick. *The Dance of the Millions.* Latin America Bureau. 1988.
24   Conference of Institute for African Alternatives. *Op.cit.*
25   C. H. Douglas. *The Policy of a Philosophy.* Institute of Economic Democracy. 1936.
26   André Gunder Frank. In Hans Singer, Sumitra Sharma. *Op. cit.*
27   Quoted in Hans Singer, Sumitra Sharma. *Op. cit.*
28   Michel Chossudovsky. *The Globalisation of Poverty.* Zed Books. 1997.
29   Jeffrey Sachs. *Theoretical Issues in International Borrowing.* Princeton Studies in International Finance. No 54. July 1984.
30   United Nations. *Financing Economic Development in Underdeveloped Countries.* United Nations. New York. 1949.
31   Vincent P. Crawford. *International lending; Long-term Credit Relationships and Dynamic Contract Theory.* Princeton Studies in International Finance. No 59 March 1987.
32   R.Robinson. *Developing the Third World; The Experience of the 1960s.* Cambridge University Press. 1971.
33   A. P. Thirlwall. *Financing Economic Development.* Macmillan. 1976.

9

The cancellation of Third World debt

'Cancel or repudiate Africa's external debt'.[1] *How* to cancel Third World debt is a distinct issue from *why* these debts should be cancelled. Before considering the options for cancelling the debts of developing nations, or in various ways reducing their impact, it is worth reviewing the grounds on which such a policy is warranted.

1   Loans were advanced as being repayable, whereas analysis of institutional debts, including mortgages, national debts and Third World debts, shows that these constitute part of the global money supply and are thus inherently unrepayable in aggregate.

2   Because these loans are unrepayable in aggregate, severe difficulty is experienced with the repayment of individual loans, as a direct function of fiscal competition.

3   Inappropriate project approval, loan criteria, risk analysis and over-liberal lending.

4   The failure to take into account that similar development projects would contribute to a collapse in commodity prices, invalidating the fiscal projections of these projects, and thereby compromising debtor nation finances.

5   The issuance of loans in dollar terms and demand for payment in dollar terms leading to excessive material loss for debtor nations.

6   The imposition of conditions that blatantly favoured the cartels and business monopolies of the industrialised nations.

7   The failure of the floating exchange rate mechanism to reflect true value, or promote a balance of trade.

8   The imposition of deflationary 'austerity measures' based on pure monetarist theory that led to sustained economic recession.

9   The insistence upon privatisation/deregulation programmes that lead to Third World debtor nation assets being acquired by powerful international commercial concerns.

10 The poor returns on sales of valuable debtor nation assets, due to (7) and (8) above.

There is, however, one over-arching argument which, above all others, calls for the cancellation of Third World debt. This is that the debtor nations have, over the decades since Bretton Woods, suffered a clear material loss by accepting loans for purposes of development. The real, physical balance of trade has involved the progressive transfer out of debtor nations of vast quantities of material wealth, as a result of sustained annual exports of increasingly undervalued primary commodities, minerals and other raw materials, devalued debt-equity swaps and the wholesale loss of infrastructure assets to foreign commerce and investors through direct and portfolio (stock market) investment.

After this massive transfer of wealth which quite dwarfs the goods and services imported as purchases by the original loans, the debtor nations of the Third World owe nothing, in material terms, to any nation or institution beyond their borders. The fact that Third World debt lacks legitimacy demands action because, although these debts do not represent any true duty or obligation on the part of debtor nations towards any other nation, debtor nations are compelled to act as if such an obligation existed. Whilst carrying an unrepayable bank debt, and having already remitted vast quantities of goods, services and assets to the more wealthy nations and their corporate sector, debtor nations are compelled to act as if their debts represented a true inter-national obligation.

The continued existence and damaging effect of these debts, in spite of sustained economic effort by the developing world, is economically unjustifiable as well as morally repugnant.

1 The cancellation of debt bonds

Whenever Third World debt cancellation is discussed, it is automatically assumed that somebody, somewhere has to suffer a loss. Either banks must cover the losses, taxes must be raised or Western governments must foot the bill. Whichever way, someone has to pay.

In fact, Third World debts could be cancelled with little or no cost to anyone. Indeed, cancellation would be not only the simplest process imaginable, but to the general advantage of the world economy. All that is involved is a bit of creative accountancy – something at which the West has shown itself highly adept when this has suited its political purpose.

To appreciate this, it is essential to recall that the dominant form of money in the modern economy, bank credit, is entirely numerical. It is an abstract entity with no physical existence whatsoever, created in parallel with debt. Debt cancellation is therefore largely a matter of numerical accountancy. This is emphasised by the fact that only one factor prevents the immediate and instant cancellation of all Third World debts – the accountancy rules of commercial banks.

Third World debt bonds form part of the assets of commercial banks, and all banks are obliged to maintain parity between their assets and liabilities (deposits).

If commercial banks cancel or write off Third World debt bonds, their total assets fall. Under the rules of banking, the banks are then obliged to restore their level of assets to the point where they equal their liabilities, usually by transferring an equivalent sum from their reserves. In other words, when debts are cancelled, normally banks suffer the loss.

There are two options for overcoming this accountancy blockage. They involve acknowledging that debt-cancellation is both desirable and possible, and *adapting bank accountancy accordingly*.

The first option is to remove the obligation on banks to maintain parity between assets and liabilities, or, to be more precise, to allow banks to hold reduced levels of assets equivalent to the Third World debt bonds they cancel. Thus, if a commercial bank held $10 billion worth of developing country debt bonds, after cancellation it would be permitted in perpetuity to have a $10 billion dollar deficit in its assets. This is a simple matter of record-keeping.

The second option, and in accountancy terms probably the more satisfactory (although it amounts to the same policy), is to cancel the debt bonds, *yet permit banks to retain them for purposes of accountancy*. The debts would be cancelled so far as the developing nations were concerned, but still valid for the purposes of a bank's accounts. The bonds would then be held as permanent, non-negotiable assets, at face value.

Such a policy would be completely effective in terms of cancellation, without affecting the accountancy of banks in the slightest. Indeed, to the extent that banks are under pressure to acknowledge the true value of Third World debt bonds (which may be as little as 10% of their face value), the accountancy position of banks would be considerably improved and confirmed. By this method, any amount of undesired debt could be permanently cancelled with immediate effect.

There are three precedents for this policy.

1   To cancel Third World debt bonds in terms of their claim on debtor nations, yet declare them valid for accountancy purposes, would place them in essentially the same category as the 'reserve assets' demanded by governments. Reserve assets are a sum of money from a commercial bank's assets that a government demands be lodged with the central bank as a commercial surety (0.5% of total liabilities within the UK banking system and 5% in the US). Banks are still permitted to account these 'reserve assets' within their total assets, but they are inaccessible and effectively 'sterile' to the bank – useless other than for their accountancy function.

2   In addition to the precedent of reserve assets, the behaviour of banks shows that they already treat and account the debt bonds they hold in this creative and cavalier fashion. Bank regulators are frequently lax in how they oversee banks, and especially in the way they allow the banks to report their net

worth. A bank can pretend on its books that a $1 million loan to Brazil is indeed worth $1 million, despite the fact that analysts might think that Brazil will pay back only one third of the loan and the market value of the debt bonds reflects this. In essence the bank is inflating the value of some of its debt assets, declaring a numerical value which those assets do not have. Any normal business that did not reflect the changing real value of its assets would find their accounts challenged.

The fact that this happens proves beyond dispute that the main function of these debt bonds is as an accountancy device. These loans are not worth their face value – the value of the original loan. The banks will not receive full repayment of these loans, and they know this. Yet the banks continue, in their assets column, to account them at full value.

3   The third precedent actually involves precisely the effective cancellation of Third World debt being discussed. During the 1930s debt crisis, a number of Latin American nations defaulted on their loans to the United States, as did Britain. To this day, the US Treasury keeps a record of a number of these debts, accounting them in full. In the words of Cheryl Payer, 'that part of the debt that was not settled was simply ignored... The US Treasury continues to carry these debts on its books, and annually publishes the principal and interest owed by each of the debtor nations that defaulted in the 1930s, which include Britain, France and Italy'.[3]

This is very revealing. The US Treasury is fully aware that these debts were officially defaulted on, and that there is no intention by the nations concerned ever to repay them. So why does it bother to record and account them? Because in doing so, the US Treasury maintains the fiction that the debt bonds are valid assets, which suits its fiscal purpose. To remove these debts from the books and acknowledge their lack of worth would require the transfer of equivalent assets from US reserves. This the US does not wish to do, and so she wisely adapts her accountancy accordingly.

Thus we have an almost exact precedent for Third World debts being cancelled with respect to the debtor nations, yet maintained as an accountancy device. Even if it were argued that Britain and the other nations might one day pay up on those debts, the fact that this form of creative accountancy has been successfully adopted for decades, and that the position could remain *ad infinitum*, demonstrates that such a policy is perfectly practicable.

The effect of debt cancellation

The monetary effect of any such a write-off would be that the $2.2 trillion dollars that has been created by the process of lending to Third World nations, would be released permanently into the world economy, where it is currently now dispersed. The position of banks would be unchanged, other than that they would not receive future interest payments on Third World bonds. Against this must be set the fact that they would be relieved of trying to account assets whose true value conflicts with their market value, and which are in some senses little better than liabilities.

Freeing banks from the obligation to transfer monies from their reserves to cover 'failed debts' allows banks to cancel Third World debt without penalty – except for a nominal loss of annual interest. In fact, to the extent that banks would no longer be constantly requested to bail out debtor nations with additional loans, the pressure on them to build up their reserves through interest receipts would diminish.

As for the wider macro-economic effects of such cancellation, there is every reason to claim that these would be very positive. If once it is accepted that the world suffers from excessive debt and that there has been an over-reliance on banking to create money, such cancellation must contribute to a more stable, less exposed global economy. Full cancellation of Third World debts would inject $2.2 trillion dollars of 'solvency' into the global economy – simply by allowing the $2.2 trillion of bank credit currently countered by equivalent debts to circulate freely.

Not only the Third World but the entire community of nations would benefit from debt cancellation. The many 'debt boomerangs', whereby Third World debt backlashes on the wealthy nations, would be ameliorated.[4] The general gain from cancellation can also be appreciated in the contribution this would make to halting globalisation and reducing the power of multinationals, as is discussed in the following chapter.

Banking and debt cancellation

To understand how such a cancellation is possible, we need only remind ourselves that modern money is almost entirely numerical – a mere book-keeping system. There is nothing of physical substance either to lend or to repay. Money, debt, assets, deposits and bank reserves are all linked in the generation of money and the accountancy of banking – but these links can be severed and the rules suspended if desired.

Understanding the accountancy rules of banking clarifies the oft-stated claim that Third World debt threatens the global financial system. As everyone knows, the global financial system is not remotely threatened (even under the conventional banking perception) by vast numbers of depositors suddenly wanting to withdraw their money. Banks would never be in the position where they had to 'call in' their loans to the Third World in order to 'pay their depositors', or face bankruptcy. Also, the past forty years have proved that the global banking system is not threatened by the repeated failure of debtor nations to actually repay their loans; indeed, the failure to repay has constantly prompted banks to advance new, larger loans to debtor nations today, so that they can make repayments on the smaller loans from yesterday. Similarly, the global financial system is not threatened by any failure to make interest payments, since this simply results in lower payments to depositors and shareholders. In addition, interest and dividend payments can accrue from a wide range of other sources of profits, including the great bulk of loans other than Third World debt bonds, which do generate steady interest payments.

The failure of the banking system is threatened by one aspect of Third World debt alone. This is the accountancy status of the debt bonds. If Third World nations *en masse* were to refuse to honour their debts, or if there were any general economic collapse that led to large numbers of debt bonds being declared devalued, or valueless, then many banks' assets would plunge to the point where there was insufficient in their reserves to cover the loss. It is the accountancy status of Third World debt that threatens banking, and thereby the financial system as a whole.

Yet the entire commercial world knows the value of many of these bonds to be minimal, and trades and sells them at fractions of their face value. These debt bonds, in fact, *already have* critically low values – this is just not acknowledged! It would be utterly perverse to argue that valueless Third World debt bonds can be treated at full value by banks when it suits them, but that the same policy should not be used for purposes of cancellation!

Debt-equity or sterile assets?

In terms of this approach to cancellation, it is worth reflecting on another cavalier policy by which banks take even more blatant advantage of Third World debt. Debt-for-equity swaps involve a bank exchanging debt bonds for commercial property in the Third World. This commercial property then replaces the debt bonds in the bank's asset column. But to acquire property in this way is not to obtain 'ready money' to 'repay its depositors'. The bank has moved appreciably away from the accountancy of monetary affairs, tacitly acknowledging that the claim that it 'must' have debt repayment in order to 'pay its depositors their money' is a myth.

Some depositors are constantly withdrawing their money, whilst other depositors are paying money in. The entire banking system revolves around the knowledge that the outflow of withdrawals and the inflow of payments allows banks to work with a small, and reasonably predictable, monetary base. The remainder of their assets can take any form: debt bonds, land, property, industrial assets. Knowing they are able to rely upon a steady monetary base, banks have swapped debt bonds – often applying their full face value – for debtor nation assets, many of which are heavily undervalued.

Before a debt-equity swap, a bank holds a loan with a definite face-value and a defined return; then it goes shopping in the Third World and uses the debt to buy – who knows what? The bank, which itself created the credit-money to advance to the debtor nation, has capitalised fully on its past credit-creation, and has now acquired a valuable asset. The bank will never have to sell this property to repay any depositor, just as banks never have to foreclose on debtor nations to obtain the money to pay any depositor. Whatever was acquired in the debt-for-equity swap has become the bank's legal, permanent property – and by what right? This is only accepted because we are, in general, conditioned into accepting bank debts as legitimate claims, and mesmerised into accepting the spurious assertion that a bank 'must' have debt repayment (or its equivalent) in order to 'pay its depositors their money'.

The point, in terms of debt cancellation, is this. If a bank can convert debt bonds with a fixed monetary value into property and industry with no fixed value, and to which it clearly has no true right or title, then a bank can accept accountancy involving sterile debt bonds which preserve its accountancy balance, but cancel its claim over developing nations – again to which it has no true right or title. Commercial banks would lose nothing to which they had any right by this method of cancellation.

2   Converting Third World debts into national debts

The greater part of this book argues that complete debt cancellation is fully justified. However there are powerful vested interests and prejudices ranged against such a policy. There is another strategy that might be used which, whilst less immediate in its effect than cancellation, is of a fundamental nature, and would certainly be an improvement on the World Bank's HIPC Initiative. It might also appeal more to the 'financial morality' of the bankers, politicians and economists actually in a position of influence. This strategy would convert the 'international' debt of Third World nations into national debts.

There are two reasons why the conversion of their 'international' debts into national debts would be of incalculable assistance to debtor nations. Both highlight the serious injustice of Third World debt.

The first reason is that the industrialised nations administer and control their national debts. By contrast, every time the developing nations need to increase their international debts, they are forced to submit to the hopeless incompetence, political bias and quasi-colonial dictates of the IMF and World Bank. The second, more fundamental reason for converting Third World debts into national debts is that national debts are accounted in the currency produced by that nation. The key feature of international debts is that they are accounted in hard currencies. Debtor nations are therefore driven to seek a surplus of export revenues for repayment.

Just to illustrate the severity of Third World debt, it is worth considering the radically different position in which the industrialised nations would find themselves if their national debts were denominated in foreign currencies. If the UK were in the position of a debtor nation, expected to pay up annually on an international debt the size of its national debt, unable to reschedule at will, this would mean either:

(a) obtaining sufficient exports to produce a trade surplus of approximately £25 billion per year; or

(b) submitting to 'structural adjustment', with detailed macro and micro economic policy set by the World Bank and IMF and no opportunity for rescheduling, with the UK government being forced to apply for permission to the IMF to run its annual deficit.

The position of the United States would be even more disastrous. In addition to the above restrictions, the ability to take advantage of the dollar's position as the *de facto* unit of international currency would vanish. At present, America runs an annual trade deficit – i.e. imports more than it exports – to the tune of approximately $150 billion. If the US money stock were not constantly replenished through government borrowing, adding to its national debt by approximately $300 billion annually, the loss of money abroad through excessive importing would bring the US economy to its knees within months, if not weeks.

The ability to produce dollars at will, and the key position of the dollar, give America the supreme economic advantage. America draws on the material wealth of the world virtually *ad infinitum* – creating dollars in exchange for goods and using its national debt to cover up its trade deficit. At the same time, the developing nations must pay their debts in a currency they cannot produce – dollars. The US can enjoy the imports of the world, exporting a stream of dollars without fear that the currency will collapse. What would the World Bank make of America's trade deficit? What would America's creditors make of the US national debt, which is in excess of 80% of GDP – a ratio that has risen every year for the past three decades? What structural adjustment, social, economic and regulatory policies would the IMF place on the US for her record of failing to settle her debts by $300 billion per year, and drifting into debt by a further $300 billion?

Converting international debts to national debts would grant developing nations the same autonomy as the industrialised nations. They would have the right to manage and, if desired, postpone or increase their debt level whatever their trading success, and without being obliged to go cap-in-hand to the multilateral institutions. Economic policy would remain in the hands of elected politicians.

Practicalities of conversion

As we saw in Chapter 7, national debts and Third World debts have an identical composition. They consist of debt bonds – paper contracts – held by the world's commercial banks and lending institutions. The method of administration of both national debts and Third World debts is virtually identical. Both national debt bonds and Third World debt bonds are 'promises to repay' money at a later date, plus interest. They thus guarantee a return to the holder of the bond. Both national debt bonds and Third World debt bonds are 'time-related' and both forms of debt have exhibited an identical pattern of escalation in the last 40 years. No country, developed or developing, can repay its bonded debts. Instead, there is a constant 'rescheduling' in which maturing debt bonds are settled at the same time as new, larger debts are taken on: i.e. there is perpetual postponement.

The structural similarity between international and national debts emphasises the ease with which conversion could take place. What actually has to be done is astonishingly straightforward. Third World debt bonds are already in the possession of commercial banks – precisely the same institutions that buy national debt bonds. All that is required is that the amounts denominated on these bonds be changed from dollars or pounds into the appropriate national currencies. The debts are then national. It is as simple as that. The current market rate conversion would provide an entirely equitable exchange.

Though apparently a more modest reform than cancellation, conversion would re-define and re-classify Third World debts as no longer 'international'. There would no longer be any pretence that these debts represent an obligation to remit goods and services to other nations. A clean sheet would be instituted in the record of the international balance of trade.

There is a precedent for this policy, which underlines the willingness of the wealthy nations to take advantage of such 'creative accountancy' when it so suits them. Currency conversion of dollar debt bonds into pesos was actually employed in the 1984 Mexico Rescheduling Package. Bergsten Cline Williamson notes the effect and the declared rationale of this policy; '... their own central bank, their lender of last resort, could more effectively come to the rescue if necessary'.[5] A general application of what has already proved a practical and successful policy is clearly possible.

Effects of conversion

The main purpose and effect of converting Third World debt into national currencies is to reduce the immediate burden of debt, and return economic and political control to the elected governments of those nations. In control of their own debts, Third World nations would be able to set their own economic priorities, which would almost certainly involve devoting less effort to exports, and developing their own agriculture, industry, infrastructure and welfare for their own citizens.

It might be objected that banks holding the converted bonds would suffer considerable losses, since debtor nation currencies might well fall from their 'conversion rate' and the bonds would therefore decline in worth. But this is an argument for stabilising currency values, not for impeding a reform of such importance. Also, as noted earlier, Third World debt bonds already trade at a fraction of their face value.

The advantage of this 'conversion policy' over cancellation is that it requires far fewer concessions on the part of creditors, and no acceptance of a monetary reform critique. Debts are not cancelled, they are simply transferred into more appropriate currencies at market value. This, incidentally, gives bond holders the option of selling these bonds and suffering no loss.

3 Supported repayment

It would, in theory, be quite possible to pay off Third World debts without using money already in existence. New money could be created *ab initio* by a process that does not involve any additional debt, and this money could be remitted to the commercial banks and other institutions holding debt bonds. The banks would receive this as full repayment of the debts, and the bonds would be written off as a consequence.

There is no great mysticism or difficulty in performing this task. Banks create new credit-money to the tune of millions of pounds every day. They have no authority to do this – only a technique coupled with cultural acceptance of this practice. Any other institution, so authorised, could perform a money-creating act, and could create money in whatever form was deemed appropriate. This includes the creation of numerical money (i.e. credits) that had no parallel debt, was not intended for repayment, and hence was 'debt-free'. There is a perfect precedent for this in the form of notes and coins which, as discussed earlier, are created *ab initio*, at no cost other than the labour and materials involved, and as a pure credit to the government's account.

There is absolutely nothing to prevent the creation of numerical money on the same debt-free basis as note and coin. There is nothing to prevent this being done on a sufficient scale to repay commercial banks for the totality of Third World debt, and so liquidate the debt bonds. Banks' balance sheets would remain in perfect order, exactly as if the debtor nations themselves had repaid the sums they were originally loaned – whereas by this approach, those revenues would be left circulating in the global economy whilst the additional money would serve simply to cancel the bonds of Third World debt.

The practical and the institutional demands of supported repayment, and the knock-on effects, are rather more problematical than simple cancellation. Money could be created, as required, by the governments in whose currencies the debt bonds were denominated. Thus the UK government would create the appropriate sum in pounds sterling to cancel the Third World debts it is owed, which could then be transferred direct to the appropriate commercial banks in full and permanent settlement.

Alternatively, and more realistically, one of the existing multilateral agencies, or some new agency, could be authorised to create the required sums in an international currency, such as SDRs. This very policy has indeed been proposed in the past. A bill was submitted in 1987 to the US House of Representatives, instructing the US Treasury Department to raise with the IMF the idea of making a one-time issuance of 'special purpose SDRs', to be allocated amongst poorer countries, with the proviso that they could only be used for the repayment of official debt.[6] The Bill was rejected. This was a full-blown policy of Third World debt-cancellation by supported repayment using a neutral but convertible currency.

It is bound to be objected that such a policy of supported repayment by money-creation is inflationary, and would have a damaging effect on currency values if creditor nations were to create this money. But it has to be remembered that, by supported repayment, money would not be passed into general circulation but would be directed to banks. There, the money would form part of their assets, and could not have an automatic inflationary effect, nor affect currency values. The only way these revenues could enter the broader economy and prove inflationary is if they became the basis of further lending, or if banks used the money to make purchases. The option of using SDRs as the basis of supported repayment is especially attractive in terms of eliminating such potential knock-on effects, since it would be a simple legislative matter to restrict the negotiability of these SDRs, requiring that they be held as non-negotiable assets. This option actually represents an overlap with the option of cancellation discussed earlier.

Cancellation – whose problem?

When discussing solutions to Third World debt, it is easy to fall into a fundamental political error. Responsibility for creating a satisfactory accountancy solution for Third World debt does not lie with either the debtor nations or those who defend them. It rests with the representatives of those institutions responsible for causing this debt in the first place, and those in positions of international responsibility and influence – mainly the G8 countries, the World Bank and IMF, the OECD and the United Nations.

If extensive debt relief presents a financial accountancy problem, either to the World Bank, commercial banks or the wealthy nations, and it is asserted in defence that they did not appreciate the intractability of the debts being created, then, as their own legal principles assert, ignorance is no defence. In fact, the matter of ignorance cannot even be claimed. The potential danger of irreversible debt due to an un-redressed imbalance of trade, coupled with lending based on fractional reserve banking, was voiced at Bretton Woods. Keynes' original proposal for an International Clearing Union and the Bancor should be recalled. Had Keynes' proposal, or one similar, been accepted, there would have been no such thing as Third World debt. As we saw earlier, the dominant American delegation rejected this scheme in favour of their own, despite widespread warnings as to the defects of their Stabilisation Fund; warnings that have been wholly vindicated.

With all the options for reform – supported repayment in national currencies, the use of SDRs, discounted buybacks, cancellation and conversion, and with actual precedents in every case – it is clear that the cancellation of Third World debt is a matter of political will, not a matter of technical or financial difficulty. Any solution will undoubtedly cause problems, but that is a reason for proceeding with caution and readiness to take compensating action, not a reason for paralysis. Failure to take action is not an option. At present, all the drawbacks, anomalies and costs of the inequity of the current system impact on the impoverished developing nations, their peoples and their commerce, which is wholly unjust.

The potential problems, such as inflation, currency values and excess bank expenditure, should be addressed. Any perceived disadvantage to creditors should be subordinated to the greater right of debtors for relief. Permissions for commercial banks with regard to old debt bonds; restrictions on commercial banks if supported repayment is used; better control of currency values; enhanced regulations on spending and lending – if a problem is perceived, it can be addressed. This is a man-made world of numerical accountancy, open to redesign and reconstruction. What is primarily required is the will to act, an assumption of responsibility, and the determination to make a new scheme work by constant review. As Keynes once said of Roosevelt's monetary reform speech, Third World debt is 'in substance a challenge to us to decide whether we propose to tread the old unfortunate ways or to explore new paths; paths new to statesmen and to bankers, but not new to thought'.[7]

Summary

The cancellation of international debts, or their conversion to national debts, is the *sine qua non* if Third World nations are to discover a path away from poverty and decline and towards more socially and culturally benign futures. The acknowledged need is for Third World countries to develop their agricultural and industrial infrastructure for their own domestic consumption and direct less effort towards export-led growth. To the extent that international debts remain, the export imperative remains.

As we have seen, the Third World cannot be said to be in material debt to the industrialised nations. The developing nations are in financial debt to international banks. But whilst not actually in material debt to the industrialised nations, because these bank debts are denominated in dollars, they are forced to behave as if they were in debt to the West, seeking a perpetual export surplus.

Third World debt thus represents a major economic anomaly. A debt towards one group of institutions (commercial and multilateral banks) takes expression as a debt towards another group of institutions (the industrialised nations), despite the fact that such an obligation does not truly exist.

Two main options for rectifying this anomaly are suggested in this chapter. The first is the 'monetary reform option', which breaks the chain between debt and money, cancelling Third World debt bonds but allowing them to serve as bank accountancy devices. The second is the conversion of international debts into national debts, placing developing nations in control of their own fiscal policy.

The monetary reform option is unquestionably the more justified policy since these debts lack economic validity. It avoids the sudden shock of debtor nations being faced with the immediate fiscal responsibility of a much-increased national debt. It also actually reduces the aggregate of global debt, contributing to the establishment of a money stock circulating free from a background of debt. As the next chapter shows, this would contribute more to halting the 'drive towards globalisation' than would the conversion option.

The second option, conversion to national debts, is more effective than it perhaps sounds. True, the debtor nations would remain in debt to commercial banks and multilateral institutions. But the denomination of these debts in their own currencies alters the balance of power significantly. Developing nations would be under no greater pressure to achieve an export surplus than is, for example, the United States, which runs a massive annual trade deficit whilst having an awesome national debt that continues to escalate. National debts, whilst a foolish institution, at least leave the majority of power with elected politicians, who decide by how much the national debt-that-will-never-be-repaid will rise each year. The export imperative is completely lifted by the conversion option.

The conversion option is also attractive because, whilst an effective reform, it neither requires acceptance of a monetary reform agenda, nor breaches the contractual obligation of debt and interest repayment. These debts are obligations formally undertaken by developing nations to banks. The validity of these debts is open to legal challenge, but involves an extensive series of complex arguments. This is where the 'conversion option' really scores.

It is an obviously 'fair' request to have international debts which do not actually reflect a genuine obligation between nations, converted into national debts in which the relationship is confined to the debtor nation and the banks concerned, via that nation's currency. This negates the pressure to export for dollars and also the obligation to seek bail-outs from the multilateral lending institutions, with all the political demands that this entails. The 'conversion' option is therefore far more likely to win broad acceptance. Incidentally, the conversion policy leaves each developing nation with the option (as yet adopted by no Western nation) of deciding to adopt a monetary reform agenda, and gradually retiring the national debt whilst instituting a controlled government money supply. This point is discussed in more detail in Chapter 12.

If extensive debt relief presents a financial accountancy problem, either to the World Bank, commercial banks or the wealthy nations, then the responsibility lies with the offending institutions to create the accountancy to deal with this. It should be remembered that the potential danger of irreversible debt due to an un-redressed imbalance of trade, coupled with lending based on fractional reserve banking, was voiced at Bretton Woods.

Keynes' original proposal for an International Clearing Union and the Bancor should be recalled. The significant features of Keynes' proposition was that the Bancor was to be a currency of issue as opposed to one multiplied via fractional reserve banking. Also, there would be an equal obligation on both debtor and creditor nations to maintain a balance of trade over time. The dominant American delegation rejected this scheme in favour of their own, despite wide-spread warnings as to the defects of their Stabilisation Fund that have been wholly vindicated.

In the end, the precise manner in which dollar debts are lifted from Third World nations is immaterial. Whether they are removed by outright cancellation, supported repayment, conversion, or by some other policy, this is a matter the international community must quickly determine. However, it should be stressed that, far from discussing how much debt should be remitted, the appalling record of the Bretton Woods institutions ought seriously to raise the question of compensation to debtor nations. Unfortunately, the havoc that has been played with their development, their economic infrastructure and indeed their entire history of the past fifty years is beyond any financial redress.

Endnotes

1   Conference of the Institute for African Alternatives. Bade Onimode (ed). *The IMF, The World Bank and African Debt*. Zed Books. 1989.
2   Jeffrey Sachs, Felipe Larrain. *Macroeconomics in the Global Economy*. Prentice Hall International. 1993.
3   Cheryl Payer. *Lent and Lost*. Zed Books. 1991.
4   Susan George. *The Debt Boomerang*. Pluto Press. 1992.
5   Bergsten Cline Williamson. *Bank Lending to Developing Countries – the Policy Alternatives*. Institute for International Economics. No 10, April 1985.
6   J. Cavanagh, D. Wysham, M. Arruda. *Beyond Bretton Woods – Alternatives to the Global Economic Order*. Pluto Press. 1994.
7   Quoted in Richard Douthwaite. *The Growth Illusion*. Green Books. 1992.

10

The drive behind globalisation

This chapter argues that, whilst many critics may recognise what is happening through the process known as globalisation, the economic forces involved are not broadly understood. The debt-based financial system, and Third World debt in particular, are analysed as key factors in the drive behind globalisation. This offers many insights into the policies needed to control globalisation. In addition, since globalisation is a very damaging process that impacts on the wealthy nations as well as the developing nations, this analysis gives additional incentive to the West to find a rapid solution to the international debt crisis.

As discussed in the opening chapter, the dominance of the international market and the recent upsurge in international trade is seen as one of the most damaging features of globalisation. Of course, it is not trade *per se* that is the focus of concern, but that involving

(a) the international exchange of near-identical products, and

(b) the importing of goods and services that could be produced locally.

This increase in 'pointless' trade is often blamed on the free trade ethic that now dominates the management of international economics. But this cannot claim to be a full explanation. Free trade principally involves the removal of barriers to trade. The deeper question is; why do goods and services flood across international borders when such barriers are removed?

There are many such trends and phenomena within globalisation for which there are currently no adequate explanations. Part of the reason is that the trends are so familiar that we do not even question them. For instance; why do 'diseconomies of scale' never seem to apply to multinationals? This is a question that is simply not asked. We have lived so long with the growing dominance of Big Business that the cumbersome success of global multinationals is simply accepted.

But contrary to popular belief, economists do not automatically accept that 'bigger is better'. As long ago as Ricardo, economists recognised that, up to a certain point, size brings efficiency – 'economies of scale'. Beyond a certain point, size creates inefficiency – 'diseconomies of scale'. Why does this not operate against multinationals and globalisation?

As a related, geographical example, why is it profitable to grow vegetables in the southern hemisphere and air-lift them to Europe? This is a vastly inefficient use of resources. Apart from the gross wastage of the transport involved, the misuse of land is glaringly apparent. Land desperately needed in southern Africa to feed indigenous populations is directed to producing foodstuffs for export, whilst in Europe 10% of land is currently out of production under set-aside and Europe's farmers are struggling to survive.

Part of the answer is of course familiar to us, and immediately highlights the significance of Third World debt. The gross inequalities between nations and the pressure of their dollar debts mean that multinationals can buy into developing Third World countries, obtaining contracts, assets and labour at disgracefully low rates. The low cost of resources and labour in the developing nations then effectively subsidises the transport of end products to the industrialised nations.

But this answer does not explain why, after decades of development, Third World nations find themselves in such a parlous financial position. Nor does it explain why UK consumers now buy strawberries that have flown halfway round the world and taste like blotting paper, rather than tastier, domestically produced varieties. Nor does it explain why European farmers have been unable to compete their way back into the market.

Globalisation and the financial system

This chapter argues that an understanding of the financial system allows us to answer more of the questions thrown up by globalisation. Many of the answers inter-relate and suggest that the financial system is a key factor driving forward the process of globalisation.

Four aspects of the financial system are particularly relevant to the process of globalisation.

1 The creation and supply of money to national economies

As we have seen, the financial system currently adopted by all nations is based on fractional reserve banking. Only the existence of permanent debt maintains the money stock in circulation. Modern debt is therefore, in aggregate, un-repayable. Furthermore, difficulty is experienced in the repayment of individual debts in all four sectors – private, commercial, government and Third World.

2 International trade imbalances

Chapter 4 discussed how, at Bretton Woods, the American delegation insisted that nations with a trade surplus should not be obliged to spend the revenues they thereby gained back into nations with a trade deficit. As a result, countries are under no obligation to maintain a balance of trade with other nations, and are permitted to seek an indefinite trade surplus. This is a key factor in the pattern of trade we see today.

3 Third World debt

The position of acute debt afflicting the developing nations is one of the main ingredients of globalisation. Multinationals operate in the 'development gap' between the poorer nations and the richer nations. Backed up by a large capital base, and negotiating with impoverished nations desperate for any influx of foreign currency, multinationals are able to secure valuable natural resources and labour at rock-bottom prices.

4 The international flow of financial capital

During the 1980s, the industrialised nations undertook extensive 'deregulation' of finance, dropping barriers to the outflow of money and seeking to attract inflows of foreign investment. The floodgates to international finance were opened. It was subsequent to this deregulation that international money markets began the switch from 95% trade-related exchanges and 5% financial speculative investment, to the current reversed position of 5% trade-related and 95% speculation.

A vast quantity of money now circulates at the international level in currency deals, stock market transactions and trade settlement. The build up of international capital, coupled with extensive further deregulation, has led to the development of a predatory international financial sector. It has been repeatedly demonstrated that the principal activity of this international financial sector is not maturing, productive investment, but short-term, speculative investment, involving extractive gain.[1]

These four factors combine to drive forward the process of globalisation. They also produce the ideal financial environment for multinational corporations to prosper at the expense of more resource-efficient enterprises. The following discussion is divided into two sections. The first examines the effect of the debt-based financial system on marketing pressures and trading patterns. The second examines the range of factors presenting the perfect environment for multinationals and their 'global growth' strategy.

Trade and a lack of effective demand

The debt-based financial system offers us a powerful insight into the drive behind globalisation, through the concept of a 'lack of effective demand'. A lack of effective demand means that consumers/customers possess insufficient money to buy outright the goods and services produced within an economy; i.e. the economy is not 'self-liquidating'.[2] This inability of consumers to purchase outright the products of their own economy has three critical effects, each of which contributes to globalisation. Lack of effective demand generates both under-consumption and constant-production, and also creates an intense competition for sales.

(a) Under-consumption

It is tempting to argue that many Western economies suffer not so much from under-consumption as over-consumption. Whilst this is a valid opinion in one sense, it rather misses the point. Under-consumption does not mean that consumers are buying too little, but that they are unable to buy all of the goods that their economy is producing.

The evidence for such a lack of effective demand in modern economies is overwhelming. All nations are locked in an impossible battle to export surplus goods they cannot sell. Meanwhile, there is widespread poverty, even within the wealthy nations. Coupled with the grinding poverty within the Third World, this constitutes a blatant 'lack of effective global demand' – an inability on the part of the global economy to sell what it can produce, to people who desire the products. There is further evidence from the industrialised nations. If consumers are unable to buy goods and services outright with the purchasing power they actually possess, the only alternative method of purchase is to borrow money – i.e. go into debt. The growth of 'debt-buying' within the developed economies in recent decades has been striking.

Chapter 6 gave details of the near-vertical rise in mortgages in recent years. Not only houses, but cars, furniture, home improvements, holidays – even the essentials of food and drink – are increasingly being bought using some form of borrowing. Firms compete by offering the most advantageous credit terms and deferred payment schemes. It is now acknowledged that the modern economy is completely dependent upon debt-buying, indeed, the vigour of an economy is often measured by the growth in consumer debt, through the euphemistic term 'consumer confidence'. The inadequacy of the disposable incomes of the majority of the population to liquidate (buy) the products of the modern economy is glaring.

(b) Overproduction

Under-consumption goes hand in hand with constant-production, since the growth in private debt ties people to full-time employment. In the UK and USA, for example, women have entered the employment market in increasing numbers over the last three decades. Sometimes this was in search of a career, often it was to provide their families with 'the extras'. But increasingly, the two-wage family is finding that the woman must work, simply to pay the bills and the mortgage. Mortgage repayments absorb over 35% of the average US wage and the two-wage family in America is standard – indeed, is occasionally a four-wage family with both husband and wife moonlighting between two jobs. This suggests both income inadequacy and a heavy consumer debt burden eroding disposable incomes.

It has often been argued that a natural and obvious development for the industrialised economies would be some form of job sharing, or job rotation. But with a population carrying a heavy burden of mortgage debt and dependent upon the wage from a full-time job, how can job sharing or job rotation ever occur? And so, since we must perpetually work, so the economy perpetually grows, producing ever more goods, which must then find a market.

(c)   Competition for sales

The market for goods in an economy suffering from debt and a lack of effective demand will be intensely competitive, since not all the goods produced can be sold. Although consumers can, to some extent, compensate for this by borrowing-to-buy, today's debt erodes tomorrow's income – so the lack of demand is merely postponed and increased.

There is abundant evidence of a lack of demand leading to intense commercial competition for sales. In the modern economy, commerce adopts a wide range of strategies to ensure survival. Advertising, image creation, low-cost credit deals, perpetual redesign, new models with the latest technological refinements – all these are essential business strategies (and major providers of employment) in the debt-based economy. A staggering 18% of the American economy is based on marketing and promotion.

Extensive marketing and globalisation

Overproduction, under-consumption and intense competition for scarce consumer purchasing power all have a critical effect on commerce, particularly on marketing. These factors constitute the main drive behind globalisation by creating an ubiquitous pressure towards extensive marketing. This involves the use of transport as a competitive strategy – a device for securing adequate sales in a cut-throat market.

This is most easily outlined at the international level. If an economy suffers from a lack of effective demand, and difficulty in selling the goods and services it produces, the obvious solution is to try to sell some of its products to another economy – i.e. to export. Another economy offers an increased customer base and additional consumer purchasing power.

Of course, this instantly creates a problem. Commerce attempting to export in search of additional sales will come into conflict with domestic commerce in another country. That nation's domestic commerce, already suffering from the lack of purchasing power within its own economy, will find its sales reduced by foreign goods. Commerce in that nation will have to respond, and one of the strategies it will use will be to attempt to find its own export outlets. But if all economies suffer from debt and under-consumption, and their commerce is seeking overseas sales, commerce is still, in aggregate, seeking sales that do not exist.

This analysis explains two phenomena. First, the conflict that is all too evident in the constant effort to 'capture' foreign markets whilst 'defending' domestic markets in a global economy dominated by surpluses and inadequate sales. Second, it explains the cross-border exchange of near-identical goods and services, since to the extent that each firm is successful in its export drive, this will inevitably lead to an exchange of customers.

This pressure to export is more accurately described, not in terms of international trade, but in geographical terms, since the export imperative also operates within a national economy. Globalisation is an extension into the international domain of trends that have dominated domestic economies for many years – released by the free trade ethic that has progressively removed protectionist barriers.

The intense competition for sales in a debt economy places pressure on firms to supply goods and services to a wide geographical area, since this will offer them a wide potential customer base. If a firm initially serves a local market, the lack of purchasing power within that local area will pressure it to seek a wider regional market. If a firm has a regional market, there is pressure to seek the additional purchasing power of a national market. If a firm cannot obtain sufficient sales from within its national market, it will be obliged to seek a foreign market for its products. Firms in all localities, regions and nations are under the same pressure – driven by the lack of effective demand within their existing market range, and in response to invasion by competitor firms from further afield.

This offers us a powerful explanation for the intense conflict over trade in the world as a whole and the trend towards the increasing 'overlap' of markets. With all firms using transport as a competitive device to seek further markets, the final result is a thin spread of national or international supply by firms, with massive transport costs incurred and shared, and near-identical goods from many different manufacturing sources available in most areas.

Reflecting on the evidence

This analysis provides a powerful understanding of the 'export warfare' that dominates world trade. It also ties in with the observable world surplus of sellers and shortage of buyers, and the glutted global market. It provides us with an explanation for the apparently bizarre exchange of similar products between nations and regions, and the importing of goods and services that could be produced locally. It also provides us with an explanation for the erection of barriers to trade. If the world beyond your borders is trading for mutual benefit, or trading in surplus goods of marginal value, there is no reason to construct barriers to trade. But if foreign competitors are constantly attempting to sell aggressively into your economy, marketing goods and services that your own workforce produces and depends upon for employment, protectionist barriers are a natural response.

The analysis also explains the involvement of governments in promoting trade. All nations trade from a position of gross insolvency, but because they are permitted to seek a trade surplus there is a great temptation for governments to direct their economies to seek an excess of exports over imports. This will not only secure employment but improve the liquidity and solvency of the overall economy by bringing in foreign revenues.

A debt of some sort is the only rational explanation for the attempt to gain a surplus of a useless artefact – money – in exchange for a net loss of goods and services. The debt-based financial system places all nations – their people, commerce and governments – in chronic debt. In such circumstances, the use of trade to gain money becomes not a pointless exercise, but completely rational – indeed a very sensible option.

This is where trade imbalances become a critical factor. Under no obligation to maintain a fiscal balance of trade, nations have an opportunity to use trade to tackle their insolvency and find markets for their surplus production. But they must also resist a trade deficit, which would worsen their already exposed financial position through their trading account. The pressure that debt exerts on governments to resist a trade deficit and pursue a trade surplus enshrines economic aggression at the heart of international trade. This in turn encourages governments to subsidise domestic goods and services, since subsidies serve to

(i)   make the goods cheaper at home and so protect the domestic market, and

(ii) make the goods cheaper abroad and help them cut into a market.

The use of subsidies to promote exports is a major factor contributing to globalisation. There are also many indirect and hidden subsidies in the form of tax concessions and different tax and expenditure regimes. Since these impact on the price of goods and services, the scope for export support is considerable.

Finally, this monetary analysis also highlights the shortcomings of one of the principal arguments used by many critics of globalisation – that the construction of road, rail and air links at public expense constitutes a hidden subsidy for traded goods. (This argument is anyway rather weak since the cost of fuel and vehicles is not externalised.) The above analysis explains the root cause of the ubiquitous pressure to export; it is not the road that causes the trade, but the pressure to use the road.

The corporate advantage

Whilst this analysis might explain the growth of pointless trading, no analysis of globalisation would be complete if it did not offer an explanation for the astonishing dominance of corporate business in the modern world economy. The extensive marketing, cross-traffic of goods and remote production of goods that could be produced more locally all point the finger at one kind of commerce – the multinational corporation.

There are two principal ways in which a debt-based financial system presents conditions that allow multinationals to prosper and drive out more efficient competitors. Everyone knows it is cheaper to buy good-quality products that last longer. But despite the fact that modern economies could produce good-quality, durable products, and although consumers naturally prefer them, in an economy riddled by debt, low-price goods enjoy a marked sales advantage. This spells success for mass production and big business.

Mass production naturally enjoys economies of scale. But there are, or should be, marked diseconomies of scale that ensure a balance between mass-production and small/medium-sized businesses. More labour-intensive methods are better able to supply what people actually want in terms of quality and durability, and should therefore be preferred by consumers. Small/medium-sized commerce can also be more distributed geographically and hence carry lower costs associated with transport and distribution. It also offers a more accessible, often more attractive work environment and should therefore be favoured by employees.

But although many mass-produced products lack quality, mass-production does allow goods to be produced at very low unit cost. The need to transport and distribute mass-produced goods obviously raises costs, but generally, mass-production and bulk transport can secure a price advantage over production on a smaller scale. The choice is then with consumers – lower prices or better quality?

In the modern, debt-based economy, there is only one winner. Consumer decisions over price, quality and what they can afford inevitably favour mass-produced goods, because lack of effective demand, or lack of purchasing power, places financial pressure on consumers to purchase low-priced products. The aggregate of consumer expenditure decisions favours mass-produced goods and services – precisely those products offered by large, centralised businesses such as multinationals. Industry thrives and changes accordingly.

Once low price becomes the dominant consideration for consumers, the green light is given to a perpetual decline in quality and durability as industry actively seeks to cut costs, increase output, transport in bulk and undercut the opposition. The term 'improved methods', rather than referring to changes that bring about improvements to the actual product, is now virtually synonymous with increasing output at lower unit cost and a declining standard of product. The decline in durability and consumer satisfaction in everything from new houses, cars and household goods to foodstuffs and financial services is well-documented. This bias in favour of cheap, mass-produced goods constitutes a major aberration, or malfunction, of the free market pricing mechanism. It has ushered in an era of competitive cheapness, declining quality and durability; of goods that require constant replacement and create mass-produced consumer dissatisfaction.

The advantage of size

Mass production naturally requires large, centralised commerce. Supplying the dominant market in low-cost goods, big business slowly squeezes out small/medium decentralised firms, both by direct competition and by gradual collapse of the networks that supply their raw materials and distribute their finished goods. Thus corporate big business flourishes with its culture of bulk manufacture, bulk growing, bulk supply, bulk delivery and even bulk retail.

The advantage to big business does not stop with the defect in pricing that unduly favours cheap mass-produced goods and services. The pressure to change and adapt, as well as mass-produce, requires research and development facilities – again larger companies are better able to compete.

Size helps multinationals access capital, since they are generally able to obtain credit more easily, at lower rates of interest and on more advantageous terms. Size also grants multinationals an advantage over smaller businesses when it comes to withstanding the pressure of debt. Banks and other lending institutions are less likely to foreclose on large debts to Big Business than they are on small business debts. It has frequently been observed that, if the standards of accountancy applied to small businesses were applied to corporations, many would be immediately wound up. The old dictum, 'if you owe the bank £100, it's your problem; if you owe the bank £1,000,000 – it's the bank's problem,' is now part of our investment culture.

Size has become an essential survival strategy for international businesses. Competition from similar corporations generates an impetus towards growth, both as a form of commercial defence and aggression. These corporations have often come into existence in the first place by mergers and acquisitions of related or competitor companies. This process has now reached a stage at which companies cannot rest for a second. If their share value falls or if they become financially over-exposed, if they are too small or if they are simply too successful, the odds are that they will be the subject of a predatory take-over. And what is the best way to ensure that you are not the subject of such a take-over? It is to become predatory yourself, adopt an aggressive, acquisitive, expansionary policy.

Multinationals are actually the creations of debt-finance; the culmination of the unfair advantage given to big business in a debt economy; the ultimate in mass-production, cost-cutting, employment-shedding, bulk transport, extensive marketing, constant change, excessive centralisation and poor product quality and durability.

Third World debt and multinationals

In the ruthlessly competitive, brutally commercial culture of the world market, any opportunity to secure an advantage will be taken. This includes the opportunity to capitalise on the desperate financial position of the Third World. Indeed, buying out the Third World is not only the best corporate investment opportunity ever, it is an opportunity that must be taken – for if one company does not, its competitors surely will.

Developing nations, desperate for foreign investment, are driven to compete to attract the multinationals. The pressure of debt and the low factor prices that prevail in those countries provide multinationals with vistas of valuable, little exploited and deeply undervalued resources, including labour that is little more than slavery. Multinationals are able to obtain cheap raw materials, cheap labour and low-priced commercial assets; they can expect (or demand) low taxes and lax labour and environmental regulation. Everything multinationals need to set up cheap manufacturing outposts for export to industrialised nations using bulk transport strategies is readily available. Meanwhile, debtor nations are desperate for foreign investment, convinced (after the blind alley of debt) that this offers a path to successful development.

That multinationals operate in this way, capitalising on the 'development gap' between the wealthy and Third World nations, is well understood. But it is not usually appreciated that there is a tie-in between the debts of Third World nations and those of the wealthy nations; a linkage that multinationals turn to exceptional advantage. This linkage offers further insight into the persistent decline in the quality and durability of goods and services, and emphasises that globalisation is an extension into the world economy of trends already witnessed within national economies.

Investment in debtor nations provides multinationals with the opportunity to mass-produce goods for export from the Third World to the industrialised nations at very low unit costs. Although the cost of transport raises the price of these goods, they are often sufficiently cheap to undercut producers in the more wealthy nations.

It should not automatically be accepted that, just because these goods carry lower price-tags, they ought to succeed in finding a market in wealthy industrialised nations. These products have, or should have, a marked disadvantage. Corporate Third World production is mass production for mass marketing; grown in bulk, harvested in bulk, manufactured, processed, assembled and transported in bulk. Many such goods, services and foodstuffs are of pronounced low quality, yet they still sell in the industrialised nations.

This is where the astonishing level of 'wealthy nation' debt comes into play. The excessive levels of national, private and commercial debt in industrialised nations create a market in which consumers and the retail networks gravitate towards low-price goods. Thus corporate production in the Third World of low-price, poor quality products finds a ready market.

The apparent preference of the world's consumers for junk – junk food, cars, furniture, electrical goods, kitchen utensils – is just that. An *apparent* preference. The cheap, throw-away culture dominating the world is the inevitable product of two factors – first, the price/value discrepancy between Third World and industrialised nations and, second, the undue advantage granted to cheap goods in a debt-based economy. Multinationals are simply business concerns that take full advantage of, and respond to, these two factors.

This analysis shows just how essential Third World debt is to multinational success and also to globalisation. It also highlights the cost to the wealthy nations of the rising dominance of multinationals. These business empires succeed not because they supply what consumers want, but what they can afford in a debt-based economy. Multinationals thereby drive out more resource-efficient, localised, quality-oriented commerce.

The commercial success of multinationals is not any measure or reflection of true productivity, or efficient use of resources. Their success is due to their ability to take advantage of the gaping financial disparities between nations. Sheer size gives them the power to hold peoples and nations to ransom; to enforce low wages and extract concessions and thus keep production costs to an absolute minimum; to find a world market for the resultant goods at a selling price which disguises the cumbersome inefficiency of their operations and covers the gross wastage of transport; and to externalise and deflect the widespread social, employment and environmental consequences of their activities.

Multinationals take advantage of the financial conditions within the individual wealthy and in Third World nations, and the world economy as a whole. Their success is thus a financial success. Corporations are financially efficient in a world where finance rules. But in terms of resources – natural and human – they are grossly wasteful and destructive.

How monetary reform could help stop globalisation

If we want to address corporate power and globalisation, there are many acts of legislation that could be passed at national and international levels. But however important this may be, it is vital to alter the peculiar fiscal conditions that create the drive to export and also grant such an advantage to corporate mass production. This is a matter of addressing causes, rather than effects.

The most important reform is undoubtedly one that would convert our economies away from being almost exclusively based on debt. The creation of financially balanced economies is absolutely vital if globalisation is to be tackled effectively. The dominant effect of a debt-based financial system is to create non-liquidating economies which means that for any given economic area, not all the goods produced can be sold.

Only financially balanced economies can hope to contain globalisation, by removing the pressure to export a surplus of goods that cannot be sold at home. If economies were financially balanced, trade between various economic areas would be based on the inherent ability to buy all goods produced, and would therefore represent an exchange of *surpluses and goods of marginal value*. In other words, trade for mutual benefit. The current price advantage enjoyed by multinationals in a debt economy, which creates and sustains these inefficient giants, and the pressure towards the exporting and extensive marketing of goods, would both be cancelled. With the advantage of excessive size and the export imperative removed, the powerful economic impetus behind the globalisation of trade would be tackled at its source.

The only alternatives to constructing a financially balanced economy are (a) to attempt protectionism – the legal regulation of international trade – or (b) to counter all the advantages currently enjoyed by multinationals, using taxation and subsidies to support local and national economies. But this latter policy involves determining which commerce merits subsidy, how much subsidy would be fair, and which big businesses should carry the burden of additional taxation. To attempt to construct a tax/subsidy regime that could successfully counteract the all-pervasive pressure to produce and export is a policy fraught with complexity and danger.

The best way to illustrate this is to consider one of the most frequently suggested proposals – the idea of raising the price of fuel to act as a disincentive to the excessive transport of goods and services. It is accepted almost without question that this would penalise multinationals, deflect distribution towards markets closer to home, and help localise the economy.

But this is very poor economics. It might seem at first glance that a tax on fuel must halt globalisation, by making transport more expensive – but it wouldn't. A tax on fuel is a unit tax and *unit taxes impact on local producers and distributors as well as international commerce.*

The whole point about bulk international distribution is that, whilst the gross cost of transport is huge, the quantities of goods involved mean that the cost per unit moved is greatly reduced. For local transport and supply, the gross cost is lower, but the small quantities involved mean that *the cost of transport per unit is higher*. In terms of a disincentive to transport, it is the impact of higher fuel prices on the price of the final product that is decisive.

A fuel tax might well raise the cost of international bulk transport significantly, but the cost of local and national distribution would also rise. Whilst the gross increase for local/national transport would be lower, this would be divided between fewer goods, so the additional cost-rise per item might well be the same as for international, bulk transport.

It must also be remembered that big corporate businesses are exactly the type of companies that could carry any tax or fuel price increases that are likely to be implemented, and survive – whilst many small local firms would be threatened. Globalisation and the dominance of big business are intimately associated with the non-viability of local industry. Anything that threatens this viability further – even a fuel tax to 'get at' the big boys – would simply have a counterproductive effect.

Ultimately, the idea of trying to construct a tax and subsidy regime to counter globalisation carries a deep contradiction within itself. Where is the monetary support for the local economy to come from? If it is derived from income taxation, this impacts upon consumers everywhere – i.e. all local economies. If it is derived from commerce, then small producers and local economies are hit just as much as the big producers. If it is derived from, or rather raised by, a government deficit, future interest payments on the national debt must raise revenues either from consumers or commerce, whilst the revenue available for local subsidy programmes is progressively cut.

The whole idea of trying to counter the trend towards globalisation, either by protectionism or fiscal measures such as taxes, is founded on the unconscious assumption that there is nothing *inherently* wrong with the financial economy – it is just a matter of redistribution and legislation to produce the desired results. But if there is a deep-rooted instability in the financial economy that creates a 'drive' toward globalisation, then it makes no sense to pursue these policies when rectification of the financial system offers the chance to tackle the problem at source.

Summary

The cancellation of the debts owed by developing nations is essential if the problem of globalisation is to be addressed. Multinationals lock into the gaping disparity in asset values and labour costs across the global economy, and also exploit the pressure on debtor nations to seek foreign revenues. The result is an increasing global traffic in goods due to a gross discrepancy in costs and pricing between nations. Third World debt thus completely distorts the rational geography, balance and power of the global economy.

The relationship between Third World debt and the multinationals is responsible for countless backlashes on the industrialised nations – the flood of cheap produce from abroad; the unemployment this creates; the pressure on domestic commerce to compete standards down; the growing pollution of the world ecosystem. The many undesirable consequences that stem from the process of globalisation emphasise that debt cancellation would be beneficial not just to the developing nations, but to the wealthy nations as well.

It must be stressed, too, that the current debt-remission programme, which seeks only *to reduce the level* of Third World debt, would be completely ineffective in tackling globalisation. If Third World nations are left carrying significant dollar-debts, they will be forced to continue to seek a surplus of exports over imports, and also forced to attract the dollar-rich multinationals.

Cancelling Third World debt would contribute substantially to halting the drift towards a global economy. In addition, reforming national financial systems from being based on debt to being based on liquidity, with an adequacy of purchasing power, would cancel the fierce export imperative that drives forward the trend towards aggressive, extensive marketing. These two elements of monetary reform, international and national, therefore address the issue of globalisation by tackling its root cause.

In the context of international trade, monetary reform to create financially balanced economies is a genuinely original policy. It acknowledges that the economic nationalism and protectionism of the past are not an acceptable model. But it also criticises and seeks to counter the deregulated export-driven commerce of today. The next evolutionary phase in economics is one that is neither nationalist nor internationalist in bias, but transcends such abstract concepts to reach the real world, seeking to restore the viability of local and regional economies everywhere, which are actually the true basis of both national and international prosperity.

Endnotes

1   Joel Kurtzman. *The Death of Money.* Simon and Schuster. 1993.

2   That modern economies suffer from a chronic lack of effective demand is not accepted by neo-classical economics. The claim that such a lack of effective demand is generated within a debt-based financial system derives from the observation that commercial debt has the effect of raising prices, since businesses must repay their debts, whilst consumer debt (including mortgages) lowers people's disposable incomes. This elevation of prices and reduction of incomes means that the goods and services available within an economy cannot be bought with the incomes being distributed for their purchase. Orthodox economics disputes this argument. The orthodox perception of the effect of debt is of a dynamic, in which interest payments are re-distributed to depositors, and debt repayments are recycled to further borrowers. The orthodox perception thus embraces debt as part of a dynamic equilibrium in which any 'lack of demand' from debt is compensated for. However, the orthodox perception fails to note that an economy is thereby reliant upon further borrowing to bring debt repayments back into circulation, and also reliant upon those receiving interest payments actually utilising this spending power. If they fail to spend these payments on goods and services, and if further borrowing does not occur, then the claim of a lack of effective purchasing power is clearly true. Orthodoxy replies by claiming that those savers who do not expend the interest they receive do actually utilise this money. Borrowers will step forward, banks will lend the accruing interest payments, a new product – 'a debt' – is thereby created. The unspent revenues will re-enter the economy through the creation of an additional 'good' – the debt – upon which the new borrower will pay interest and the lender receive interest, and so on. However, the orthodox perception fails to take into account that, by this arrangement, borrowers cannot be termed 'willing agents'. The withdrawal of money by debt repayment and the overall requirement that this be re-circulated means that borrowing overall is compulsory, and that borrowers represent those people least successful at obtaining the money they need from the existing circulating stock. The orthodox perception also fails to consider the difference between an economy that is entirely based upon debt, and an economy where a substantial proportion of the money stock circulates free from a background of debt and the need to borrow is inherently lessened, and the pressure to maintain this dynamic borrowing cycle considerably reduced. A broader discussion of this analysis can be found in *The Grip of Death* by Michael Rowbotham. Jon Carpenter. 1997.

3   Michael Rowbotham. *The Grip of Death.* Jon Carpenter. 1998.

11

Blaming the Third World

E conomic incompetence, corruption, capital flight, and excessive military spending by debtor nations; these are the four explanations generally offered to the public as the causes of Third World debt. However, a number of authoritative studies have investigated these issues and, although the details vary, have generally concluded that the above factors have not been the root cause of endemic Third World debt. Dharam Ghai and Cynthia Hewitt de Alcantara offer a general comment;

> There has been a tendency, especially by economists, to single out inappropriate policies as the main culprit in the crisis. While they have played roles of varying importance in different countries at different times, it stretches credulity to attribute a dominant role to them in the intensification of the crisis in the 1980s.[1]

Jacques Gelinas is more emphatic;

> We should ignore the causes highlighted by the media (such as corruption of Third World elites, their low education level and their inherent financial incompetence) as well as the equally hollow official explanations supplied by the International Financial Institutions... Instead we must look for causes that stem from the system's very nature and act as components of the international financial structure.[2]

Economic incompetence

The alleged economic incompetence of debtor nations centres on one observation; that they have failed to meet the repayments on their debts. Such accusations seldom mention specific projects, or what mistakes were made, or by which countries; just 'incompetence' – and all the Third World nations are guilty.

There are two main reasons for this astonishingly presumptive vagueness. First, in the complex, contradictory and jargon-ridden world of macro-economics, there is always plenty of room for vague, across-the-board allegations. Indeed, it is often safer to generalise, since to be specific is to ask to be shot down in flames by an economist with a different view. Secondly, the involvement of the World Bank and IMF in the management of debtor nation economies has been so great, that any specific examples or charges of incompetence automatically and deeply implicate them!

Currency values offer a perfect example of the latitude within economics for policies which, although they might appear to have substance, actually carry a deep-seated contradiction within themselves.

Over the years, debtor nations have been repeatedly advised that their currencies are over-valued. This advice stems from the argument that, to boost exports, those exports must be cheap enough to compete in the world market; if a currency is over-valued, exporting will be difficult because goods will be over-priced relative to others on the world market. But as was discussed in Chapter 6, lowering a currency's value typically has a negligible effect on a nation's trading account. Even if the volume of exports rises, these exports earn less per unit, whilst the cost of imports rises. Also, in a global market of surpluses, the act of currency devaluation by one nation automatically puts a pressure on other competitor nations to devalue *their* currency so as to make *their* goods cheaper. The end result is a series of competitive currency devaluations by developing nations all attempting to make their goods cheaper. But so convinced are economists in general, and World Bank economists in particular, of the importance of 'export success', that currency devaluation is constantly urged as a rational technique for improving trade revenues.

In assessing the value of currency devaluation, it is worth reflecting on why debtor nations receive so little for their exports. It is not that they are exporting in insufficient *quantity*, but that they do not receive *a fair price per unit* for their goods. What is the effect of currency devaluation? To make these goods even cheaper on the world market. And what is the effect of competitive devaluation by debtor nations exporting similar commodities? To make these goods cheaper still to buyers from the wealthy nations, while reducing the return per unit and increasing the material loss to developing nations! Nevertheless, employing an economic model of export-led growth that 'should work because we want it to work', the World Bank has repeatedly argued that debtor nation currencies are generally over-valued.

The issue of currency values is discussed at length as one example amongst many of deeply flawed economic advice, which in turn highlights the lack of substance behind the accusation of 'economic incompetence' on the part of the developing nations. The incompetence would appear to rest rather closer to the Washington headquarters of the World Bank and IMF.

Development literature is full of case studies that emphasise time and time again that 'debtor nation incompetence' is an easy scapegoat for the World Bank and IMF, an evasion of self-critical analysis and a cover-all for the weaknesses within neo-classical free market economics. The following are representative of the many comments from development literature that stress the genuine efforts of debtor nations to undertake economic improvements, and the complicity of the Bank/Fund in the debt crisis.

In **Africa**, 'there is a very broad consensus among African governments that the IMF and World Bank terms are often harsh and unsuitable [and have] generated severely adverse effects on the overall economies of these countries, especially with regard to agriculture, manufacture and foreign trade'.[3]

The **Philippine** economy collapsed in 1998, after accepting structural adjustment, and despite the fact that 'the government had implemented nearly all the [Bank's] recommendations on export promotion [including] the most important and difficult actions required'.[4]

In **Yugoslavia**, 'in the last ten years, the whole IMF policy has been nothing but a failure. All its prognoses were proved wrong, and its policies and measures had an opposite effect from what had been expected'.[5]

In **Latin America** during the 1980s, 'it is hard to find a single case where IMF programmes of adjustment have halted the [economic] decline'.[6]

In **Chile**, 'the total collapse by 1981 of the monetarist experiment in Chile is a salutary lesson in the failure of IMF prescriptions, even when applied in their most rigorous form and by a government totally committed to their success'.[7]

In **Jamaica**, since the first IMF loan was granted in 1977, a survey showed that the economy has cumulatively declined; 'it is undoubtedly the case that the economic medicine prescribed by the IMF has, even by the latter's own limited criteria of "success", palpably failed in Jamaica. Indeed the effects of the IMF measures upon the vast majority of the Jamaican people have been far more disastrous than the calamities of droughts and floods that nature has seen fit to inflict upon them in recent years'.[8]

Blaming it on 'flight capital'

The most convenient 'get-out' for the international lending agencies is the claim that the money loaned to Third World nations never actually went on development projects, but ended up in the overseas bank accounts of a corrupt ruling class. The channelling of money abroad is termed 'capital flight' and has been extensively studied, both in terms of the amounts of money involved and the factors influencing it.

The first point to make is that the record shows that the bulk of loans were not mis-spent in the way often suggested – siphoned off into the pockets of elites. Flight capital there certainly has been, but in the main this has not been directly from the sums loaned to Third World nations. Flight capital has been sent abroad from earnings by the business and wealthy classes in developing nations.

This immediately raises a fundamental issue. To claim that such capital flight, is responsible for Third World debt involves a glaring double-standard. One study opens with the question;

Why is it that when an American puts money abroad it is called 'foreign investment' and when an Argentinian does the same it is called 'capital flight'? Why is it that when an American company puts 30% of its equity

abroad it is called 'strategic diversification' and when a Bolivian busi-
nessman puts only 4% abroad it is called 'lack of confidence'?[9]

When our pensions are invested overseas, either in stock markets or to take
advantage of better interest rates, this is called portfolio investment and is a *good*
thing. When the small numbers of middle classes in developing nations place
their savings in wealthy nation stock markets, or in secure currencies, this is called
corrupt profiteering and is a *bad* thing. So although foreign direct investment and
foreign portfolio investment bring back revenues into the country, businessmen in
the debtor nations and the members of the wealthy/middle classes clearly have
'no right' to follow the trend that dominates modern economics.

A false impression of the amount of money sent abroad is often created by
media stories claiming that leaders of debtor nations hold massive overseas
fortunes. By investing abroad, some individuals have indeed become comparatively wealthy. But this does not mean they took this wealth out of the debtor
nations. As we all know, clever investment, successful capital investments,
buying and selling foreign stocks and shares and constantly rising stock markets
can make a person very wealthy. But this means that whatever wealth these
allegedly traitorous classes in the debtor nations may now hold, it does not follow
that they took all this wealth, in the form of money, out of the countries in the
first place.

In addition, the decline of debtor nation economies means that these people,
whose wealth is locked into the stronger economies and their currencies, appear
vastly wealthy by comparison with the economic ruin around them, which again
creates an impression of gross profiteering and corruption.

For years it was contended that flight capital 'never returns' and is lost to a
developing nation's economy, again imputing nothing but greed towards the
holders of overseas wealth. But one of the most comprehensive studies on the
subject concluded that, contrary to the popular notion that flight capital never
returns and produces no returns, there were frequent flow reversals back into
debtor nation economies, and subsequent investment, usually when economic
conditions were conducive.[10]

That there has been a political desire to inflate the sums involved in capital
flight is well recognised. An infamous study by the bank, Morgan Guaranty,
contains figures which more impartial and authoritative studies have described as
'egregiously misleading'[11] and 'exaggerated'.[12] Lessard and Williamson point out
that many such studies of capital flight have omitted to take account of 'offshore
intermediation' (in which foreign money markets are used prior to funds entering
the economy) and 'round-tripping' (where funds are invested abroad for a
period, then brought back into the economy). Some measures of flight capital
often include cross-investment between debtor nations – i.e. capital flight is paralleled by inward investment, and no net loss of capital is actually involved. Capital
withdrawn from a developing economy by international banks involved in

financing the private sector has also often been accounted as flight capital. This, as Lessard and Williamson point out, is a glaring error, since it is no more than a withdrawal of previous foreign investment! Even the working capital of debtor nations' own banks and multinationals, engaged in foreign trade, have been included as flight capital.[13]

The general conclusion has been that, considering the actual sums that can genuinely be defined as flight capital, this loss of revenue may have exacerbated the debt crisis, but has not been a major causative factor.

Leaving aside the amounts involved, what is most significant about the many studies on the subject is the analysis of the causes of capital flight. Capital flight has not been a constant phenomenon, has not affected all nations equally, and most of the developing nations have had periods when there was virtually no loss of capital abroad at all. All studies found that capital flight was dramatically affected by the economic conditions and policies of the country. 'What we generally understand to be flight capital is for the most part a symptom rather than a cause'.[14]

Rudiger Dornbusch argues; 'Surely the lack of a hospitable investment climate is the basic reason for capital flight'.[15] Eduardo Conesa's study in 1986 found growth to be the single most important deterrent to capital flight.[16] Miguel Rodriguez agrees;

> As a preventative to capital flight, there seems to be no substitute for sound expansionist macro-economic policies ... these appear to be preferable to old-fashioned orthodox budget-cutting and anti-inflationary policies, since the induced recession creates an environment in which capital flight will ensue.[17]

Rodriguez points out that debtor trade liberalisation, freely convertible currencies and IMF-induced recession were major causes of capital flight. John Cuddington agrees, adding;

> In many cases, however, capital flight is a direct private-sector response to ill-conceived or poorly executed domestic policies. In such circumstances, it would be more appropriate to condemn the controversial policies than the capital flight.[18]

It appears that we have a rogues' gallery of factors promoting capital flight – low growth, lack of a hospitable investment climate, trade liberalisation, freely convertible currencies, poor domestic policies and IMF-induced recession. The last, general point about IMF-induced recession in fact covers all the others. The fact is that these causes of capital flight are *all* the undisputed result of World Bank/IMF conditionality. These economic policies and conditions were all the direct result of demand restriction, free trade and deregulatory conditions that have been imposed on developing nations since the late 1970s.

IMF austerity programmes and structural adjustment involved such punishing deflationary policies that debtor nations were thrown into grinding recession, often with zero or even negative growth. Can the wealthy and middle classes in those countries be blamed for sending their capital abroad under such circumstances? When your own national economy is collapsing around your ears, what is the sensible thing to do with your money? Invest abroad – just as the French and Germans did when *their* nations were hit by recession in pursuit of the Maastricht criteria. The application of double standards over flight capital is disgraceful.

Financial deregulation has been a key factor in capital flight. In the early days, debtor nations tried to maintain capital controls, and ensured structural diversity by developing their own banking and financial sectors, which they protected. But most have been forced by the IMF and World Bank to open their borders to capital flows and deregulate their financial sectors to allow foreign competition.

This has had three effects. First, as multinationals have bought out domestic industries, domestic investment has declined since it cannot compete with the capital strength of these giants. Naturally, investors then tend to send their money abroad; they are better off putting their money into Monsanto shares than trying to compete with that company through the local economy! Second, as banking and other financial institutions were similarly taken over, the opportunity for the wealthy classes to invest in the financial structures of their own nation was removed. Third, precisely the same pieces of legislation imposed by the IMF, World Bank and OECD – allowing the unregulated flow of investment capital – also made it easy for the rich to invest their money abroad.

The experience of Venezuela provides a perfect illustration of the combination of Bank/Fund recession/deregulation policies. In 1979, after a decade of growth in which 'capital flight was minor and the private sector invested at record levels in a booming economy', the new government under the direction of the IMF 'started to introduce contractionary policies. Private investment collapsed, and private domestic savers hurriedly started to shift their wealth abroad'.[19]

Another example of a policy that has contributed to capital flight was the demand on debtor nations that failing commercial debts be transferred to the state rather than allowed to proceed to bankruptcy under normal commercial law. The study by Lessard and Williamson concluded that the assumption of private debt as sovereign debt by governments has the triple effect of presenting a commercial advantage to foreign investors, deterring domestic investors, whilst also encouraging investors in debtor nations to search for the same advantage by themselves investing abroad. Result – more capital flight.

In view of the powerful disincentives to domestic investment caused by Bank/Fund policies, capital flight is, as John Cuddington points out, a perfectly sensible and rational response. Lessard and Williamson even express the opinion that 'what may be surprising is not the extent of capital flight, but the extent to which residents of less developed countries hold local assets'.[20]

It is not the intention to defend or ignore the instances where there has been gross sequestering, and foreign investment for private profit, of revenues that might have helped with debt repayments. But the proven instances of this are nowhere near enough to account for the massive failure of debt repayments. That there has been capital flight from the developing nations is not in dispute. But the suggestion that this accounts for Third World debt involves:

- ignoring the fact that recorded flight capital/foreign investment has been far too small to account for Third World debt;
- ignoring the fact that the economic endeavours of the developing nations were such that a degree of capital flight should have been supportable;
- a cynical application of double standards;
- ignoring the fact that the IMF and World Bank themselves created the conditions in which flight capital/foreign investment was made possible and encouraged.

Corruption

The allegation that debtor nation governments are corrupt – or more corrupt than politicians in the wealthy industrialised nations – is perhaps the most shameful slander of all. Corruption within debtor nations there has certainly been. But once again the charge is general, not specific. Vague allegations of 10% backhanders on every financial transaction; overseas bank accounts held by tin-pot dictators; images of luxurious lifestyles and reckless spending on military hardware ... and all Third World nations are guilty of it ... they must be because they haven't paid their debts. The presumption is quite outrageous.

Everyone has read the stories of the Marcos dynasty, Amin, Suharto and the like. But for every developing country with a greedy big-spender at the helm, there have been a dozen without such figures. Even in these notorious cases, the sums actually known to have been sequestered have been nowhere near sufficient to account for each nation's overall debt total.

Logic also argues that corruption should not automatically be seen as a causative factor in the debt crisis. If the borrow/invest/export/repay development model is recalled, the endeavours of developing nations were intended and expected to generate a surplus of wealth from the 'added value' that debtor nations contribute to the investment. This surplus wealth ought to have been sufficient to sustain a degree of corruption, before this impacted so heavily as to drive a nation into debt. Also, it was the *funded projects* that were supposed to generate the revenues for debt repayment – not the entire economy. The effort that has gone into development in these economies has been prodigious, which emphasises yet further that they ought to have been capable of supporting a degree of corruption, undesirable though this clearly is.

However, the main reason for rejecting the allegation of broad corruption as a cause of the debt crisis is that it constitutes a blatant re-writing of history. The benign, educated and popular leaders who led developing nations in their early optimism fell as a direct *result* of the poverty and cultural collapse sweeping their nations. Often, corruption and military dictatorship *followed* the debt-induced poverty, and did not cause it.

Far from being motivated by selfishness and greed, many Third World leaders were accused during the 1950s and 1960s of being too philanthropic and generous, although as Chapter 4 notes, the welfare spending they undertook was (until the advice was changed) absolutely in line with the advice they received. But as the development crisis took hold, these leaders shouldered the blame. The struggle against intractable debt led to economic chaos; the export imperative drove their domestic agriculture and industry into decline and then decay. Displaced from land given over to export crops, the dispossessed flooded to cities, where they erected pitiful shanty towns. Obliged to contend with increasing social unrest, the early rulers were gradually replaced. Dharam Ghai records the transition in post-war Latin America, where country after country was forced to reschedule its debts;

> In a growing number of Latin American countries, the early years after the War were characterised by a national consensus represented by the emerging alliance of the political elite, the state officials, industrialists and the urban working classes... However, even as these groups gained ascendancy ... and as the industrialisation-based process strategy consolidated itself, many countries were subjected to social strains [including] the persistence of mass poverty and widespread under- and unemployment... The response to such development was the adoption of increasingly repressive methods and the replacement of civilian governments by military regimes in a growing number of countries so that, by the early 1970s, the majority of the Latin American countries found themselves in the grip of authoritarian and repressive regimes.[21]

The double standards involved in this 'corruption' smear campaign against the Third World are quite amazing. If we actually search the record for evidence of corruption and incompetence, it is not the debtor nations that are implicated. Any corruption within the debtor nations has been more than matched by the disgraceful conduct of the international agencies and business community.

We have seen that at Bretton Woods, Keynes argued that it was vital to establish a mechanism to maintain a balance of trade between nations. Despite his warnings the American delegation, who feared a major recession in the US, insisted that the balance of international trade should be left to 'free market commercial forces' and that the IMF and World Bank should promote a free trade agenda.

How can we find words to describe this degree of economic incompetence and self-seeking corruption? Important aspects of trade theory were ignored. The warnings of economists past and present, who emphasised the dangers of aggressive trading by commercial interests in wealthy nations, were also ignored. The security and advantage of a single nation, the United States, was favoured over the mutual interests of all other nations. Is this not incompetence? Is this not corruption on such a scale that the 'money-in-a-brown-envelope' corruption in the poorer nations just does not even *register*?

Since Bretton Woods, the actions of the World Bank and the IMF have betrayed a continuing refusal to accept the defects in their own agenda. Joined by a growing number of similar international bodies such as GATT and WTO, these organisations have shown persistent favouritism to the wealthy nations and their commercial interests.

Since the 1950s, increasing numbers of debtor nations on the verge of collapse have been forced to ask for their debts to be re-scheduled. Did the World Bank question its free market programme or the terms of its loans? No; it demanded that trade barriers be dropped as a condition of the bail-outs.

As debts mounted, more and more nations were forced to seek loans – not for *development* – but simply to pay the *interest* on their earlier loans. Did the World Bank reflect on the possibility that Third World debts might actually be *unre-payable*? No; they issued more loans and instituted more free trade demands under 'Programme Aid'.

Debtor nations were by now exporting raw materials and products from indus-tries that had received no direct loan assistance. This extended to the point where, in some nations, virtually their entire economic resources were directed towards getting dollars from abroad. Did the World Bank and IMF reflect on the fact that it was the *funded projects* that were supposed to produce the revenues for debt repayment – not the entire economy? No; they instituted Austerity Programmes, insisting that debtor nations cut welfare, cut food subsidies, cut education budgets, etc. etc. etc.

Did the World Bank and IMF do anything to support falling commodity prices? No. They allowed the monopoly power of corporations to dominate, and when developing nations attempted to form alliances that would allow them to stand up to the corporations, these moves were deemed 'unfair competition'.

Did the World Bank and IMF listen to the many economists and critics who were screaming at them that their debt-funded, export-led growth model was a catastrophic failure, responsible for appalling famine and social instability, and that developing nations needed to develop their agriculture and industry for their own needs? No. They instituted Structural Adjustment.

Throughout, the judgement has been that it cannot be the economic model, first offered to and later imposed on debtor nations, that is responsible. Free market neo-classical economics has achieved such a powerful grip on the minds of economists and politicians that they cannot think outside it, not perceive its weaknesses. Any failures must mean that the free market ethic has not been applied effectively enough: but have faith, it will work in the end… and we hold the debts so you are going to go through with it.

Crony capitalism

A recent variant of the 'corruption' allegation directed at the developing nations is that their governments are guilty of appointing friends and relatives into positions of power, or of granting them financial favours. This is 'crony capitalism', and as usual a few examples are offered, whilst the entire community of debtor/developing nations is smeared.

In terms of Third World debt, crony capitalism is a ridiculous concept. A family or a surname cannot cause debt. It is policies, not personalities that contribute to debt. It has been known for years that certain extended families in the developing nations constituted an 'intelligentsia'. Their sons and daughters, who were seen as destined for political service, a professional or a commercial role, were sent for education in the West. It is hardly surprising, therefore, that little more than a generation after independence, these families should figure in positions of prominence.

The desire of ruling families and cliques to consolidate their power is understandable in another sense. Whenever an economy is so undermined that their wealth is threatened, ruling classes have sought, throughout history, to protect themselves by acts of greed. Viewing the appalling poverty around them that increasingly threatened not only their livelihoods, but their lives, the ruling classes in debtor nations have evolved into, or been replaced by, an elite that identifies more closely with international financiers and the World Bank. This is hardly surprising.

To the extent that corruption does exist, the Bank and Fund must again assume a large measure of the blame. Their structural adjustment policies were deliberately aimed at the poor majority, requiring cuts in wages, welfare, education and those subsidies that kept basic food prices low. The Bank and Fund refused to make their loans conditional upon policies involving either the redistribution of land or wealth, or progressive taxes that spread the burden of adjustment. The World Bank and IMF have actually *fostered* the creation of a callous elite in the Third World. 'Corrupt practices and embezzlement too often are presented as cultural, even genetic characteristics of Third World leaders. In fact, a careful study of the phenomenon reveals that they are inherent features of the foreign aid industry, a system Third World leaders willingly adopted, but did not invent'.[22]

George Corm argues that corruption is 'a rational economic response to a socio-economic environment devoid of logic and clear economic rules'.[23] Acknowledging the identification of Third World elites with 'the international set', Jacques Gelinas recognises a 'global power elite' which includes the native elite of the underdeveloped areas.[24]

What is so astonishing yet again is the application of double standards. Little more than a century ago, when Western nations were undergoing their 'development', class and status were dominant mindsets. It was considered perfectly normal for friends and relatives of the political classes to be favoured with patronage. Indeed, you were considered a bounder and a cad if you didn't get your cousin a post at the Foreign Office. But the developing nations are somehow supposed to leapfrog all the faults, failings and restrictions of a rapid change in culture. 'Crony capitalism' is just another convenient scapegoat for the scandal of Third World debt.

Western nations are, even today, far more guilty of cronyism than the developing nations. For real crony capitalism, consider the favouritism of the international agencies – World Bank, IMF, GATT and WTO – towards international corporate big business. The GATT and WTO agreements have made no efforts to limit the powers of multinational corporations. This is despite calls for legislation on take-overs, power of monopoly, profit repatriation, driving out smaller competitors by temporary price cutting, and tax avoidance through transfer pricing. Yet whilst refusing to act on these, GATT and WTO have been pursuing to the last minutiae agreements on patent rights of genetic material, intellectual property rights, corporate property and trading rights – in which the wealthy nations and their corporations dominate. A farmer who saves patented seed grown from his previous crop for replanting will be in breach of international patent law. Meanwhile, the power of multinationals to asset-strip smaller domestic competitors and use corporate raiding to acquire control of a small nation's industrial lifeblood has not been touched. One can see exactly what the priorities of GATT and WTO are, and where their allegiance lies.

This favouritism reached a new high with the attempt to institute the Multilateral Agreement on Investments (MAI) in 1998. This was nothing but a charter for multinational power, profit and protection. The MAI did not attempt to prevent, or even comment on, the massive 'investment sweeteners' and tax concessions that multinationals extract by playing national governments against each other. But the MAI expressly forbade any nation to make payments to its own industries that were not also made to the multinationals!

Under the MAI, multinationals were to have unfettered and unconditional investment rights. No nation state could exclude a foreign investor from any economic sector. If a country passed new environmental laws, multinationals must be given compensation to cover the cost. Finally, there was provision under the MAI for a tribunal whereby multinationals could take countries to court, but it was expressly stated that this court could not be used by countries against multinationals.

Before the MAI was due to be signed, OECD countries were allowed to register national exemptions to the treaty. It is worth noting that America insisted on a clause removing all US state assets and natural resources from the agreement. Once signed by the 29 OECD nations, the poorer nations outside the

OECD would have had no opportunity to seek any exemptions whatsoever. Although discussions on the MAI were halted after public protest, the WTO has expressed its intention to pass international legislation in the field of investment and the agreement is expected to resurface, this time under the aegis of the WTO.

Does crony capitalism come any bigger than the powerful influence exerted by corporate business over GATT, the WTO, the OECD, the World Bank and the IMF? Does corruption come any more scandalous than using the tier of international government to secure your own commercial and national advantage? Does corruption come any more unspeakable than exposing entire nations to starvation by permitting corporations to demand, on contract land, the use of seeds genetically manipulated so that the crop seeds, even if saved, will not germinate?

Dictatorships and military spending

In the current media consensus over Third World debt, excessive military spending is constantly cited as a major causative factor. In terms of channelling funds away from development, it is again worth keeping a sense of proportion. Are we saying that within their entire economic effort, the developing nations should have no spare capacity with which to arm themselves? According to the borrow/invest/export/repay model, it was the funded projects that were supposed to generate the revenues for debt repayment, not the entire economy. The effort that went into development in these economies was prodigious, and that development ought to have been sufficient to support a degree of military spending. Or are we saying that the only purpose of development is to pay back debts?

Once again, the accusation of excessive military spending involves a blatant rewriting of history, and reversal of the actual events. Certainly military spending is expensive and has added markedly to the debt crisis since the 1970s. But the debt crisis was then already in full swing, and moreover it was the debt crisis that prompted the massive recorded rise in military spending. One can even get the words from the horse's mouth. Robert MacNamara, former President of the World Bank, stated;

> There is a direct and constant relationship between the incidence of violence and the economic status of the countries afflicted... since 1958, 87% of the very poor nations, 69% of the poor nations and 48% of the middle income nations suffered serious violence... There is a relationship between violence and economic backwardness and the trend of such violence is up, not down.[25]

Susan George's book, *The Debt Boomerang*, contains a chapter devoted to analysing the relationship between war and debt. 'Of the 25 world states with the biggest debts, 12 were at war in 1990 or early 1991... Of the 41 states involved in war in 1990 or 1991, 25 have heavy debt burdens... Of 24 states involved in decade long wars, 18 had heavy debt burdens.'[26]

War is fed not only by the pressure on ruling elites and governments, but by the fact that it offers attractive employment opportunities for an often starving peasantry. We should also remember that the 'militarisation' of debtor nations, particularly in the years between 1950 and 1980, had as much to do with the drive for arms exports and the desire for political influence by the great world powers, as it had with private armies and civil wars. In 1971, R. Robinson observed; 'Too much [aid] is designed to subsidise the donor's exports or serve his diplomatic strategic or military purposes abroad... We believe that, if the aid used misguidedly hitherto to promote the donor's individual strategic and commercial interest directly, were used specifically to develop the recipient's economy, these interests would be much better served than they have been.'[27]

Summary

Once the essentially unsound and invalid nature of Third World debt is accepted, the political history of the developing nations takes on an entirely new light. Many of these now impoverished societies were once predicted to have a prosperous future, enjoying considerable natural advantages of climate, geography and natural resources. The struggle against intractable debt has led to their development into chaos, as the export imperative has driven their domestic agriculture and industry into decline. Blame for this is habitually placed upon corrupt political regimes and their financial indulgence in military hardware. In fact the typical order of events has been that the benign and popular leaders who led developing nations in their early optimism fell as a result of the poverty and cultural collapse sweeping their nations. Corruption and military dictatorship followed the debt-induced poverty, and did not cause it. The burden of guilt falling on the West for its construction of an unsound international financial system is truly vast.

It was one thing for the wealthy industrialised nations to base their own economies on fractional reserve banking – a manifestly foolish decision. But to decide at Bretton Woods that the accountancy of international trade and development aid were both also to be based upon bank-created credit was a decision of such culpable, blinding stupidity and cupidity as to leave one gasping for words.

To base the global financial system on debt and then express wonder, dismay and disapprobation when debtors fail to make payment from within a debt-based financial system – is this not the final word in economic incompetence? Or maybe the final word in corruption, since debtor nations have been forced to pay a tribute – in the form of interest – on debts that are inherently un-repayable.

Much study and analysis has gone into investigating the claim that debtor nations are responsible for their own economic predicament, because of political corruption, economic incompetence, capital flight and military spending. The lack of substance behind these accusations directs attention back at the World

Bank and IMF, inadequate trading conventions and a financial system in which debt is endemic and coalesces around the poor. As R. Robinson states, the burden of responsibility for action over Third World debt lies with the wealthy nations;

> Originally it was the advanced economies that imposed the international economy on the underdeveloped societies. It would be almost indecent therefore for the advanced countries to reject their historic responsibility for making the enforced relationship work constructively today.[28]

Endnotes

1   Dharam Ghai (ed). *The IMF and the South – The Social Impact of Adjustment.* Zed Books. 1991.
2   Jacques Gelinas. *Freedom from Debt.* Zed Books. 1998.
3   Conference of the Institute for African Alternatives. Bade Onimode (ed). *The IMF, The World Bank and African Debt.* Zed Books. 1989.
4   Robin Broad. *Unequal Alliance. The World Bank, the IMF and the Philippines.* University of California Press. 1988.
5   Hans Singer and Sumitra Sharma (eds). *Economic Development and World Debt.* Macmillan. 1989.
6   Latin America Bureau. *The Poverty Brokers.* The Latin America Bureau. 1983.
7   Latin America Bureau. *Op. cit.*
8   Latin America Bureau. *Op. cit.*
9   John T. Cuddington. *Capital Flight.* Princeton Studies in International Finance. No 58, Dec. 1986.
10   Donald R. Lessard and John Williamson. *Capital Flight and Third World Debt.* Institute for International Economics. 1987.
11   Bergsten Cline Williamson. *Bank Lending to Developing Countries – the Policy Alternatives.* Institute for International Economics. No 10, April 1985.
12   Donald R. Lessard and John Williamson. *Op. cit.*
13   Donald R. Lessard and John Williamson. *Op. cit.*
14   Ingo Walters. In Hans Singer and Sumitra Sharma (eds). *Op. cit.*
15   Rudiger Dornbusch. In Hans Singer and Sumitra Sharma (eds). *Op. cit.*
16   Donald R. Lessard and John Williamson. *Op. cit.*
17   Miguel Rodriguez. In Donald R. Lessard and John Williamson. *Op. cit.*
18   John Cuddington. *Op. cit.*
19   Miguel Rodriguez. In Donald R. Lessard and John Williamson. *Op. cit.*
20   Donald R. Lessard and John Williamson. *Op. cit.*
21   Dharam Ghai. *The IMF and the South – The Social Impact of Adjustment.* Zed Books. 1991.
22   Jacques Gelinas. *Op. cit.*
23   Quoted in; Jacques B. Jelinas. *Op. cit.*
24   Jacques Gelinas. *Op. cit.*
25   Robert S. MacNamara. *The Essence of Security; Reflections in Office.* Hodder and Stoughton. 1968.
26   Susan George. *The Debt Boomerang.* Pluto Press. 1992.
27   R. Robinson. *Developing the Third World. The Experience of the 1960s.* Cambridge University Press. 1971.
28   R. Robinson. *Op. cit.*

12

The future of development

The accountancy of international trade has always been one of the most difficult areas of economics. There is a general desire for there to be open trading between nations. But the fact that nations function as discrete economic units, each with their own currency, and that trade is not in the main conducted between nations but between businesses in one country and consumers in another, whilst currency exchanges have to be conducted – all these factors play havoc with this goal.

History and logic both emphasise that it is vital that the concept of a balance of trade is incorporated in the future rules of international trading. An imbalance of trade means that a given nation or economic region is acting as either a net *supplier* of goods and services or a net *recipient* in relationship to other nations or economic regions. Either situation implies an injustice.

Keynes proposed an International Clearing Union for the accountancy of trade, using a neutral unit of international exchange – the Bancor (see page 39ff). There would be an obligation on all nations to maintain a zero account with the ICU, denoting a true balance of trade, while interest would be charged to nations running a trade deficit and similar penalties levied on 'creditor nations'. The concept of penalties against creditors might seem novel, but is justified by the central importance of a balance of trade, since this places an equal responsibility on all nations to maintain that balance. Indeed, it was never expected that creditor nations would suffer the penalty of having their surplus Bancors confiscated, since they would naturally prefer to spend them. Thus, the concept of penalising creditor nations was intended to rule out the policy of seeking a perpetual trade surplus, and to direct creditor nations to adopt policies that coincided with those of debtor nations.

Keynes did not challenge the right of commerce to trade freely and was implacably opposed to protectionism; however he recognised that the context in which trading took place was centrally important. The beauty of his proposal, and surely the primary requirement of any constructive replacement to the current system, is that it was intended to allow trade to be completely free and open at the commercial level. Meanwhile, the overall fiscal balance of trade impacted on governments, who were given the responsibility for maintaining a zero account with the Clearing Union. They could achieve this by a number of means. Modest currency revaluations were permitted to help restore a trade balance. Domestic taxation could be adjusted, either to raise or lower costs, thus affecting prices. Alternatively, the government itself could act as buyer, spending surplus Bancors, or subsidising domestic goods to encourage exports that would earn Bancors.

All such actions, including the use of Bancor subsidies, would in the final analysis be inherently non-aggressive. Since, in global terms, trade deficits and surpluses equate, the aggregate desire to spend excess Bancors would equal the aggregate desire to earn additional Bancors. Thus the actions of deficit countries promoting exports and the actions of surplus countries accepting additional imports would be complementary.

It was this self-adjusting mechanism, coupled with commercial freedom, that so excited those who understood Keynes' ideas, and won him the admiring tribute from Lord Robbins quoted in Chapter 4. The ICU appeared to promise an end to the trade aggression that had so destabilised the inter-war years. Keynes had devised a mechanism that managed to embrace both levels at which trade operates – the commercial and the international. It left commerce with the freedom it requires if consumers and producers in different nations are to be of mutual service, whilst placing governments under an obligation that only they could fulfil, since by their position and power they alone were placed to undertake policies that would lead to trade adjustment. And the goal was a balance of trade.

A measure of the brilliance of his proposal is that, over the last forty years, Keynes' ICU and Bancor have been acknowledged as the foundation of numerous proposals for reform of the Bretton Woods institutions and the conduct of international trading. A. P. Thirlwall provides an excellent survey of some of the early variants, including the Stewart plan for a Clearing Union and an international currency which he called Rocnabs (Bancor spelt in reverse).[1] Thirlwall relates these schemes to a discussion of the use of SDRs to construct an updated system of liquidity based on the same Keynesian principles. Graham Walshe describes the 1969 Modigliani-Kenen plan for tackling debt and reforming trade, another clear descendant of the ICU; 'The heart of the plan is the provision that countries respond symmetrically to deficit and surplus imbalances.'[2]

Elegant though Keynes' proposal and its variants may be, the history of the debt crisis suggests a potential problem. Although these proposals would appear to address the matter of a *fiscal* balance of trade, a discrepancy in the *material* balance of trade is not covered (as occurs, for example, when the Third World is under persistent pressure to sell commodities below value). The possibility that this might again result from any new system cannot be ignored. In an effort to address this matter, certain economists (including Keynes himself) have argued that currencies should be evaluated in relation to a 'basket of commodities', such as oil, steel, wheat, meat and fruit. But this reduces the scope for currency revaluations, one of the key policies of the ICU and its descendants.

This discussion again emphasises the tremendous complexity of this area of economics. There is no space in this book to investigate the full range of possibilities for the accountancy of world trade, and the many drawbacks involved. It is not intended as an evasion, however, simply to say that this is a crucial area of international economic reform and that all the issues, institutions and conventions must be addressed. The role of the IMF and World Bank; floating exchange rates; how a constructive balance of trade can be maintained that has regard for both the fiscal and physical (or value) dimensions; international investment capital; international trade capital – all these matters inter-relate and should be considered in combination, as well as separately.

It is also worth noting that monetary reform, if it were ever broadly adopted, would contribute markedly to the fostering of a balance of trade by creating financially balanced economies. This would remove the current pressure on economies to achieve an export surplus, and may in the end be an essential ingredient of a truly equitable world economy. But even monetary reform has its limitations. Individual firms might still export aggressively in pursuit of greater profit, since trade is not actually conducted between nations, but between producers and consumers.

Monetary reform is also invoked in the matter of supplying money to the international arena. As has been discussed, nations have all suffered a heavy net loss of money to the international arena, money that has been created mostly within their own domestic economies. This leaves a severe burden of debt within domestic economies. Several economists have called for a 'supply of liquidity' for the international economy, usually suggesting SDRs for this purpose. If a neutral, convertible currency such as SDRs formed the basis of international settlement and exchange, there would be a number of clear gains. National currencies would be less prone to 'leak' from national economies. The 'commodification' of money, in which currencies are traded directly against each other, would be reduced. No one nation would be in a position of advantage through being able to produce at will the international unit of exchange. Finally, where international lending does take place, this could be in a neutral currency where a debtor nation places itself under an obligation to the community of nations rather than any one nation and its currency.

It is worth noting however that the primary purpose of such a currency should be that of trade settlement. The institution of an international currency that supplanted national currencies, or that centralised political or economic control, is the very antithesis of the philosophy implicit in the concept of stable, balanced and democratic economies.

For this reason, the nature and terms of issue of such a currency are vital. If it were issued as a debt against a nation on the basis of that nation's trading account (as Keynes suggested) it is very likely that it would then prove impossible for nations in aggregate to maintain zero accounts. This is simply because, as with any currency, at any one time and therefore at all times, a given quantity of the currency would necessarily be in circulation, or in the case of an international trade currency, involved in transactions and clearances. Thus, the paradoxical situation might well arise in which, instead of global accounts balancing, the community of nations carried an aggregate debt. This could prove very damaging to trade and place all nations in a position of exposure. In a sense, Keynes and others allowed for this in permitting nations a degree of latitude in their trading account before penalties were applied. But it would be essential to consider the possible need actually to create, issue and circulate an amount of the international currency *ab initio* and free from debt, in sufficient quantity to allow the community of nations to show an overall balance of trade.

It is probably true that no mechanism will ever be perfect, but awareness of the appalling malfunction of trade accountancy over the past half century underlines the importance of reform. Third World debt *is* the great failure of world trade accountancy. With a genuine political will, it would be impossible for such a blatant injustice and economic malfunction to occur, whatever mechanism(s) and conventions were agreed. But frequent review would clearly be essential.

International investment

International capital flows have proved highly destabilising in recent years and reform is urgently needed. To institute international controls over capital flows would be to grant considerable additional power to an already unaccountable tier of remote governance. However, an area of great potential for policy-making is to differentiate between portfolio investments (buying into foreign stock markets) and true investment, where financial capital is actually committed that helps create capital assets and improve productive ability within the host economy.

(a) Portfolio investment

When a company issues shares and sells these on the stock market, it receives the revenue raised from this share issue, providing it with funds for investment. From this moment on, the buying and selling of shares on the stock market brings no monetary gain whatsoever to the company. The bulk of stock market activity involves this buying and selling of shares, with no passage of funds to the companies concerned. It is this trading in shares on stock markets that is broadly termed 'portfolio' investment.

This secondary market in shares is vital in maintaining their value and so ensuring any future share issues are successful. However, the recent effect of large foreign portfolio investments in destabilising national economies suggests that foreign portfolio investment, rather than investment *per se*, should be the focus of international financial regulation.

In other words, the case exists for constructing suitable regulations for evening out foreign portfolio investment, but leaving the transfer of capital by companies for the purposes of true investment undeterred, or at least subject to different regulations.

Portfolio investment is a clear instance where a ban on leveraged funds is warranted. In other words, the desirable process of restricting bank credit creation could be coupled with the protection of stock markets from excessive short-term, speculative investment.

The intelligent use of a Tobin tax on portfolio investments might also be considered. A Tobin tax is a levy on international money transfers, intended to act as a deterrent to short-term, aggressive investments that simply extract profit rather than create wealth. Such a tax can be graduated, with a sliding scale from heavy penalties on short-term investment to lighter penalties for longer term investments. It is thus a very flexible policy instrument, applicable to different areas, at different rates and taking into account the critical factor of time.

A graduated Tobin tax on international portfolio investment could be levied either on profits secured by dealings on foreign stock markets, or on the total stock market investment transaction. The first scenario is perhaps more just, while the second would ensure that sudden, destabilising monetary influx/efflux – even if it generated no profit – was discouraged.

There would be no impact upon true investment, for if a foreign company is undertaking a true investment it will bring capital into the country, by-passing the stock market and all such disincentives.

(b) Currency speculation

The relative value of national currencies is of the utmost importance for healthy, equitable international trade. Any practices that distort currency values and cause undue fluctuations are very undesirable.

Without question, the most pressing area for regulation involves the activity of 'hedge funds'. These are investment funds managed with the express purpose of targeting and profiting from changes in currency values. They usually operate on short-term deals, buying and selling currencies in anticipation of a sudden change in value. This is not, in essence, a problem. What is a problem is that hedge funds leverage, or borrow from, commercial banks up to *one hundred times* the amount of money they actually hold. This gives them colossal financial power and the mayhem that can result was demonstrated during the Asian financial crisis as well as on 'Black Monday', when the British pound came under attack and was forced to leave the European Exchange Rate Mechanism.

Hedge funds can take particular advantage of a currency whose value has been allowed to 'float' on the money markets by mounting a concerted attack. Yet this is in direct conflict with the original purpose of a floating exchange rate mechanism. The primary intention of the convention of floating exchange rates is to act as a feedback mechanism for the maintenance of a balance of trade. Thus, floating exchange rates are intended to be influenced by trade-related currency exchanges. But if hedge funds attack a currency, it can be destroyed within hours, after a sequence of events that has not the remotest connection with the balance of international trade.

From this, it might appear that there should be an outright ban on hedge fund speculation. However, it has always been accepted that hedge fund activity would impact upon currency values, and provided this is not excessive, it serves to even out the effect of trade-related currency deals.

In view of the current imbalance of 95% speculative, 5% trade-related currency transactions, the level of hedge fund involvement is clearly excessive. A constructive restriction on hedge fund activity could take the form of a ban on the use of leveraged funds for currency deals. It is the leveraging of funds that magnifies their financial strength so considerably. A ban would impact on all hedge funds equally and therefore not interfere with the competitive balance between them. However, there would be a considerable and welcome reduction in their total influence on currency values. This would contribute to allowing the primacy of trade-related currency transactions to re-emerge, and thereby help foster an equitable balance of trade between nations.

Multinational investment and democratic governments

The recently proposed Multilateral Agreement on Investment (MAI) was quite unacceptable in terms of the balance of power between elected governments and international commerce. There should certainly be a code of conduct regulating international investment. However, the damage caused by recent aggressive corporate activity suggests that this should first address the many excesses and unjust practices carried out by multinationals, such as demanding grants from national governments, transfer pricing, corporate raiding, asset-stripping, monopoly buy-outs, unjust patent rights and so on.

A potentially useful guide for investment is the abandoned ITO/Havana Treaty. This was the third element of international economic affairs discussed at Bretton Woods. The treaty eventually foundered when the American delegation refused to agree to its terms, which included inter-governmental agreements on commodity prices and preferential trading arrangements for developing nations. The treaty also contained measures against restrictive practices by multinationals. Applying such principles today might result in legislation such as the following;

1   An international ban on multinationals accepting/requiring cash inducements from governments, unless pro-rata equity-ownership of the investment is granted to the government.

2   An international ban on transfer pricing, with heavy fines for goods and services sold internally, or between corporations, at rates that differ from those charged to the wider market.

3   National governments to retain the right of subsidy to domestic firms, and

for foreign firms to qualify for equivalent subsidy only if they can demonstrate that there has been no capital injection or support transferred from abroad within the previous five years.

4   The right of national governments to declare chosen sectors of their economy the complete or partial province of ownership by domestic companies.

5   The source of, and repatriation of, corporate profits to be subject to international audit.

6   The right of governments to set environmental standards that they deem to be appropriate, irrespective of the impact on individual companies whether foreign or national.

7   The right of governments to seek agreement regarding the sharing of technological expertise (including patent transfers) and the training and employment of nationals as conditions of inward investment.

8   The institution of an International Court of Commercial Conduct, accessible to governments, private commerce and individuals, for the submission and hearing of complaints against international corporations.

In other words, any international agreement on investment should seek to regulate in favour of elected governments, supporting them in the responsible management of their economies, *before* it seeks to secure the rights of overseas investors and corporations. Constructive reform would return the element of risk to investors and restore sovereign power to governments. This need not mean that foreign investment would, in aggregate, be deterred; simply that it would take place within a different framework. Since the purpose is a more resource-efficient form of economic activity, there is every reason to argue that such investment would be intrinsically more productive and ultimately more financially rewarding for investors.

Sources of development capital

The subject of foreign investment leads to one of the key issues of development economics; sources of capital to fund economic growth. Foreign investment and/or loans from the World Bank or IMF have long been relied upon as essential sources of finance. The regulation of international capital and writing-off of international debts would, according to the conventional development model, consign the poorer nations to perpetual underdevelopment.

Even if a conventional economist agreed that Third World debts could be written off, a worried look would spread across his face as he asked, 'What about moral hazard?'

'Moral hazard' is the term used to describe the reluctance of lenders to advance loans to borrowers who either default or have their debts cancelled. They are bad credit risks and future loans are in doubt. The threat of moral hazard is constantly raised as a downside to any form of debt cancellation, and this would surely apply to the creative accountancy suggested in Chapter 9. One could not expect banks to lend money in the knowledge that the bonds they hold would constantly be turned into non-negotiable assets. Such debt cancellation would have to be 'once and for all'. But it still raises a question mark over the ability of debtor nations to repay any future loans.

Of course, new systems of trade accountancy based on a *balance* of trade would contribute greatly to the repayment of debts, since the loans would register as an imbalance and adjustment ought to follow. But considering the difficulties of equitable trade accountancy, it may well be that reforms in other areas are needed to complement the objective of balanced trade. The issue of loans to the Third World, itself a critically important area of the development debate, could contribute markedly to balanced trade accountancy.

Borrowing 'capital'

Cheryl Payer points out that there exists within the discipline of economics a single word for two concepts – capital.[3] Financial capital is not the same as the physical capital of productive assets, such as machinery. But the confusion between the two has led to a damaging assumption. The fact that the developing nations needed to obtain physical capital from industrialised nations was taken to mean that they needed to borrow financial capital to buy it with. In fact, in terms of maintaining a balance of trade, this assumption is quite false. Third World nations ought to have purchased foreign goods for development, such as machinery, with their own currency, since to restore the balance of trade would require the industrialised nations to buy back goods from developing nations – which would require the use of developing nation currencies. In short, *Third World debt ought never to have been denominated in dollars or pounds in the first place*. Restoring a balance of trade means returning money to where it started from, and the only logical arrangement is for developing nations to import what they need using their own currency.

This argument is even stronger when a floating exchange rate mechanism is in operation. Floating exchange rates rely upon currency surpluses to promote a balance of trade. If loans to the Third World are denominated in dollars, this is hardly going to generate surpluses of debtor nation currencies that will reduce their currency values and so promote their exports! The contradiction is glaring.

However, the issue of capital and currency denominations goes far deeper than this. The lending of financial capital to the Third World does have its own ratio-nale. But this rationale not only ignores the issue of the currency required for a balance of trade, it is deeply flawed in another sense. Lending to the Third World has been justified on the grounds that the best way to stimulate development is to take advantage of the 'natural' tendency of financial capital to flow from industrial to undeveloped nations. Cheryl Payer summarises this theory succinctly;

> Conventional economic theory holds that the so-called developing countries
> are poor in capital, and that because capital is scarce, returns to capital
> investment are higher in the Third World countries than in capital-surplus
> developed countries. According to this theory, private capital should natu-
> rally flow from developed to underdeveloped countries.[4]

Many writers and analysts have agreed with Payer in faulting this theory of
'capital flows from rich to poor', and some have advocated the generation, by
developing nations, of their own capital. This is obviously very relevant to the
'moral hazard' argument. By creating their own financial capital and using this
to mobilise their own resources, developing nations can become less dependent
upon international capital. There is a strong theoretical tie-in between this
concept and the basic monetary reform proposal, whereby a state is recognised
as having 'the right and responsibility to create its own currency and furnish its
people with a sound medium of exchange'.

Without this concept, development theory has dwelt on two options. Either
financial capital must come from abroad, or Third World nations must generate
sufficient 'surplus savings' within their own economies to provide the capital for
investment. Borrowed capital has led to Third World debt. Surplus savings in
developing countries are slow to accrue. This has left developing nations in a
'capital quandary'; they have abundant resources, they have the labour and the
world markets are there – but they have not got the money, so these elements
cannot connect. They have the natural capital, but not the financial capital with
which to mobilise it. The introduction of a third option – capital creation by Third
World governments – offers a dramatic change in development theory.

The trouble is, such capital creation constitutes full-blown monetary reform,
and as we have seen, monetary reform is the issue that cannot be named, the great
taboo amongst economists. It is interesting as well as perplexing to see just how
carefully the following commentators – leaders in the field – will avoid stating
openly that Third World governments can create their own financial capital for
development, whilst implying this very policy.

> The only way to prevent future debt crises is to drastically limit unbalanced
> international capital flows, which means abandoning the dangerous myth
> that Third World countries need to import foreign capital... It is quite
> possible for poor countries to develop by relying mainly on their national
> resources, and there is no real alternative to this.[5]

> ... development strategies in those countries should increasingly rely upon
> their own nationally generated resources for funding development and must
> avoid patterns of development intensive in foreign exchange that will
> remain scarce for the coming years.[6]

The potential importance of government-created capital is so great that a diversion into capital theory is justified at this point.

Banking capital or social capital?

Conventional theories assert that investment capital must come from savings. The more traditional theory asserts that investment should come from savings to avoid inflation, arguing that the lending of savings for investment does not constitute an act of money-creation. Investment is deemed to involve an act of simple lending, of savings that are 'tied up' on deposit. Thus, it is argued, the active, circulating money stock is not increased by the lending of savings.

More advanced equity theory accepts that investment must come from savings, but asserts that when a loan is made, money creation has taken place. It argues that a new product – debt – has been created. This new product generates a return, in the form of interest, for the lender. Thus, lenders profit through the action of banks making loans to borrowers.

Both theories are profoundly false. The falsity of the traditional theory is reasonably obvious and confirmed by every book on the practice of banking and every piece of monetary data available from the global economy. Bank lending involves money creation.

The falsity of the equity theory is not so immediately apparent. Deposits of money used as the collateral for lending do indeed accrue interest from borrowers. But this is not the entire story. Ultimately depositors do *not* gain from the action of banks in using their deposits as the basis of lending. We all know this is the case. A monetary deposit of £1000 left untouched, gathering interest, for a decade or so may have grown to £2000. But the *purchasing power* of that sum can actually have fallen, due to inflation. Whilst the empirical evidence that savers who hold monetary deposits actually lose out is fairly widely appreciated, and whilst inflation is recognised as the culprit, the full analysis of this phenomenon is not widely understood. Why do depositors, despite receiving interest payments, ultimately lose money?

The answer was first spelled out by the Nobel laureate, Professor Frederick Soddy,[7] who demonstrated that it is the banking system that is responsible for the constant erosion of depositors' wealth, and the banking system that is the ultimate beneficiary of capital/money creation.

The cause of the inflation that devalues all deposits is, of course, the act of monetary creation by banks. The money stock is inflated by every act of lending and this constantly devalues money. Soddy pointed out that it was *banks* who actually gained as a result of their lending activities. True, the depositor receives a nominal amount of interest. But the valuable new product created – the debt bond – is deemed the property of the bank, not the depositor against whose money the loan was advanced.

This debt bond represents both the quantity of money created and the degree by which the money stock has inflated. The depositor receives interest. But the money stock is inflated by the totality of the loan, whilst the depositor receives only a fraction of this amount annually. Therefore his gain will not be as great as the bank's for many years. Meanwhile, because the bank keeps issuing further loans to other borrowers, the first borrower finds his monetary deposit eroded by constant inflation. The rate of payment of interest rarely keeps pace with the rate at which the money stock is inflated. And all the while, banks are accumulating assets, held in their own name, using their depositors' money as collateral and constantly devaluing it. As for the interest payments, these derive not from the bank, but from the borrower. The summary of this rather complex relationship is that depositors make a gain at the expense of borrowers, whilst the banks gain at the expense of both. Indeed, the banks gain at the expense of the entire community since they increase their wealth by the full amount of each loan. Thus, Soddy argued, banks lay claim to the 'virtual wealth' of the community.

There is abundant confirmation of the fact that banks are the true beneficiaries of the act of lending. By lending against their depositors' money, banks and building societies now possess legal title to 35% of the UK housing stock and 48% of US housing. Banks also hold increasing title to global commerce as a result of the steady increase in commercial debt. Meanwhile, the aggregate of privately held wealth (including savings) has declined steadily. The fact that debt constitutes material gain for the banking system is highlighted by the debt-equity swaps, through which international banks have secured valuable debtor nation assets on their books.

The fact that banks cannot freely sell the wealth they hold as assets, since their assets must equate with their liabilities, is quite immaterial. The ownership they exert might be termed 'latent'. But the point is that the banks *do* own these assets, which means that people do *not* own them. Banking thus creates a situation of gross dependency, as witnessed by the growth of mortgages, commercial and government debts and Third World bonds. And, crucially, whilst the wealth they hold is not immediately accessible to them, the existence of debt allows banks to determine the policy of their debtors. Debt is about power, rather than wealth.

Banks achieve this power by the act of creating money as a debt repayable to them, securing this by a debt – a claim against an asset. By this process, banks have come to possess legal title to, and hold latent ownership over, an increasing proportion of the total of national and international wealth. The monetary reform argument is that, rather than banks 'monetising the wealth of the community', the government should undertake this function *as a social service*, and supply money in adequate quantity to serve as a medium of exchange, thus reducing the need to borrow.

This is not the occasion to expand on the monetary reform agenda. However, it clearly has considerable relevance to Third World development and should be thoroughly examined as a potential source of capital. It is possible to conceive of a development model in which government-created money, which cannot be issued in unlimited quantities, forms the 'first resort' for investment capital, and international lending – denominated in SDRs or developing nation currencies and brokered by a reconstituted World Bank – is used as a back-up. This would reduce the burden of debt and, alongside reforms to ensure a balance of trade, could form a constructive basis for capital supply to developing nations. It would acknowledge that the source of financial capital should be two-fold; to tie in with both the natural capital of the developing nation and the physical capital imported from abroad.

It is also worth pointing out that most 'Third World' nations are now well on the road to development, in the sense of having a scientific, technological and industrial base. This is a basis of 'real wealth' upon which future development can build. In this sense, the need for developing nations to import *physical* or 'real' capital from the more wealthy nations is far less than it once was. To the extent that such real capital is needed, as discussed earlier, it should be purchased with the nation's own currency to avoid the dangers of unrepayable debt. The fact that much of the physical capital established in the developing nations is currently deemed the property of foreign corporations is a problem best addressed by appropriate taxation and other legislation.

Monetary reform

The principles of monetary reform were outlined in Chapter 8, and in the present chapter the subject has been discussed in relation to capital sources for developing nations. However, monetary reform does not have to be based just on the 'national model' advanced earlier, nor is the international sphere the only other arena in which monetary reform is relevant. There is also scope for a local dimension to monetary reform which is of relevance to developing nations. One option is to attempt to stabilise the many 'micro-credit' schemes operating in developing nations. Another is to adopt and develop the system of government finance used by the Channel Islands.

Micro-credit schemes

Micro-credit schemes have, at times, proved highly successful co-operative ventures in the developing nations. Small loans have been made to individuals and family groups to allow them to buy seed or livestock, start up small enterprises, or simply run drains to their houses. Micro-credit offered through schemes such as the now famous Grameen Bank has rejuvenated entire regions.

However, these schemes have often run into difficulties after a period of apparent success. This is hardly surprising since, whilst they are decentralised, offer loans at low rates of interest and attempt to be sensitive to local needs, they are still *debt*-based. Like a national debt-based economy, such schemes succeed whilst they are growing, but there comes a point at which the need to repay loans, or interest on the loans, is no longer compensated by sufficient new borrowing. Liquidity drains, the fiscal competition heightens, selling becomes difficult, those who have borrowed experience repayment problems, new borrowers are deterred and the revival simply collapses. This has happened repeatedly to micro-credit schemes. There is a clear need for a supportive money supply – a carefully regulated input of debt-free money – to compensate for the principal and interest payments that threaten these ventures. It would be simple to administer, distributing small quantities of credit (created debt-free and not subject to repayment) to maintain liquidity and demand in the system, but insufficient to cause inflation. Various simple indicators could be used to judge the quantity of additional money thus required, including the volume of current borrowing, the rate of current repayment and turnover.

Distributed money creation

For over a century, the Channel Islands have operated a system of government finance that is unique. Most of the money supply is, as usual, created by commercial banks as a result of 'lending to borrowers'. However, the island governments do not run a national debt. If one of the islands' administrations wishes to fund a new project or public service, but does not have the revenue from taxation to do so, it creates money as a government issue for the specific purpose. This is used to fund the project and is thereby spent into the economy. In subsequent years the money is gradually taxed back, then cancelled out or 'destroyed'.

The rationale behind the process is that the monetary economy is, or should be, subordinate to the 'real' economy. The questions that the islands' administrations consider are:

(a) is there a genuine need for this project?

(b) do we have the materials necessary to complete the task?

(c) do we have unemployed workers who want employment?

If the answer to all three is 'Yes', then the Governors feel justified in creating the money to allow the various resources to be mobilised, and the project completed. Once the job is completed, the money involved has completed its function – hence it is withdrawn by taxation and destroyed.

Whilst obviously not an adequate basis for national monetary reform, since the need is for a permanently circulating, stable money stock, the Channel Islands practice offers an excellent model for regional monetary reform within larger nations.

It is one of the great complaints of monetary reformers that the local absence of money leads to the immobilisation of resources. The raw materials are lying idle in a builder's yard; a new community centre is needed; builders are unemployed – but 'we haven't got the money', so the community centre cannot be built.

There is no guarantee that national monetary reform would eliminate this problem, even though there would be a greater monetary adequacy within the economy as a whole. The opportunity exists to take the Channel Islands model and use it as a basis for restricted local money creation by local authorities or similar civic bodies.

Thus, a local authority might be granted the right to create and issue money (simply in the form of a credit allowance) on a temporary basis, using this power to mobilise resources for specific additional projects or services, with an obligation to regain that revenue in subsequent years and cancel it. Such local authority monetary issue would thus have an overall neutral effect on the total money stock, with local councils equipped to compensate for temporary regional shortages of revenue needed to undertake specific policy measures.

Such a reform distributes and decentralises the money-creating powers of government, and would help counter the tendency of investment and economic activity to aggregate in geographical clusters, leading to areas of localised over-investment and other areas of localised stagnation.

Summary

Many of these reforms overlap in their intention and policy. However, this is not undesirable, since the reforms would complement and reinforce each other. Nor are these reforms exhaustive of the need and scope for financial/economic reform at the regional, national and international levels. They are presented as examples of the legislative direction that is necessary to address the severe malfunction of modern economics, and the specific disasters of Third World debt and globalisation. The intention is to provide a stable and supportive framework for the regeneration of local and international economies.

Endnotes

1   A. P. Thirlwall. *Financing Economic Development*. Macmillan Studies in Economics. Macmillan. 1976.

2   Graham Walshe. *International Monetary Reform*. Macmillan Studies in Economics. Macmillan. 1971.

3   Cheryl Payer. *Lent and Lost*. Zed Books. 1991.

4   Cheryl Payer. *Op. cit.*

5   Conference of the Institute for African Alternatives. Bade Onimode. *The IMF, The World Bank and African Debt*. Zed Books. 1989.

6   Hans Singer, Sumitra Sharma. *Economic Development and World Debt*. Macmillan. 1994.

7   Frederick Soddy. *Wealth, Virtual Wealth and Debt*. Omni Publications. 1933.

13

The legal and moral challenge

It is unlikely that the wealthy industrialised nations and relevant multilateral institutions have either the determination, the desire or the degree of co-operative dialogue necessary to tackle Third World debt in the ways described in this book. Western governments would have to be placed under considerable pressure to entertain such reformist policies – just as when broad Third World default threatened in the early 1980s. For this reason, it is vitally important to consider the legal status and contractual validity of Third World debts so that they may be challenged.

The legal status of Third World debts

Financial contracts can be declared invalid and many precedents exist for this. André Gunder Frank raised the possibility of such a legal challenge;

> Normal contract law provides that contracts are invalid or can be invalidated by a court if they were signed without full cognisance by both contracting parties.[1]

Although advanced under the banner of 'aid', loans to developing countries are a financial product producing a significant return for the lending agencies involved – the World Bank, the IMF and commercial banks. As market-based products, the terms and contract of these loans are therefore subject to rules governing commercial financial practice. Where it can be shown that there has been mis-selling or misrepresentation, or if interested parties have acted or failed to act in such ways as to compromise the interests of other parties to a contract, there are substantial grounds for legal redress. All these considerations apply to the debts suffered by the Third World.

One of the main grounds in any action for substantial debt relief must be that loans were advanced to Third World nations on the understanding that these were repayable. That this is not the case is shown by the evidence of history and proclaimed by the bulk of debt/development literature, as well as being demonstrated in the monetary analysis of this book. The legal point is that the developing nations were encouraged to undertake debt by lending agents who *themselves* presented these loans as part of a development model where loans were repayable. Jacques B. Gelinas states;

The World Bank in particular and the regional development banks have, since the 1960s, dazzled Third World leaders with irrefutably logical arguments whilst promising the development aid programmes. Many people were convinced by the ideology of credit-based development.[2]

In addition, many loans were only advanced after the projects, and the fiscal projections accompanying them, were approved by World Bank or IMF economists. This places a heavy responsibility with those institutions. Their failure to carry out an assessment of their own net lending activities, and thus anticipate the fall in commodity prices suffered by the many nations to whom they were lending, was clearly a gross omission. These last two considerations make the World Bank and IMF culpable as advising institutions, and present major grounds for revision, if not the nullification, of many loan contracts. Finally, any survey of conditionality can only conclude that the World Bank and IMF have acted throughout to secure the interests of wealthy nations at the cost of debtor nations, and have deeply disadvantaged the efforts of debtor nations to manage repayment.

The insistence by the World Bank and IMF that failing loans made to private enterprises in the developing nations should not be allowed to follow a standard bankruptcy process, but should be converted into official government debts, was sheer *force majeure* and had no legal justification.

The small-print clauses, inserted during the 1970s, which permitted interest to be charged at variable rates, have also been widely condemned as a breach of fair contract.

Why has the nominally high interest component of Third World debts, which accrued without the knowledge or knowing agreement of the damaged contracting parties, not been declared legally null and void? Legal provisions to do so can and should be made... Applying this legal norm to the floating interest rate small print of these 1970s debt contracts would substantially reduce the amounts nominally owed.[3]

The resort to additional loans to fund repayments of earlier loans that were in danger of default involved a clear breach of the accepted development model, in which loans and debts represented a measure of material gain to the borrower through the purchase of foreign goods and services for development. New loans to fund repayment of bad old loans simply meant that money advanced by the Bank/Fund returned to the Bank/Fund as interest or capital repayments, incurring an increase in the total of debt without any material gain whatsoever for the debtor nation. André Gunder Frank comments;

Much of the present nominal debt was not properly contracted and certainly was never received by the debtor as an equivalent flow of real capital or resources from abroad.[4]

The essentially false representation of these loans as repayable, the co-responsibility of project approval, failure to assess the impact of similar development projects on world prices, severe binding conditions that deeply compromised the chances of debt-repayment, the demand that commercial debts be converted to government debts and the levying of unspecified variable interest rates; these factors constitute the most powerful legal grounds for the voiding of all debts, and even for claiming both relief and redress.

Conditional or unconditional cancellation?

Some critics might object that the blanket cancellation of international debts is not justified – that in terms of economic management and human rights records there have been 'good' debtor nations and 'bad' debtor nations. However, there are many reasons to argue for complete remission of the debts owed by all developing nations.

(a) The judgement of political rectitude and economic competence introduces a range of very subjective criteria into the discussion.

(b) Most debtor nations have, over the past half century, experienced both benign and oppressive regimes.

(c) The growth of debt has itself frequently contributed to the establishment of authoritarian, oppressive regimes.

(d) Even if a judgement of unacceptable or inhuman political actions by a particular government could be agreed, it should be remembered that debt impacts mainly upon the oppressed and dispossessed within countries. Such a government would, by definition, be of a character likely to attempt to continue to deflect the remaining debt overhang to impact mainly on the poor majority.

(e) The attempt to tie debt remission to conformity with certain social and environmental policies would place considerable, possibly excessive power with international agencies. The present agencies – the UN, OECD, IMF, World Bank – have proved incompetent, remote, heavily influenced by corporate interests and doctrinally biased towards a free-market ethic which, as this book argues throughout, requires complete re-examination. There is no guarantee that the administration of 'social/environmentally tied debt remission' would be any more successful or more just than previous agendas emanating from this remote tier of international governance.

(f) Any attempt to trace back the economic record to adjudge economic competence in the past would become enmeshed in an endless debate over 'true commodity values', 'fair currency values', IMF/World Bank co-responsibility for failed projects, etc. Such evaluations would prove impossible of agreement.

(g)   Endemic international debt is counter to all trade theory. The persistence of any appreciable level of debt would continue to force debtor nations to seek surplus export revenues. This would present foreign corporations with the continuing opportunity of securing resources and labour at rates that deeply distort the global economy.

(h)   The persistence of any appreciable level of debt would continue to pressure developing nations to gain revenues by exporting – in other words, the export imperative would remain in place. Since this is one of the root causes of rapid environmental degradation and social neglect, the 'tied debt remission' policy carries a deep contradiction within itself.

(i)   Finally, and perhaps most importantly, there can be no dispute that most debtor nations have repaid their debts in real terms (in the form of goods and services exported) many times over. This is such a primary and indisputable point, and casts such a shadow on the economic competence and political rectitude of the industrialised nations and their international representatives, that any policy other than total debt cancellation constitutes the continuation of a grave international injustice.

The frequent suggestion that debt should be cancelled only on condition of political conformity, environmental rectitude and evidence of economic responsibility has not just a hollow ring, but resonates with the very same self-righteous economic imperialism that has attended Third World debt for the past forty years. Tempting as it may be to impose conditionality on debt remission, the goals of such conditionality – environmental protection and more democratic political structures – are far more likely to be achieved by a complete and unconditional removal of the burden of debt.

If debt is merely reduced and conditionality imposed, developing nations will still be obliged to struggle for surplus export revenues in a world of debt. The orientation of their economies to the competitive pursuit of exports will ensure that the needs of the environment, political and social progress, along with agricultural and industrial development for domestic needs, will all continue to be secondary considerations.

Whilst apparently an attractive option, the administration of debt relief, conditional on agreed standards of social and environmental behaviour, holds far more perils than any real likelihood of success. We should accept that, in the overall analysis, complete debt remission is by far the fairest and most constructive policy. It removes the export imperative entirely and permits debtor nations to establish their own development priorities. No blame could then be placed on the more powerful nations for the institution of 'environmental and social imperialism' via 'tied debt remission'. The governments of developing nations would be held fully responsible for the social, environmental and economic priorities they pursued. The concerted pressure of the international community, acting not through the invidious channel of tied debt remission but through customary economic, political and diplomatic sanctions, holds far more likelihood of effective influence and pressure.

The HIPC Initiative

Before considering the political forces arrayed against debt cancellation, it is worth summarising the approach to debt forgiveness suggested by the World Bank. The World Bank and the IMF are 'deeply concerned' over Third World debt. They are so concerned that they have come up with a programme to tackle the problem – known as the HIPC (Highly Indebted Poor Countries) Initiative. This has been described as 'debt relief the poor can bank on'.

Much has been made of the 'change of heart' by the World Bank that the HIPC initiative is alleged to represent. The bank claims it is now firmly committed to a social and environmental programme of development priorities involving education, welfare, environmental regulation, debt relief and restricting debt to sustainable levels.

Michel Chossudovsky has accused the Bank of covering up its policies with empty promises and offering a public relations 'counter-paradigm'. Whilst the Bank's expressed intentions have altered, he points out, the key political and economic demands on debtor nations have not.

> While the Bretton Woods institutions have acknowledged 'the social impact of adjustment', no shift in policy direction is in sight. In fact since the late 1980s, coinciding with the collapse of the Eastern bloc, the IMF-World Bank policy prescriptions (now imposed in the name of 'poverty alleviation') have become increasingly harsh and unyielding. [The Bank now offers]...a 'counter-paradigm', embodying a highly moral and ethical discourse. [This] focuses on 'sustainable development' and 'poverty alleviation' [but] rarely challenges neo-liberal policy prescriptions.[5]

In fact, the position is worse than Chossudovsky suggests. What the HIPC Initiative does is retain the Bank's basic economic premises and model, whilst demanding that debtor nations undertake social and welfare reforms. The nations will be offered additional loans, plus nominal interest relief on their current debts, to fund these demanding programmes, with debt remission as a later reward. Thus the HIPC Initiative transfers the responsibility for elaborate welfare and environmental goals to the debtor nations, whilst these are to be funded by little else than allowing debtor nations to borrow yet more, whilst keeping the interest payments that they cannot assemble at present!

What the HIPC Initiative actually says is revealing. The 1997 World Bank document, which still serves as the framework of its poverty alleviation and environmental programme, refers to 'sound economic policies' on over *thirty* occasions.[6] The stated intention is to help the debtor nations reach a position of 'sustainable debt'. After six years, debtor nations will be eligible to apply for remission of a portion of their 'unpayable' debts, providing they have followed these 'sound economic policies'. But these policies are nowhere defined in the document. In absence of any statement suggesting a change in the Bank's previous definition of 'sound economic policies', the HIPC Initiative requires debtor nations to adopt

(1)   free and open trading and investment,
(2)   the phasing out of subsidies on domestic products,
(3)   a deregulated financial system,
(4)   free entry and exit for capital,
(5)   floating exchange rates,
(6)   privatisation to attract foreign investment, and
(7)   deregulation of all commercial sectors of their economies.

In short, what debtor nations are being offered is eventual modest debt reduction, after six years of further compliance with the standard IMF and World Bank agenda of 'adjusting' to the world economy. Institutions with a proven track record of the most abysmal failure in development advice, known to be influenced by the international corporate sector and prepared to impose austerity and structural adjustment in pursuit of a misplaced free-trade ethic – these same institutions are to adjudge the compliance of debtor nations to *further* free-trade demands and preside over the remission of debts to 'sustainable levels'. At the end of the programme debtor nations may, or may not, be eligible for a portion of their debt – that which the World Bank decides is 'unpayable' – to be remitted. The HIPC Initiative represents a complete failure to address Third World debt, whilst once again placing debtor nations in a position where they are bound to collect the blame for the failure.

The most revealing word in the entire HIPC programme is the most apparently harmless – debts will be 'sustainable'. Such use of a term coined by the environment movement in criticism of modern Western economics is repugnant. But it also reveals the true extent of concern for the developing world. For sustainable in this case means *permanent* – and permanent debt fits the corporate agenda far better than critical debt levels. It will suit corporations perfectly if Third World debt is reduced from its current rather 'embarrassing' total.

As long as they remain in debt – call it sustainable debt if you prefer – the developing nations will be driven to compete for scarce export revenues in a world of frenzied export competition. This in turn will continue to grant multinational corporations the power to say 'OK… list the concessions you will offer us, and we might invest in your country…!' It is in the 'development gap' between the North and South that multinationals flourish. The gap can be lessened, and still be effective.

The HIPC Initiative repeats the mistakes and the failed promises of previous attempts to tackle the debt crisis. The 1985 Baker Plan offered $12 billion of new funds and enhanced 'surveillance' to ensure less 'corruption'. It was conditional upon the usual adjustment policies. The 1989 Brady Plan offered debt-service reduction plus new finance packages on a voluntary case-by-case approach. Some debtor nations were allowed to buy back their debt. But this too was conditional upon the usual structural adjustment policies.

In short, powerful representatives of the Western nations continue to demonstrate a clear unwillingness to act constructively on Third World debt. They maintain at all times their basic economic premises and continue to impose this agenda on debtor nations. There has never been any assumption of co-responsibility or any admission of the flaws in the trading conventions and institutions that preside over this debacle. From the Bretton Woods Conference, the rejected UN Declaration calling for a New International Economic Order (1974), the Arusha Initiative (1980), the Baker Plan (1985), the Brady Plan (1989), through to the current HIPC Initiative, there has been no concession, financial or verbal, that the smallest measure of blame lies elsewhere than with the debtor nations. This position is enshrined once again in the HIPC Initiative, which contains no review of trade conventions, accepts no blame for the actions of multilateral or commercial lenders or Western governments, and considers debt remission solely on the grounds of alleged unsound economics and corruption, coupled with the flawed concept of sustainable international debt.

Jubilee 2000 and debt remission

This discussion helps to explain the failings of the Jubilee 2000 Campaign. The old saying, 'if you sup with the devil, you should use a long spoon', could not be more apposite, since the campaign demonstrated a lamentable lack of political acumen. As they struggled to press the issue of debt relief on behalf of the debtor nations, Jubilee 2000 accepted at the outset that the focus of attention should be on a single category of debtor nations – the Severely Indebted Low Income Countries (SILICs). These nations then became known as the Heavily Indebted Poor Countries (HIPCs). This meant that less than 20% of the total of Third World debts – only those of the small, low income nations – was under consideration from the outset. India, for example, with its international debt of $93 billion, and Brazil's debt of $258 billion, do not qualify for debt relief under the World Bank's HIPC plan. No plan exists to tackle the poverty of the Brazilian Favelas or Indian slums.

Having excluded the majority of impoverished nations, the campaign's second mistake was to accept the terms under which the World Bank agreed to consider debt remission. Remission would be considered where there was evidence of political corruption and/or economic mismanagement, provided that the Bank and Fund's criteria of 'sound economic management' were followed thereafter. This was a clear political trap – whether intended or not. The apparent concession excluded what are without doubt far more substantial grounds for debt remission – the co-responsibility and culpability of the Bank and Fund themselves. The powerful but complex argument that the terms and accountancy of world trade had led to decades of expropriation was advanced as a mere complaint, urging that the developing nations had received rather a raw deal. Meanwhile, the shameful historical record that ought to exclude both the Bank and Fund from all right to define 'sound economic management' was completely ignored.

The mistake was compounded. Having obtained the apparent concession that incompetence and corruption were grounds for debt 'forgiveness', advocates of debt relief sought to maximise these factors and attribute debt to incompetence and corruption wherever possible. In so doing they denigrated the efforts of a generation of Third World leaders and mobilised public opinion behind a wholly fallacious analysis. They also consigned the debtor nations to debt relief at the hands of two of the institutions justly vilified for their economic programmes and development advice in the past.

The campaign's final mistake was to accept the concept of 'sustainable' debt. Only the 'unpayable' debts of the most impoverished small countries would be tackled, whilst the evidence of the last five decades is that Third World debt is an institution that is *inherently* unrepayable. For the majority of debtor nations, the entire period has been one of persistent escalation and failed repayment. As was argued in Chapter 8, the concept of endemic international debt is wholly fallacious in terms of international trade accountancy. However, the term 'sustainable debt' allowed the Bank and Fund to project the image of crisis management of the debt problem, purloining an adjective from the green vocabulary, whilst completely failing to address fundamental institutional failings.

Jubilee 2000 literature scarcely mentioned the problems associated with trade accountancy and the future world economic order. In addition the campaign offered no analysis of debt and money. Yet no analysis of Third World debt that fails to take into account the present debt-based financial system can either claim to understand debt, or hope to inform a policy that addresses the problems caused by debt.

Persuaded, like the public, to accept the promises of the HIPC Initiative, Jubilee 2000 lacked the economic guile to check the policies. The Campaign decided to accept the concessions, run with the World Bank and get what debt relief it could, on the grounds that something is better than nothing. As a result, it ignored the evidence that did not square with the presumption of incompetence and corruption; the historical record was re-written in front of the entire world whilst the Bank and Fund managed the most astonishing feat of political resurrection.

Sadly, the Jubilee 2000/Christian Aid effort demonstrated political naïveté. It was a classic case of tackling symptoms, not causes. By tackling debt as a series of unpleasant numbers to be reduced, while failing to address the true causes and nature of that debt, the long-term injustice perpetrated against the developing nations has been totally overlooked. Debt remission has become a whitewash; political consciences have been salved and public sympathy used up whilst the critically high levels of debt will inevitably recur.

It might seem a dreadful judgement, but the fact is that by acting as a focus for protest, monopolising the opportune moment and yet failing to insist upon effective levels of debt cancellation, Jubilee 2000 has done far more harm than good. It is actually serving the needs not of the debtor nations, but of the commercial interests that benefit from Third World debt, which will be more than happy to see the institution of a process that accepts a definition of 'sustainable debt' whilst continuing to exercise control over debtor nations. The Third World will remain sufficiently financially exposed for their purposes, levels of debt critical enough to cause outright collapse will be avoided, the 'embarrassments' of the past will have been addressed and the institution of Third World debt will be secured for the future.

The next move

As was discussed in Chapter 9, the cancellation of international debt presents no great technical difficulty. It may well be that accompanying trade reforms are necessary, but this too emphasises that in discussing international debt and globalisation, we are deep in the realm of power politics rather than economics. It is all a matter of political will.

Whether or not the developing world was deliberately brought into its current state of dependency we may never know. But there are certainly interests and aspirations that now benefit from the majority of nations of the planet being in a state of permanent financial exposure. The following statement makes reference to American corporate power. In reading it, it should be borne in mind that 20% of US citizens now live below the official poverty line.

America is run largely by and for about 5,000 people who are actively supported by about 50,000 beavers eager to take their places. I arrive at this figure this way; maybe 2,500 mega-corporation executives, 500 politicians, lobbyists and Congressional committee chairmen, 500 investment bankers, 500 partners in major accounting firms, 500 labour brokers.[7]

Of course, such commercial power and material gain are not confined to America but are now global, with similar beneficiaries to be found in all nations. If commerce represents the material gain of Third World debt and globalisation, the political dimension must not be forgotten. Third World debt may, in some degree, represent a series of mistakes or an accident of history denoting human institutional failing. But there can be no doubt that the push towards globalisation constitutes a clear policy. The cautionary arguments warning of the danger to democracy of complex political amalgamations on the scale represented by the

WTO, the European Union and NAFTA have been persistently ignored. There is a clear determination to develop the tier of international governance at the expense of democratically elected and accountable national governments.

Behind the growing corpus of institutions wielding global power, a number of informal but very influential 'consensus groups' are known to hold meetings in great secrecy, with key representatives from banking, commerce, the media and politics. Such people wield a shocking degree of power. It has to be recognised that there is a new imperialism governing modern politics and economics. This is not an imperialism that can, ultimately, be identified with any one nation.

We are seeing the emergence of an international elite that sees the world as its duty of care, its constituency and its market. It has its more obvious commercial and political dimensions, with key players among the corporate moguls and political delegates.

But the best way to appreciate this new imperialism is to recognise that it is *also* fully represented within the NGOs and voluntary sector. The intelligentsia in the West has shown how easily it is enticed into the arrogant mindset of benign dictatorship in seeking to make debt relief conditional upon environmental and social changes. There are any number of people, concerned and knowledgeable about debt and globalisation, who will go all the way with the analysis of this book, but balk at the notion of complete debt cancellation. Whilst perceiving the injustice of debt, they cannot acknowledge that the developing world can put its own house in order and should be entrusted so to do. The developing world needs 'guidance' and debt provides the opportunity for leverage and control over the agenda – which of course should be environmentally sound, culturally attuned and socially conscious. This is the imperialist mentality. It is precisely the mentality that dominates the upper echelons of the WTO, the EU, NAFTA, etc. and it plays right into the hands of the more avaricious global elite. But, ultimately, it demonstrates that this is a form of mental imperialism; a conviction of superiority and competence; a statement of a lack of trust in others.

The injustice of Third World debt will not be tackled adequately without an attitude that accepts that the citizens and political representatives of the developing nations are no more or less capable and competent than others, and far better placed to determine the meaning of progress for them. Some may do this worse than others; but some will do it better. And that is the way forward, rather than the imperialism of tied debt remission.

Pressure for change

The political forces and prejudices ranged against such reforms are indeed frightening. Certainly, debt cancellation will not come without considerable pressure. From where might this emanate?

First, supportive Western public opinion is vital. Without sufficient popular outrage, politicians will continue to refuse to take on the powerful and remote tier of international government, banking and commerce whose interests dominate today's global economy. NGOs are proving a vital aspect of modern democracy. Not only are they capable of informing and motivating public opinion, but they undertake research and present analyses that present a serious challenge to many mistaken or outdated orthodoxies. In recent years, a growing number of new economics movements have become established, with their basis in environmental concern and social justice. They are to be found in the United Kingdom, Canada, the United States, Australia, New Zealand, South Africa, Brazil and many European countries. The quality of the challenge they present to the political and economic status quo is rapidly improving.

However, the under-funded voluntary sector cannot present this challenge on its own. What is also needed is support from the ranks of established economists, including the powerful media and academic figureheads of this discipline. There is a responsibility on establishment intellectuals in the West to embrace a fuller understanding of the causes of Third World of debt and the nature of globalisation. Support from those with professional expertise in economics is particularly important, since it is into their province that the matters of 'debt' and the genuinely efficient use of resources naturally fall.

Acknowledgement of the wasteful and destructive character of much global commercial activity is long overdue whilst the economics profession surely cannot further defer the critical analysis of the institution of money. The decrease from 20% to 4% of government-produced notes and coins in the money stock, and the fact that this represents an equivalent decrease in the quantity of money circulating free from debt, is a major shift in the financial basis of the modern economy. Outside the monetary reform movement, this factor is completely unstudied, indeed has passed almost unnoticed.

We must also recognise the lack of a coherent theoretical basis to government national debts and the fact that these have proved to be cumulative and unrepayable, not cyclical. Within these considerations alone is huge scope for enquiry. There is abundant empirical evidence to support such study, in the pattern of private, government and commercial debt; the growth of consumer debt, especially mortgages; the increased monetary pressure to secure full-time employment; the growth of different sectors of commercial debt and its impact on business viability, the direction of industrial development; and changes in production techniques and product quality. At the theoretical level there are grounds for a complete re-examination of monetary theory including capital generation and equity theory, the constitution of the money supply, the nature of inflation, the sources of government funding and, not least, development theory. There is opportunity also for the evaluation of different monetary systems and the policy options these present. Academic involvement and an end to the media embargo on such issues are vital if monetary reform is to gain the respectability that it clearly deserves.

The refusal of professional economists to challenge the dated conventions of neo-classical economics constitutes a gross abrogation of responsibility. There is an understandable readiness on the part of the public to defer to expert opinion. But there is a wholly unacceptable cowardice on the part of experts in refusing to expose themselves to censure by challenging a mistaken orthodoxy. All these factors play into the hands of the current consensus-makers. But if even a few economists exposed the injustice of expecting the emergent nations to repay dollar debts within the context of a debt-based global economy and under the most adverse terms of trade imaginable, the effect could be dramatic.

Repudiation by debtors

The final factor that needs to be considered may well prove to be decisive. Pressure from the Third World itself might well emerge from a coalition of debtor nations determined to take unilateral action in repudiating debts that have no economic, legal or moral status. This is precisely where the debtor nations are strongest. International debt is acknowledged to be largely unenforceable, with payment depending entirely upon the acceptance by debtors that it is in their best interest to pay. Any significant level of default or repudiation by even a small group of debtor nations, accompanied and backed up by a legal challenge, would transfer the onus of responsibility for solving the accountancy problem of Third World debt to where it truly lies – the Western nations, their multilateral agencies and their vulnerable, over-exposed banking sector. This would concentrate the relevant minds wonderfully.

Against this, many governments in the Third World are now often seen as closer to the international elites than to their own people, seeking approval from this quarter of global power more avidly than they defend the welfare of their citizens. But this shift has been a gradual process, and Third World politicians should not be wholly condemned for what has happened. They have been subject to such internal unrest, external pressure, economic persuasion and political temptation that it was inevitable that they would embrace the priorities of global free trade and absorb the belief that through 'sound economics and good governance' the poor will one day be better off. Belief in their own ability at governance has been perpetually eroded ... there appears to be no other game in town than the free trade scrum-down ... everyone says it will work in the end ... and there's that shiny limousine arriving to take you to the World Bank convention where everyone prefers it if you fit in...

But there are a number of political figures within the Third World with the mental and moral integrity to challenge the dictates and tendentious advice emanating from the grey-suited international governance lobby. The responsibility on these politicians to rekindle the flame of protest that flared during the 1980s cannot be overstated. Another vital factor will be the readiness with which a 'second wave' of political leaders in the emergent nations desert the Washington

Consensus and re-assert the rights of their own citizens if any significant challenge should arise.

With sufficient determined, intelligent and courageous action by those who represent the millions who have been exploited and thrust into profound poverty, the Third World has hope. It is a profound irony that citizens in the developed world, threatened as they undoubtedly are by globalisation, might ultimately depend on the impoverished Third World nations to present an effective challenge to the global rule of debt.

Summary

Third World debt represents the gravest imaginable failure and bias of our economic/trading system. Instituted by the powerful nations, it has led to the subjugation of many sovereign nations and the acquisition by powerful international commercial interests of valuable assets that rightly belong to those sovereign nations and their subjugation to economic policies that are against their best interests.

It is all the more reprehensible that this modern economic imperialism should be conducted by subterfuge, under the banner of 'aid' and 'trade'. After four decades of such development, continually distorted by prejudiced Western economic institutions and flawed economic ideology, if the concept of 'forgiveness' is to be discussed, it is without doubt the North who should be seeking it of the South.

Cancellation or repudiation of the international debts carried by the emergent nations would allow them to set their own economic priorities. They would then be free from the obligation to follow the pro-corporate agenda of the World Bank and IMF, whilst multinationals would have to adjust to a world where countries were more economically independent. The desire on the part of corporate business to invest in developing nations would be met by the demand that such investment should provide real, material benefits for the citizens of that nation. The conduct of multinationals would have to change considerably or many doors would be shut in their faces. In addition, the developing nations would have a chance to co-operate economically with each other in a way that has been impossible whilst they carry permanent dollar debts. Competition from new companies in these nations would rapidly lead to the slimming down of many of today's multinationals and the likely fragmentation of many corporate monopolies.

The potential impact of cancellation on corporate business and the diversification of economic policy suggest that a satisfactory solution to the debt crisis is a vital policy, and presents possibly the best starting point for tackling globalisation. To encourage us in this direction, and in view of the terrible environmental damage being caused by globalisation, the following statement seems a fitting warning to a world based on debt. Simon Bolivar, the nineteenth-century liberator of the Andean Spanish colonies, once wrote;

I despise debt more than I do the Spanish! ... that's why I warned Santander that whatever good we had done for the nation would be worthless if we took on debt because we would go on paying interest until the end of time. Now it's clear: debt will destroy us in the end.[8]

Endnotes

1   André Gunder Frank. In *Economic Development and World Debt*. Hans Singer and Sumitra Sharma (ed). Macmillan. 1989.

2   Jacques B. Gelinas. *Freedom From Debt*. Zed Books. 1998.

3   André Gunder Frank. *Op. cit.*

4   André Gunder Frank. *Op. cit.*

5   Michel Chossudovsky. *The Globalisation of Poverty*. Zed Books. 1997.

6   Anthony R. Boote and Kamau Thugge. *Debt Relief for Low Income Countries. The HIPC Initiative*. International Monetary Fund. 1997.

7   Robert Townsend, 1972, CEO of Avis Car Rental. Quoted in Titus Alexander. *Unravelling Global Apartheid*. Polity Press. 1996.

8   Jacques B. Gelinas. *Op. cit.*

Bibliography

Alexander, Titus. *Unravelling Global Apartheid*. Polity Press. 1996.

Bank of England. *Annual Statistical Releases*. 1995, 1997. HMSO.

Barnet and Muller. *Global Reach; The Power of the Multinational Corporation*. Simon and Schuster. 1974.

Bjorset, Brynjolf. *Distribute or Destroy*. Stanley Nott. Ltd. 1936.

Boote, Anthony R. and Thugge, Kamau. *Debt Relief for Low Income Countries. The HIPC Initiative*. International Monetary Fund. 1997.

Broad, Robin. *Unequal Alliance. The World Bank, the IMF and the Philippines*. University of California Press. 1988.

Brown, Brendan. *The Flight of Capital International Capital, A Contemporary History*. Croom Helm. 1987.

Building Societies Association. *A Compendium of Building Society Statistics* (Eighth Edition). The Building Societies Association. 1990.

Cahn, Jonathan. *Challenging the New Imperial Authority*. Harvard Human Rights Journal 6. 1993.

Cavanagh, J., Wysham, D and Arruda, M. (eds). *Beyond Bretton Woods – Alternatives to the Global Economic Order*. Pluto Press. 1994.

Chossudovsky, Michel. *The Globalisation of Poverty*. Zed Books. 1997.

Clarke, Tony, and Barlow, Maude. *MAI*. Stoddart Publishing (Canada). 1997.

Conference of Institute for African Alternatives. Bade Onimode (ed). *The IMF, The World Bank and African Debt*. Zed Books. 1989.

Crawford, Vincent P. *International lending; Long-term credit relationships and dynamic contract theory*. Princeton Studies in International Finance. No 59 March 1987.

Crocket, Andrew. *Money*. Nelson. 1997.

Crowther, Geoffrey. *An Outline of Money*. Thomas Nelson and Sons Ltd. 1950.

Cuddington, John T. *Capital Flight*. Princeton Studies in International Finance. No 58, Dec. 1986.

Dimancescu, Dan. *Deferred Future*. Ballinger and Co. 1983.

Douglas, C. H. *Dictatorship by Taxation*. Institute of Economic Democracy. 1936.

Douglas, C. H. *The Policy of a Philosophy*. Institute of Economic Democracy. 1936.

Douthwaite, Richard. *Short Circuit*. Green Books. 1996.

Douthwaite, Richard. *The Ecology of Money*. Green Books. 1999.

Douthwaite, Richard. *The Growth Illusion*. Green Books. 1992.

Emmanuel, Arghiri. *Unequal Exchange*. Monthly Review Press. 1972.

Fetter, F. W. *The Development of British Monetary Orthodoxy.* Harvard University Press. 1965.

Gelinas, Jacques. *Freedom from Debt.* Zed Books. 1998.

George, Susan. *The Debt Boomerang.* Pluto Press. 1992.

George, Susan and Sabelli, Fabrizio. *Faith and Credit.* Penguin Books. 1994.

Ghai, Dharam (ed). *The IMF and the South – The Social Impact of Adjustment.* Zed Books. 1991.

Greider, William. *One World, Ready or Not.* Penguin Books. 1997.

Grey, John. *An Effective remedy for the Distress of Nations.* 1842.

Gunnemann, Jon P. *The Nation State and Transnational Corporations in Conflict.* Praegar. 1975.

Hayter, Teresa. *The Creation of World Poverty.* Pluto Press. 1981.

Hicks, J. R. 'Free Trade and Modern Economics'. In *Essays in World Economics.* Oxford: Clarendon Press. 1959.

Hutchinson, Frances. *What Everyone Really Wants to Know About Money.* Jon Carpenter. 1997.

Holloway, Sir Edward. *Money Matters.* The Sherwood Press. 1986.

Irwin, Douglas A. *Against the Tide; An Intellectual History of Free Trade.* Princeton University Press. 1996.

Jalée, Pierre. *The Pillage of the Third World.* Monthly Review Press. 1968.

Johnston, Thomas. *The Financiers and the Nation.* Methuen. 1934.

Khan, Mohsin. *The Macroeconomic Effects of Fund-Supported Adjustment Programs.* IMF Staff Papers, Vol 37, No 2, 1990.

King, Edward. *Considerations on the Utility of the National Debt.* 1793.

Korten, David. *When Corporations Rule the World.* Earthscan. 1995.

Kurtzman, Joel. *The Death of Money.* Simon and Schuster. 1993.

Lal, Deepack. *The Poverty of Development Economics.* Institute of Economic Affairs. 1997.

Larrain, Felipe and Velasco, André. *Can Swaps Solve the Debt Crisis?* Princeton Studies in International Finance. No.69. November 1990.

Latin America Bureau. *The Poverty Brokers. The IMF and Latin America.* Latin America Bureau. 1983.

Lessard, Donald R. and Williamson, John. *Capital Flight and Third World Debt.* Institute for International Economics. 1987.

Lever, Lord Harold and Huhne, Christopher. *Debt and Danger.* Penguin. 1985.

Macleod, H. D. *The Theory of Credit.* Longman Green. 1984.

MacNamara, Robert S. *The Essence of Security; Reflections in Office.* Hodder and Stoughton. 1968.

Maital, Shlomo. *Minds, Markets and Money.* New York Basic. 1982.

Myrdal, Gunnar. *Economic Theory and Underdeveloped Regions.* Duckworth and Company. 1957

Nafziger, E. Wayne. *The Debt Crisis in Africa.* Johns Hopkins University Press. 1993.

Norberg Hodge, Helena. *Small is Beautiful, Big is Subsidised.* International Society for Ecology and Culture. 1999.

Nunnenkamp, Peter. *The International Debt Crisis of the Third World.* Harvester Wheatsheaf Press, 1986.

Payer, Cheryl. *Lent and Lost.* Zed Books. 1991.

Payer, Cheryl. *The Debt Trap.* Monthly Review Press. 1974.

Robinson, R. *Developing The Third World. The Experience of the 1960s.* Cambridge University Press. 1971.

Roddick, Jackie. *The Dance of the Millions.* Latin America Bureau. 1988.

Rowbotham, Michael. *The Grip of Death.* Jon Carpenter. 1998.

Sachs, Jeffrey. *Theoretical Issues in International Borrowing.* Princeton Studies in International Finance. No 54. July 1984.

Sachs, Jeffrey and Larrain, Felipe. *Macroeconomics in the Global Economy.* Prentice Hall International. 1993.

Schatan, Jacobo. *World Debt. Who is to Pay?* Zed Books. 1987.

Simmons, Patrick A. (ed). *Housing Statistics of the United States.* Bernan Press. 1997.

Singer, Hans and Sharma, Soumitra (eds). *Economic Development and World Debt.* Macmillan Press. 1989.

Soddy, Frederick. *Wealth, Virtual Wealth and Debt.* Omni Publications. 1933.

Soros, George. *The Crisis of Global Capitalism.* Little, Brown and Co. 1998.

Still, Bill and Carmack, Patrick. *The Money Masters.* Royalty Production Co. 1998.

Sutton, Mary, Sharpley, Jennifer and Killick, Tony. *The IMF and Stabilisation – Developing Country Experiences.* Heinemann Educational Books. 1984.

Thirlwall, A. P. *International Monetary Reform.* Macmillan Studies in Economics. Macmillan. 1976.

United Nations. *Financing Economic Development in Underdeveloped Countries.* United Nations. New York. 1949.

United Nations. *World Economic and Social Survey.* United Nations. 1996.

Van Dormael, Armand. *Bretton Woods – The Birth of an International Monetary System.* Macmillan Press. 1978.

Walshe, Graham. *International Monetary Reform.* Macmillan Studies in Economics. Macmillan. 1971.

Wilcox, Steve. *Housing Review 1996/7.* The Joseph Rowntree Foundation. 1997.

Williamson, Bergsten Cline. *Bank Lending to Developing Countries – the Policy Alternatives.* Institute for International Economics. No 10, April 1985.

Williamson, John and Lessard, Donald R. *Capital Flight – the Problem and the Responses.* Institute for International Economics. No 23. Nov. 1987.

World Bank. *Adjustment in Africa.* Oxford University Press. 1994.

Index

The Grip of Death

A study of modern money, debt slavery and destructive economics

This lucid and original account of where our money comes from explains why most people and businesses are so heavily in debt. It explodes many myths about subjects very close to home: mortgages, building societies and banks, food and farming, transport, worldwide poverty, and what's on the supermarket shelf.

It explains —

- why virtually all the money in the world economy has been created as a debt; why only 3% of UK money exists as 'legal tender'; and why in a world reliant upon money created as debt, we are kept perpetually short of money.

- how and why mortgages are responsible for almost two-thirds of the total money stock in the UK, and 80% in the US.

- why consumers can't get quality products.

- why business debt is at its highest level ever.

- why debts mean that a small farm can be productively very efficient, but financially not 'viable'.

- why national debts can never be paid off — without monetary reform.

- how debt fuels the 'need to grow', revolutionising national and global transport strategies, destroying local markets and producers and increasing waste, pollution and resource consumption.

- how 'Third World debt' is a mechanism used by the developed nations to inject ever-increasing amounts of money into their own economies, and why debtor nations can never repay the debts.

- why politicians who rely on banks to create money can't fund public services.

- why 'debt-money' is undemocratic and a threat to human rights.

The author proposes a new mechanism for the supply of money, creating a supportive financial environment and a decreasing reliance on debt.

Michael Rowbotham is a teacher and writer.

£15 pbk   352pp   1 897766 40 8

To order post free in the UK, phone 01689 870437 or 01608 811969